Endtime Survival Crusades And Prophecy Evangelism

ESCAPE MINISTRIES

"Our soul is escaped as a bird out of the snare of the fowlers: the snare is broken, and we are escaped." –Psalms 124:7

ENDORSEMENTS

What a blessing to know that God has given His Word to tell us not only how we got here and why we're here but where we're going when it is over. The Bible contains a lot of information about the future and prophecy. I'm excited to see Mr. Meadows use his intellect to share his insights of the scriptures with others. I pray this will be a great blessing to you.

In Christ,

Kent Hovind
Creation Science Evangelism

I endorse Evangelist Gary D. Meadows end time book and study. Brother Meadows is a wonderful man of God who loves Biblical Truths.

Dr. Clinton Willis

REVELATION OF THE END

Volume 1

Correcting the Misinterpretations of End Time Prophecy
The Greatest Mysteries of Prophecy Revealed

Betrayed by My Own Doctrine

GARY D. MEADOWS

Revelation of the End, Volume 1
Correcting the Misinterpretations of End Time Prophecy
the Greatest Mysteries of Prophecy Revealed
Copyright 2020 by Gary D. Meadows

ISBN: 978-1-7332670-0-7 (ebook)
ISBN: 978-1-7332670-2-1 (print)

Published by:
Endtime Publishing

escapeminps1247.com
info@escapeminps1247.com

All texts from the Old and New Testaments are taken from the authorized King James Version, originally published in 1611.

All rights reserved. Without limiting the rights under copyright reserved above, no part of this publication may be reproduced, stored in or introduced into a retrieval system, or transmitted, in any form, or by any means (electronic, mechanical, photocopying, recording, or otherwise) without the prior written permission of both the copyright owner and the above publisher of this book.

BOOK DEDICATION

I dedicate this book to my wife, Pamela. She loves me. She is my soul mate. She believes in me and in my ministry. She has contributed to my insights throughout my writings. She loves God with all her heart. She testifies that Jesus is the best thing that has ever happened to her! She hears God's voice. She has been tried in a "furnace of fire" and has survived. She is quiet, but deep. She is the greatest woman of God I have ever known.

Prophecy is a sizzling topic on the lips of millions across the globe, because there is a foreboding of impending doom on the horizon. The movie industry has chimed in to satisfy this thirst with a long list of climactic end time scenarios. But when it's all been said, there is a mass of people who turn back to find a Biblical witness to either substantiate or relieve their fears. That is why prophecy books are flying off the shelves, but we've ended up having a library full of prophetic revelations from authors parroting each other. Frightfully, one false interpretation built on anther can lead to a landslide of misconceptions leaving the church vulnerable to the future. So the very thing the Lord has meant for a safeguard has ended up becoming a liability for destruction.

For the person who thinks he can correct the misinterpretations of other experts surely has a firing squad waiting to shoot him through with a million holes. It's quite a gamble, but it's worth the risk. So this book will unfold a view that, admittedly, is not widely held, but seriously Biblical. The reader will hopefully be left with the haunting question, "Could this be true?" Each will have to answer that for themselves, and only God knows if it will miraculously alter the landscape of accepted Biblical interpretation. If the interpretations of the past have become stale and boring, get ready for a fresh, new, biblical look. The verses that are about to be explored will lead into a whole new arena of end time understanding. Controversy? Very likely, but this book will throw several subjects back onto the table for discussion and ultimately, it will be healthy!

DISCOVER THE ANSWERS TO THESE QUESTIONS

1. Prophecy is hard to understand. Should we even study it?
2. Who was the first prophet?
3. Who are the 4 Beasts and the 4 and 20 Elders?
4. Who are the Two Witnesses, the Two Olive Trees, and the Two Candlesticks? Absolute proof!
5. Why are there so many "2's" found in scripture?
6. Who are the 144,000? It has been conjectured forever—now a full disclosure.
7. What is meant by "the end" and how much time do we have left until it comes?
8. Does God have a calendar? What does it say?
9. What is meant by the "third day indicator", and how does it indicate how much time we have left?
10. How long is a generation? It seems everybody has their take on it, but does the scripture actually tell us?
11. How long does the Antichrist reign, three and a half or seven years?
12. What is preterism, and should we accept it?
13. Does anybody ever deal with the 2300 days of Daniel 11? What is meant by it?
14. Does anybody ever deal with the 1290 days of Daniel 11? What is meant by it?
15. Does anybody ever deal with the 1335 days of Daniel 11? What is meant by it?
16. What is the "Abomination of Desolation"?
17. Everybody says the "Abomination of Desolation" is set up in the middle of the week. Seven proofs why this is not true! If you get this timing wrong, you get everything wrong!

Now, after almost 50 years of study, Gary D. Meadows has come out of the "mountains" of obscurity to bring the reader the golden nuggets of the truths of prophecy and to answer these questions and more!

CONTENTS

PREFACE 1

1: HOW IMPORTANT IS PROPHECY? 12
   It is so hard to understand; should we even study it?

2: THE FOUR BEASTS AND FOUR AND TWENTY
   ELDERS 77

3: WHO ARE THE TWO WITNESSES? 96
   If it is not Moses, Elijah, or Enoch, then who is it? Will knowing this reveal that the rapture will happen after the tribulation?

4: WHO ARE THE 144,000? 167
   If these are not 12,000 from the twelve tribes of Israel, who are they?

5: THE END — WHEN IS IT? 265
   *Does the Bible say? Does the Bible tell us how long a generation is? The 1290, 1335, and the 2300 days of Daniel, which few explain, fills in the endtime time line. Absolute proof that the Abomination of Desolation is set up at the **end** of the week, **not** in the middle!*

6: THE END — HOW BAD WILL IT GET? 442
Does the Bible say? The world will be turned upside down. Apophis and Planet X are coming. The woman clothed with the sun in the constellations. Few men left. The great earthquake. Watch Yellowstone. The U.S. will be diminished.

    Each chapter closes with an open-book quiz with answer key.

STUDY GUIDE 514

ALTERNATIVE READING 527

LIST OF QUOTES 529

PREFACE

Paul wrote in II Corinthians that there were those who questioned whether the Lord was really speaking through him.

> 2 Co 13:3: "Since ye seek a proof of Christ speaking in me, **which to you-ward is not weak...**"

In the previous chapters to this verse, that is chapters 11 and 12, Paul lists different aspects of why he feels justified in exercising authority over the brethren at Corinth and why they should diligently heed his words. Likewise, it is important that the child of God be careful who they allow to have authority over them. Therefore it is only prudent to lay out a little background of who I am and what kind of beginnings I have had that has set the stage for this ministry, this book and those books to come.

I can't brag of any pedigree. Like Amos I wasn't the son of a well-known preacher. Similarly, as Elijah came out of nowhere, so it is my lot, as it were, to not have graduated from any seminary, little lone, a well-known one. Paul had a degree, but the 12 apostles did not. Acts 4:13 says "they were unlearned and ignorant men", but the Pharisees took note "that they had been with Jesus." These are the ones who started and established the early church, and they were trained by Jesus Himself. Like them, it's not that I haven't had training, but four years of Bible school somehow doesn't equate to a doctorate of eight years, and no one is knocking a doctorate here, but in real life, God doesn't always require that to be His catalyzing agent. It is of greater importance to have heard the Lord speak and to have heard the Lord's call to share those words with the body of Christ.

This has been a life long journey for me. A year ago did I say to myself, "I want to write a book, so I better get real close to God, so I can show that I love the Lord, so this book will be received"? No, the Lord began speaking to my heart at the tender age of 8 or 9, but even at age 5, I was already wondering if I might be able to contribute something great to society or to this world before I passed away for the privilege of having been born. The Lord at times will speak to children when they are very young and that is what happened to me at 8 or 9. I heard a prophecy message in the Nazarene Church that startled me out of my skin. Jesus was coming back in my day and taking those who were saved to be with Him forever. The question, "Was I ready?" eliminated any semblance of peace in my heart until I found myself two hours later, locked in my bedroom, on my knees, face pointed upward, and praying ever so earnestly, "Lord, I don't know if I'm ready. I want so bad to go with you when you come. Some way, somehow, before I die will you help me to be ready? Please, work it out. Amen." It was like the air was charged with electricity and I knew, that I knew, that I knew, that He had heard me and without a doubt, everything was going to be okay.

Accepting the Lord as savior of my life one or two years later at vacation Bible school didn't affect me as much as what happened at age 13. My dad had my two brothers and I and a step brother, visit him and help build a house in Merced, California. Through a series of events we ended up having a Bible study in our home from a young apostolic preacher and his wife. After the 3rd lesson we ended up falling on our faces, crying out to God, and repenting of our sins. We couldn't get baptized in the name of Jesus fast enough. After two days and two more services, I got it—the wonderful gift of the Holy Ghost. Yes, the thing some call "hocus pocus" and others say, "It's of the devil," happened to me. (Now it is more accepted, but back then it wasn't.) I spoke in tongues for the first time in my life. Ooooh was my life changed from center to circumference. It was truly God. He heard my prayer and my life was changed forever!

Does God speak today? Can people hear God's voice as though one would speak to another? David in Psalms 45:1 said, "...my tongue is the pen of a ready writer." In other words, does God speak TODAY so clear that it could be written down with a pen as David describes? Many shy away from admitting the mere possibility, though it says, "Jesus Christ the same yesterday, and today, and forever" (Hebrews 13:8). Some say, "God doesn't operate that way today. The Bible's been written and we have everything in it that we need." People, and ministers, in the church say such things, and I'm not talking about adding to the cannon of scripture, here, but God can give special revelations that bring insights into His word. Much of what is contained in this book is not mine. He sovereignly revealed it to me and it is His. If there is any glory locked in these pages, He gets it all. I am just trying to obey Him. If I fail to share what He has given to me, then I fail the grace of God. I Corinthians 9:16 says it best, "For though I preach the gospel, I have nothing to glory of: for necessity is laid upon me; yea, woe is unto me, if I preach not the gospel!" The same goes with sharing God given insights into His word, and thus I share with you what He has given to me.

Why would God speak to me? Maybe God would speak to me because He spoke to my dad at various times and places. I know that because he told me. One example is at one time in his life the Lord told him, "Go find the gold." He didn't listen, but after hearing it the third time and shaking him to his core, he obeyed and took off with his brother and my grandpa to go find the gold. There had just been a gully washer rain storm and unbelievably they found the gold in a river bed! They filed a claim, but my uncle aced my dad and grandpa out of the picture and ended up, after a lot of "maneuvering", with one of the largest gold mines in the United States. Did my dad really hear from God? My uncle lays in a grave today from an early demise to prove it. (God even spoke to my uncle the night before he died and warned him it was going to happen.) Why would God let all that happen? It's hard to know, but it proves people really do hear God speak, and my dad heard God that day. Oh yes, somebody else got that gold mine, but my dad still had the real gold and nobody was able to take it away from him and that was the "gold" of hearing the voice of God. Just maybe that spiritual gold was to pass to his children. Maybe that is just one reason why God has chosen to speak to, and through me—because of my dad. It's a legacy.

Without knowing anything about my dad's experience, which I learned late in life, I had my own encounter with God. I don't remember how I acquired the book, the Silver Chalice, but after wading through part of the book I became fascinated with these men who heard the voice of God. Would it be possible for ME to hear God's voice? Above all the gifts of the Spirit, I felt like to hear God's voice would be the greatest thing in the whole world. While others my age were getting into drugs I was getting into God! It became my quest. I didn't know of anybody who claimed to hear God's voice, directly, so I felt like if I prayed long enough and hard enough, maybe, just maybe, He would speak to little ole me, and speak to me He did. Finally, I heard Him, but as Samuel of old, I didn't recognize Him until later. After returning home from school one day, He came to my bedroom. I heard Him,

> "You think you're pretty doctrinally sound, don't you?"
> (I had given myself to studying doctrine for a long time. Pretty rare for a young man, huh? That's what God can do.)
> What was I to say? Should I answer it? This was too

weird. It sounded like someone was in the room with me. I guess it would be okay... "Yeah."

As fast as lightning, I heard it as clear as a bell, as though it was a fact, "Your doctrine on the tribulation is going to change."

(Please, understand. We were taught pre-tribulation rapture and my brothers and I had discussed it at length.) It came as I kneeled to pray. It came out of nowhere, so I filed it in the round file, but it happened. (It was a year or two later when I remembered the voice.) My own doctrine had betrayed me. My doctrine was spoiled, turned upside down and inside out. For 6 months I wrestled with the question until the truth of His return after the tribulation popped off the page, again, as clear as a bell and the course for my life was set at the ripe old age of 17.

The Lord has used several life events, starting when I was quite young, to indicate He had a special purpose for my life:

1. He began using me in the gift of prophecy during testimony service at church. People would come up to me after the service and thank me for my words and tell me that is exactly what they needed.

2. A field trip to a Bible college before graduation, in one of the prayer rooms, through tongues and interpretation, yielded a startling declaration, "I have called

you to the lost house of the children of Israel... I have called you before many people..."

3. From the school years after the Lord came into my life, that is from 8th through 12th grade, the Lord made me a witness to students and teachers alike. One morning, shortly before graduation the class adviser and class president showed up at my desk and admitted that at graduation they normally have a minister give the invocation and benediction, but they wanted to know if I would do it for the class. I told them I would be honored to do it. Until then I was a little unsure how my Godly influence was received by my classmates, but this little indicator let me know God had used me.

4. The Lord led me into Bible quizzing at a young age. During this time He developed my concentration skills in Bible study and memorization. The Lord forged, probably, the smallest team in history of three young men, into a formidable force that took the district, regional, and finally the national quiz tournament over the book of St. John in an organization of close to 3500 churches.

5. The organization started another new program called International Youth Corp (IYC). In this very first trip they were going to visit the continent of Africa, including East, South, and West Africa all in one sweep. It was designed to expose young people to the foreign mission field. The Lord graciously granted me

the privilege of being one of ten young people from across the country to enjoy this great adventure. This set the stage for two more excursions—one to Korea, and one to Australia. By the time I was 23 the Lord had allowed me to travel three quarters of the way around the world. That wasn't too bad for a poor boy from Spokane, Washington. That's what God can do!

6. After Bible college the Lord opened up doors of opportunity to teach outside the country. I taught in a small Bible college in New Westminster, British Columbia for a year and then in a small Bible college in Accra, Ghana, West Africa in 1986 for a year.

7. As far as the ministry is concerned, I started out in 1974 with a local license and upgraded it to a general license in 1975. I was ordained before going to the foreign field in 1985 and my ordination was accepted by another organization in 2006.

8. I was a Youth pastor, assistant pastor, associate pastor, and co-pastor over a period of 25 years in one church, until I started evangelizing, which I did for six months. The Lord helped me re-establish a work in Moses Lake, Washington. He helped me start a church plant in Union Gap, Washington, and in Moriarty, New Mexico. I had a television program in Albuquerque, NM for over six months.

9. You could say I was an unwanted baby at birth with no name. My mother, unwillingly, had gotten pregnant two and a half months after her second child was born and she was wanting a girl, but I was a boy and there I was. The nurse held me in her arms and asked if she wanted to hold me and if she had a name for me. No, she didn't want to hold me and no, she didn't have a name picked out. The nurse suggested the name, Gary, and my mother thought that was nice, so that became my name. The nurse instinctively placed me beside my mother and when she looked into those blue eyes (at that time) and saw the dark hair, she instantly fell in love with me, and we started to bond.

    There are interesting things about my name, which was given to me by that nurse. Gary is an offshoot of Gerald and means "Spear-carrier, Spearman", "Bold Spearman" or "Brave spearman". I trust in spiritual warfare I can be a bold and brave warrior for God and bring victory over false doctrine and false interpretations of God's word. My brother-in-law found my name in the Bible code with no "w" as there are no w's in the Hebrew language. It appears as Gary Dean Meadows in the King James version of the Bible in Jeremiah 5:31-6:4. The passage it is found in declares that the prophets are prophesying falsely. That is interesting because isn't that what this book is declaring? One could also say that false doctrine has betrayed many besides myself.

10. To write a book like this, one should know the scriptures quite well. While I didn't go the eight years to get the doctorate, as I said, the Lord impressed on my heart to memorize the entire book of Revelation and chapters 7-12 of Daniel. Like Ezekiel and John, in a certain sense of the word, I ate the scriptures. Since I don't have a photographic memory Revelation alone took me four years and twenty days. As it turns out, my degree is, actually, in knowing the scriptures. Since then I have quoted the book of Revelation over 1000 times and the last half of Daniel over 600 times. (For a boy who flunked first grade and couldn't remember how to spell "is" and "why", that's not too bad, but, let me say, only by the grace of God). It was my regimen to quote eleven chapters a day, most often, six days a week. That means for several years I quoted Revelation every two days. It's possible that I have quoted those prophetic scriptures more than any other living individual for which, again, I give all the glory to God, but just memorizing and quoting the scriptures alone does not prove one has insight into them, as Skip Heitzig, pastor of Calvary of Albuquerque, has said.

The reader will have to judge whether the insights locked in these pages are from God. One thing is for certain, this book and the ones to follow will not be like any other books on prophecy you have ever read. Enjoy.

Gary D. Meadows coming out of the wilderness of obscurity to share the golden nuggets of scripture.

Chapter One:
HOW IMPORTANT IS PROPHECY?

WHAT IS PROPHECY?

Does everybody know what prophecy is? Maybe not. Understanding the term is paramount before catching it's importance. The Hebrew word in the Old Testament is "nebuwah" pronounced "neb-oo-aw'". It means a prediction spoken or written. In the Greek the word is "propheteia" pronounced "prof-ay-ti'-ah" and it means prediction scriptural or other. UNGERS BIBLE DICTIONARY, 1970, 16th edition, page 890, doesn't give a meaning for the word prophecy, but refers you to the word "prophet", instead. So isn't a prophet one who prophesies? Ungers says it is "one who is divinely inspired to communicate God's will to his people, and to disclose the future to them." Unger also tells us that a prophet is one who is announcing and pouring forth the declaration of God. He says it is one who "sees". "Sees" what? You could say he sees God's will and sees the future, thus he is called a seer. In classical Greek it especially signifies one who speaks for a god and so interprets his will to man. Hence, its essential meaning is "an interpreter". You could say then, a prophet speaks on the behalf of God and declares his will for man in a present or future sense. He has eyes to see what is good and bad. You could say, prophecies are the words of the prophets, and they interpret God's will to man.

You could describe prophecy as an office of which few men have entered into. Unger on page 891 of his book, says, "The prophets are described as deriving their prophetical office immediately from God, and not to have attached much importance to a series of incumbents, each receiving his commission from another, or from others." He continues, their "mode of life...seems to have been subject to no uniform and rigid law, but, doubtless, changing according to circumstances. Nor from their manner of living, are we to conclude that all adopted an ascetic mode of life. Sometimes, perhaps as an example, or because of persecution they lived in poverty. Their persecution and consequent suffering did not arise from opposition to them as a distinct class, leading an unsociable, ascetic mode of life, but from opposition to their faithful ministry. The prophets had a practical office to discharge. It was part of their commission to show the people of God 'their transgressions and the house of Jacob their sins' (Isa. 58:1; Ezek. 22:2; 43:10; Mic. 3:8). They were the watchmen set upon the walls of Zion to blow the trumpet, and timely warning of approaching danger (Ezek. 3:17; 33:7,8,9; Jer. 6:17; Isa. 62:6)."

I must continue with more quotes from Unger. On page 892 he continues, "Prophecy is not intended to open the future to idle curiosity, but for the higher purpose of furnishing light to those whose faith needs confirming. The revelation of future events may be needful in times of discouragement to awaken or sustain hope, to inspire confidence in the midst of general backsliding, and to warn of evil threatening the faithful. The predictions against Babylon, Tyre, Egypt, Nineveh, and other kingdoms, were delivered to the people of God to comfort them, by revealing to them the fate of their enemies."

The Bible tells us how prophecy came to individuals in II Peter 1:

> 2 Pe 1:21 "For the prophecy came not in old time by the will of man: but holy men of God spake as they were **moved by the Holy Ghost.**"

Unger continues, "The modes of communication between God and man are clearly stated on the occasion of the sedition of Aaron and Miriam: 'And he said, Hear now my words: If there be a prophet among you, I the Lord will make myself known unto him in a vision, and will speak unto him in a dream. My servant Moses is not so, who is faithful in all my house. With him will I speak mouth to mouth, even apparently, and not in dark speeches; and the similitude of the Lord shall he behold' (Num. 12:6). Three modes are here given: (1) Vision; (2) dream; (3) direct communication and manifestation; the highest form being the last, and reserved for Moses." Unger continues on page 893, "The diviners of the heathen world were supposed to be, when under the influence of inspiration, in a…trance, their being faculties held in complete abeyance… The Hebrew prophets were not distinguished by such peculiarities. They were not subject to amentia. They did not lose their self-possession, but spoke with a full apprehension of existing circumstances." They, many times, would precede their words with such phrases as:

> "The hand of the Lord was upon me…" Ezek. 1:3, 3:14; 33:22

> "Isaiah saw…" Isa. 1:1

> "Thus saith the Lord…" Jer. 1:8 19; 2:19; 30:11; Amos 2:11; 4:5; 7:3

> "The word of the Lord came unto…" Jonah 1:1; Joel 1:1

When they uttered such phrases, the people knew that the next words out of their mouths were from God Himself.

ARE THERE PROPHETS TODAY?

When we think of prophets, our mind immediately goes to the Old Testament, because that is where the majority of the prophets were, but were there prophets in the New Testament? Yes there were, but are there prophets today? Yes there are. Look at Ephesians 4:

> Eph 4:11 "And he gave some, apostles; and some, **prophets**; and some, evangelists; and some, pastors and teachers;"

We call this the five-fold ministry. He gave these ministries to the church and has never taken them away. If there are evangelists and pastors and teachers, then there are apostles and prophets today, also. Yes, there are apostles and prophets today, but modern apostles and prophets are not the same as the original apostles and prophets. We consider the words of the original apostles and prophets to be inspired and "God breathed", but not so with the words of present day apostles and prophets. They have to prove themselves. Sorry. That is just the way it is. We cannot afford to be duped by a so called apostle or prophet. Jesus said through Paul, "prove all things". Have you ever seen or met an apostle or prophet? Maybe you haven't, but that doesn't mean they don't exist. Consider, you may have met one and didn't know it. They don't go around in today's society with a cape on their back or clothed in a gunny sack. They dress and look like regular people. Understand this also, prophets today not only foretell the future, they also do what we call "forth-tell". Most Bible scholars understand this and part of it comes from how Paul talks about prophesying in I Corinthians 14:

> 1 Co 14:3 "But he that **prophesieth** speaketh unto men to **edification**, and **exhortation**, and **comfort**."

You can see from this that one doesn't always have to be speaking of the future when one edifies, exhorts, or comforts others. But, how do you know a "bad apple" when you see one? Believe you me it is very difficult to separate the true from the false. It is almost like trying to divide the soul from the spirit, but it is much like the Old Testament. Any prediction a prophet makes must be 100% accurate or it's a sign that they are a false prophet. Second, if they speak forth a message from God, it must not violate the written word of God. We have that as a guide to go by. That is what Paul meant in I Corinthians 14. He says it this way:

> 1 Co 14:29 "Let the **prophets** speak two or three, and let **the other judge**."

Whatever they say they must not violate the word of God. That is why others were to judge and make sure of that. Any prophet who gets angry because you want to check him out is giving you a red flag to really check him out. If you don't know the word of God very well, then you are not in a position to judge, or even know if one is a true prophet or not. Also, there is no room for the "lone ranger" here. We lean on each other to make sure we are not missing something, and that is why the church is so important. The bigger question here is, what if the "church" labels someone or some doctrine as illegitimate and they are not? That is when we are in big trouble and thus the reason for one subtitle, BETRAYED BY MY OWN DOCTRINE. Parts of Christian doctrine may be wrong in some of its exegesis of prophetic scripture, but right in lots of other subjects, so don't misunderstand this point.

In summary, then, prophecies are the words of the prophets. Watch out for false prophets. Check them out! Much of the Old and New Testaments have to do with future events. How much of the Bible is prophecy? Kerby Anderson in July of 2012 on his radio broadcast, Point of View made the following statements about prophecy: "There are 578 prophecies in the New Testament, and 1239 in the Old Testament. That equals 1817 prophecies in the Bible. 25% of the Bible was at one time written in advance. Prophecy is history in the future, and history is our past in print." Since prophecy takes up so much space in the Bible, it speaks for itself that it must be pretty important. Future events always affect us and if we know what is coming, then we can prepare for them mentally, physically and spiritually. This will have a large bearing on the will of God for us, and may even determine if we survive when everything else is falling apart. From this I hope you can see that prophecy is VERY IMPORTANT and the rest of this chapter will demonstrate that very thing.

THE EARLIEST PROPHETS

The Lord introduces mankind to prophecy in the Garden of Eden when He is about to expel them for their disobedience. It is only chapter three of Genesis and already, the Lord is showing how prophecy can comfort. As it turns out, it is part of the judgment against the serpent, but it brings hope at the time of sorrow, because it reveals the seed of the woman will eventually bruise the head of the serpent. The Lord is implying that when it is all said and done, He will bring man and woman back to the place where He can have fellowship with them again as He did at the beginning. It reads as follows:

> Gen 3:15 "And I will put enmity between thee and the woman, and between thy seed and **her seed; it shall bruise thy head**, and thou shalt bruise his heel."

Again, what is He saying by this? First remember He is speaking judgment to the serpent or the devil. He is saying, "Yes, the woman (and man, by the way) has caused the fall of the whole human race, but this is what I am going to do: I have a plan and in this plan I am going to use the woman and her seed, (specifically Jesus), to win the victory over you, the devil, and bring the whole human race back to Myself." The whole rest of the Bible is an unfolding of how He is does just that. As you can see from this, the Lord has it recorded that He Himself is the first prophet.

The second prophet is Enoch who is the seventh generation from Adam. He walked with God, and was so close to God that God took him off the earth without dying. We wouldn't have even known that he was a prophet unless Jude had recorded it in his book:

Jud 1:14 "And **Enoch** also, the seventh from Adam, **prophesied** of these, saying, Behold, the Lord cometh with ten thousands of his saints,"

As you can see, these are the first prophets, but only nine chapters later, more prophecies will be given.

ABRAHAM BELIEVED GOD'S PROPHETIC WORD AND WAS REWARDED

In the book of Genesis God continues to introduce mankind to prophecy. We don't usually think of Abraham as a prophet, but that is what God calls him in Genesis 20:7 and He does that because He is always revealing the future to him. The Bible records how the Lord spoke to Abraham when He first called him in Genesis 12, and in that first conversation the Lord is speaking to him of the future:

Gen 12:1 "Now the LORD had said unto Abram, Get thee out of thy country, and from thy kindred, and from thy father's house, unto a land that I will shew thee:"

Gen 12:2 "And **I will make of thee a great nation, and I will bless thee, and make thy name great; and thou shalt be a blessing:**"

Gen 12:3 "**And I will bless them that bless thee, and curse him that curseth thee: and**

in thee shall all families of the earth be blessed."

The Lord reveals the future to Abraham as He is giving him various promises. The Lord does this a lot as He also did to Isaac and Jacob. That is why it is so important to know prophecy. If you don't know prophecy you will not know the promises that God has for His children. Misunderstand prophecy and you will misunderstand His promises. Look at the following conversations between God and Abraham:

Gen 12:7 "And the LORD appeared unto Abram, and said, **Unto thy seed will I give this land**: and there builded he an altar unto the LORD, who appeared unto him."

Gen 13:14 "And the LORD said unto Abram, after that Lot was separated from him, Lift up now thine eyes, and look from the place where thou art northward, and southward, and eastward, and westward:"

Gen 13:15 "**For all the land which thou seest, to thee will I give it, and to thy seed for ever.**"

Gen 13:16 "**And I will make thy seed as the dust of the earth: so that if a man can number the dust of the earth, then shall**

thy seed also be numbered."

Gen 13:17 "Arise, walk through the land in the length of it and in the breadth of it; for I will give it unto thee."

These were tremendous promises, and they came prophetically. Almost every time they talked, the Lord was revealing to him something in the future. The entire 15th chapter of Genesis is a conversation with God. I am not going to give the entire chapter but part of it is very revealing:

Gen 15:3 "And Abram said, Behold, to me thou hast given no seed: and, lo, one born in my house is mine heir."

Gen 15:4 "And, behold, the word of the LORD came unto him, saying, This shall not be thine heir; but **he that shall come forth out of thine own bowels shall be thine heir."**

Gen 15:5 "And he brought him forth abroad, and said, Look now toward heaven, and **tell the stars, if thou be able to number them: and he said unto him, So shall thy seed be."**

Gen 15:6 "And **he believed in the LORD; and he counted it to him for righteousness."**

> Gen 15:7 "And he said unto him, I am the LORD that brought thee out of Ur of the Chaldees, to give thee this land to inherit it."

The Lord told Abraham two chapters earlier that his seed would be, in number, as the dust of the earth. Now, He tells him that his seed will be as the stars in heaven for a multitude. What does he do with this information? Does he laugh at God or question Him further like people today would do? No! Abraham BELIEVED the Lord. This so impressed the Lord that He counted him righteous for doing so. Wow!

GOD WANTS YOU TO KNOW AND BELIEVE THE PROPHECIES OF THE FUTURE LIKE ABRAHAM

Do you believe the prophecies of the Bible? Do you even know them? He wants you to know them and believe them. Look at II Chronicles:

> 2 Ch 20:20 "And they rose early in the morning, and went forth into the wilderness of Tekoa: and as they went forth, Jehoshaphat stood and said, Hear me, O Judah, and ye inhabitants of Jerusalem; **Believe in the LORD your God, so shall ye be established; believe his prophets, so shall ye prosper.**"

Believing in God and believing in His prophets is like one and the same. Is this important? It sounds like it to me. You will be established and you will prosper. That is a great promise. I think all believers want that. When Jesus was walking incognito with the two disciples on the road to Emmaus, He opened up their understanding of the scriptures (of prophecy) after he said the fateful words: "O fools, and slow of heart to believe all that the prophets have spoken: … " Basically, Jesus wants us to believe ALL that the prophets have spoken because it has a lot to do with the future! But, if we twist the words of the prophets to our own destruction, then that is just as bad as being "slow of heart", isn't it? I'm sure the Lord wants us to be extra careful that we do neither one, huh?

Let's get back to Abraham. I am not going to go over every prophecy that the Lord gave to Abraham, but I want to go back to chapter 15 and give one more:

> Gen 15:13 "And he said unto Abram, Know of a surety that **thy seed shall be a stranger in a land that is not theirs, and shall serve them; and they shall afflict them four hundred years;**"

> Gen 15:14 "**And also that nation, whom they shall serve, will I judge: and afterward shall they come out with great substance.**"

Gen 15:15 "**And thou shalt go to thy fathers in peace; thou shalt be buried in a good old age.**"

Gen 15:16 "**But in the fourth generation they shall come hither again**: for the iniquity of the Amorites is not yet full."

The Lord again reveals the future to Abraham in regards to the Israelites going down to Egypt for four hundred years, and about Abraham dying in a good old age. It all happened just like the Lord said and Abraham knew the future over 430 years in advance. You can know the future by knowing and believing the prophecies of God's word. The Lord wants you to know His secrets about the future by studying the prophets. Look at Amos 3:

Amo 3:7 "Surely the Lord GOD will do nothing, but **he revealeth his secret unto his servants the prophets.**"

Again, by studying the prophets you will know God's secrets. We, as humans, are naturally interested in the future. I think the Lord made us like that. Does He want us, as His children, to know the future of mankind in our day and in our time? Most definitely. Look at John 13, 14, and Revelation 1:

Joh 13:19 "Now **I tell you before it come**, that,

when it is come to pass, **ye may believe** that I am he."

Joh 14:29 "And now **I have told you before it come to pass**, that, when it is come to pass, **ye might believe**."

Rev 1:1 "The Revelation of Jesus Christ, which God gave unto him, **to shew unto his servants things which must shortly come to pass**; and he sent and signified it by his angel unto his servant John:"

These verses tell us that He is revealing the future to His followers, and it tells us why? It is evident He does not want us to be surprised by the future. He wants us to be ready for it, but above that, He wants our faith to be strengthened in Him as a result of it. No, it is even more than that. As Chuck Missler puts it, someone outside our time domain has seen the end from the beginning. Who is Chuck talking about? It is God. He is the I AM. That is what He is saying in John 13:19. The "he" in the King James version is in italics. That means the translators inserted it and it can be removed if it changes the meaning. Folks, Jesus wants us to know that He is God, and it really is God in Jesus that is telling us the future. When everything does come to pass as He has said we will doubly know that He is God.

Is there any verse that says it's okay to inquire about the future? Yes. Look at Isaiah 45:

> Isa 45:11 "Thus saith the LORD, the Holy One of Israel, and his Maker, **Ask me of things to come concerning my sons, and concerning the work of my hands command ye me.**"

You could say the Lord invites you to ask, but it is stronger than that. He, actually, is commanding you to ASK Him OF THINGS TO COME. "Things to come" is definitely referring to things in the future. What is wonderful about this passage is that He gives a second command. He commands us to command Him to reveal to us things in the future. Please, do not be confused here. He is not imploring you to ask about ANYTHING in the future. One must have some discretion, and not be frivolous about the matter. There are boundaries. There is a direct reference to knowing the future about His redeemed ones. This could be about knowing the future of God's people in general.

The question is why would the Lord put this in His word unless He meant it? With that said, why would the Lord tell us the future, at all, if He didn't want us to know it? If it's important enough for God to put it in the Bible in the first place, then it is important to Him for us to know what He has written. The main idea is that He DOES want you to know the future about His people no matter what anybody says.

DANGERS

As soon as I say the Lord wants you to know the future, I must also say in the same breath that He does not want you to try to find out the future through the powers of darkness, through the devil, or through anything else, except the Lord Himself! This is important. Let me say it again. If you want to know the future, you must ask HIM to show you His secrets. In specific terms, do not go to fortune tellers, palm readers, tarot cards. Don't meditate to find spirit guides. Don't get involved in witchcraft, séances, Ouija boards, or such like or get involved with people who do. It almost goes without saying that all these things comes from the devil and his agents.

God's opinion on this matter is revealed to us by looking in the Old Testament. Look at Deuteronomy 18:

> Deu 18:9 "When thou art come into the land which the LORD thy God giveth thee, thou shalt not learn to do after the abominations of those nations."

> Deu 18:10 "There shall not be found among you any one that maketh his son or his daughter to pass through the fire, or that **useth divination, or an observer of times, or an enchanter, or a witch**,"

Deu 18:11 "**Or a charmer, or a consulter with familiar spirits, or a wizard, or a necromancer.**"

Deu 18:12 "**For all that do these things are an abomination unto the LORD**: and because of these abominations the LORD thy God doth drive them out from before thee.

Deu 18:13 Thou shalt be perfect with the LORD thy God."

Deu 18:14 "For **these nations**, which thou shalt possess, **hearkened unto observers of times, and unto diviners: but as for thee, the LORD thy God hath not suffered thee so to do.**"

Deu 18:15 "The LORD thy God will raise up unto thee a Prophet from the midst of thee, of thy brethren, like unto me; unto him ye shall hearken;"

Deu 18:20 "**But the prophet, which shall presume to speak a word in my name, which I have not commanded him to speak, or that shall speak in the name of

other gods, even that prophet shall die."

Deu 18:21 "And if thou say in thine heart, **How shall we know the word which the LORD hath not spoken?**"

Deu 18:22 "**When a prophet speaketh in the name of the LORD, if the thing follow not, nor come to pass, that is the thing which the LORD hath not spoken, but the prophet hath spoken it presumptuously: thou shalt not be afraid of him.**"

Notice in this passage that the Lord goes right from dealing with hard core black magic, into talking about false prophets. Most of God's people would NEVER even consider approaching the powers of darkness for any help whatsoever. That's why the passage is constructed as it is. The Lord warns His people to beware that not only are there wizards and agents of the dark world who will want to bring you into servitude to them, but there will be people who will impersonate themselves as the true servants and prophets of the Lord, but they will be fakes. He warns his people, in so many words, "Don't be gullible." Oh, no, we wouldn't overtly listen to the devil but under the guise of religion, we might inadvertently do that. The devil is a sly old fox. To put it succinctly, don't believe anybody—even preachers from your own church—unless what they are saying can be verified from the word of God. As the saying goes, "Everything that glitters isn't gold." Bottom line, everybody who claims to be a prophet, a preacher, or a man of God, isn't.

I must put a disclaimer in here. Who is perfect? Who has it right in every area? Is there any man? "Not I said the fly", but I strive for it. Can a saint of God understand the Bible for himself or herself? This is the day of knowledge and I believe they can and they can hold their ministers accountable to the word of God. In the Medieval era the Catholic church didn't want their people to own a Bible because they didn't think they could interpret it properly for themselves. All that has changed. The saint of God can read the Bible and understand it for themselves and if enough saints confront the pastor every time he gets off track, maybe he'll correct himself. And then again, if the pastor tries to ostracize you for causing division, maybe it is time to leave to find a more "truth preaching" preacher. Sorry pastors, but it's the truth. There are a lot of glorified "gods" behind the North American pulpits.

LESSONS FROM THE PAST

There is a saying, that those who do not know history are doomed to repeat it. It is true that we can learn from what happened in the past, if we even know about it. Here is the point: Israel as a nation had a promise that someone would come and restore their nation as a dominant world power as it was in the days of David and Solomon. This individual that was coming was called the Messiah. Their Messiah came in the person of Jesus Christ, and they did not recognize Him as such. Why? I will explain it in greater detail, but simply it was because they did not know the prophetic scripture, and the prophecies that they did know, they misunderstood. Largely the nation got their views from their religious leaders who received them from their predecessors who had received them from their predecessors, etc. Basically, then, the way they looked at prophecy became a tradition that they handed down from one generation to each successive generation, and eventually the tradition itself got off the word of God, but became set in concrete until it became the standard to measure all other false prophecies. But it was false itself and became a stumbling block to the whole nation of Israel. They felt okay, but they were deluded. They were God's CHOSEN PEOPLE. They enjoyed a false sense of security. They felt God was going to save them regardless, but they missed their calling! They missed their salvation. They missed the paradigm shift and as a result they missed being the true children of God. Jesus came to help them be born again, spiritually. He had come to give them a NEW PLAN. It was the new plan of being born of water and spirit, and because they missed Him as Messiah they also missed being saved. Let's not condemn them too much before examining ourselves. Have you been blinded by tradition? Are you sure you have prophecy right? Prophecy affected their salvation and it could affect yours. Are you sure you have salvation right? It pays to check up on ourselves. Paul told us to do that very thing. Look at 2 Corinthians 13:

> 2 Co 13:5 "**Examine yourselves, whether ye be in the faith; prove your own selves. Know ye not your own selves, how that Jesus Christ is in you, except ye be reprobates?**"

Again the Lord encourages us to search the scriptures to make sure we have the right plan of salvation. Look at John 5:

> Joh 5:39 "**Search the scriptures**; for in them **ye think ye have eternal life**: and they are they which testify of me."

It is important for us to stop, reflect, learn from their failure, and make sure we do not fall in the same pit they fell into. As I stated, they didn't recognize their messiah and they didn't accept Him, but that is not to say, nobody accepted Him. A small minority did recognize Him for who He was, but the majority did not. Those who accepted Him were definitely blessed, but those who didn't were doomed to utter destruction. Look at what the people said at the crucifixion in Matthew 25:

> Mat 27:25 "Then answered all the people, and said, **His blood be on us, and on our children.**"

Truer words were never spoken. As a result, the city of Jerusalem was leveled in 70 A.D. and hundreds of thousands were killed then. More punishment came hundreds of years later at the hands of Hitler. Six million were destroyed. Wow, pretty terrible! Does history repeat itself? Could it happen again? Yes! Look at Ecclesiastes 3:

> Ecc 3:15 "**That which hath been is now; and that which is to be hath already been**; and God requireth that which is past."

Knowing and understanding prophecy can save a person or a nation from a world of hurt, but let's talk about this in more detail. As I stated, Israel was blinded by their traditions, but their traditions were founded on the prophetic word. That seems to be a paradox, but it's true. What were the verses that blinded them? They were prophetic verses. It's not my purpose to go into too much detail here, but I want to give you a flavor of what happened to the nation of Israel. What caused them to miss their messiah? It was misunderstanding prophecy. They thought their messiah would come in glory and power, and He did, but not the kind of glory that they were expecting. Let me give you a few of the verses that they were concentrating on:

> Eze 37:21 "And say unto them, Thus saith the Lord GOD; Behold, I will take the children of Israel from among the heathen, whither they be gone, and will gather them on every side, and bring them into their own land:"

Eze 37:22 "And I will make them one nation in the land upon the mountains of Israel; and one king shall be king to them all: and they shall be no more two nations, neither shall they be divided into two kingdoms any more at all:"

Eze 37:23 "Neither shall they defile themselves any more with their idols, nor with their detestable things, nor with any of their transgressions: but I will save them out of all their dwellingplaces, wherein they have sinned, and will cleanse them: so shall they be my people, and I will be their God."

Eze 37:24 "And **David my servant shall be king over them**; and they all shall have one shepherd: they shall also walk in my judgments, and observe my statutes, and do them."

Eze 37:25 "**And they shall dwell in the land that I have given unto Jacob my servant**, wherein your fathers have dwelt; and they shall dwell therein, even they, and their children, and their children's children **for ever: and my servant David shall be their prince for ever**."

Eze 37:26 "Moreover I will make **a covenant of**

peace with them; it shall be an everlasting covenant with them: and I will place them, and multiply them, and will set my sanctuary in the midst of them for evermore."

Eze 37:27 "My tabernacle also shall be with them: yea, **I will be their God, and they shall be my people.**"

Eze 37:28 "And the heathen shall know that I the LORD do sanctify Israel, when my sanctuary shall be in the midst of them for evermore."

Amo 9:11 "In that day **will I raise up the tabernacle of David that is fallen**, and close up the breaches thereof; and **I will raise up his ruins, and I will build it as in the days of old**:"

Amo 9:12 "That they may possess the remnant of Edom, and of all the heathen, which are called by my name, saith the LORD that doeth this."

Amo 9:13 "Behold, the days come, saith the LORD, that the plowman shall overtake the reaper, and the treader of grapes him that soweth seed; and the mountains shall drop sweet wine, and all the hills shall melt."

Amo 9:14 "And **I will bring again the captivity of my people of Israel, and they shall build the waste cities, and inhabit them**; and they shall plant vineyards, and drink the wine thereof; they shall also make gardens, and eat the fruit of them."

Amo 9:15 "And **I will plant them upon their land, and they shall no more be pulled up out of their land** which I have given them, saith the LORD thy God."

There are many other verses, if you are interested. I will list them here, but understand, this may not be a complete list: Gen. 49:10; Isa. 1:26, Isa. 9:6-7; Jer. 23:5-6, Jer. 33:15-17, Jer. 33:26; Dan. 7:27; Hos. 3:4; Joel. 3:16-21; Oba. 1:17-21; Mic. 5:2; Zep. 3:15-17; and Zec. 9:9. These are the verses that the disciples of Jesus were referring to in Acts 1:

Act 1:6 "When they therefore were come together, they asked of him, saying, **Lord, wilt thou at this time restore again the kingdom to Israel?**"

Oh, yes, they saw these verses very clearly, but what they didn't see were the verses that had to do with His suffering. Their messiah would have to suffer FIRST. There are many passages that have to do with His suffering, but because of time restrains, let's just look at one, Isaiah 53:

> Isa 53:1 "Who hath believed our report? and to whom is the arm of the LORD revealed?"
>
> Isa 53:2 "For he shall grow up before him as a tender plant, and as a root out of a dry ground: he hath no form nor comeliness; and when we shall see him, there is no beauty that we should desire him."
>
> Isa 53:3 "**He is despised and rejected of men; a man of sorrows, and acquainted with grief**: and we hid as it were our faces from him; he was despised, and we esteemed him not."
>
> Isa 53:4 "Surely he hath borne our griefs, and carried our sorrows: yet **we did esteem him stricken, smitten of God, and afflicted.**"
>
> Isa 53:5 **"But he was wounded for our transgressions, he was bruised for our iniquities: the chastisement of our peace was upon him; and with his stripes we are healed."**
>
> Isa 53:6 "All we like sheep have gone astray; we have

turned every one to his own way; and the **LORD hath laid on him the iniquity of us all**."

Isa 53:7 "**He was oppressed, and he was afflicted, yet he opened not his mouth: he is brought as a lamb to the slaughter, and as a sheep before her shearers is dumb, so he openeth not his mouth**."

Isa 53:8 "**He was taken from prison and from judgment**: and who shall declare his generation? for he was **cut off out of the land of the living: for the transgression of my people was he stricken**."

Isa 53:9 "And he made his **grave with the wicked, and with the rich in his death**; because he had done no violence, neither was any deceit in his mouth."

Isa 53:10 "Yet it pleased the LORD **to bruise him**; he hath put him to grief: when thou shalt make his soul an offering for sin, he shall see his seed, he shall prolong his days, and the pleasure of the LORD shall prosper in his hand."

> Isa 53:11 "He shall see of the travail of his soul, and shall be satisfied: by his knowledge shall my righteous servant justify many; for he shall bear their iniquities."
>
> Isa 53:12 "Therefore will I divide him a portion with the great, and he shall divide the spoil with the strong; because **he hath poured out his soul unto death: and he was numbered with the transgressors; and he bare the sin of many, and made intercession for the transgressors.**"

The nation of Israel knew well the prophecies of the restoration of the Davidic kingdom, but they did not know that their Messiah would first have to suffer. They did not know that the Lord had to come and bring spiritual liberty before physical or political liberty could come. Their scriptures also foretold of the light of the gospel coming to the Gentiles. What is interesting is, in the same verse that mentions Israel being restored, and in the same sentence, it talks about salvation coming to the Gentiles. Look at Isaiah 49:

> Isa 49:6 "And he said, It is a light thing that thou shouldest be my servant to raise up the tribes of Jacob, and **to restore the preserved of Israel**: I will also give thee for **a light to the Gentiles, that**

thou mayest be my salvation unto the end of the earth."

When would the Gentiles have salvation preached to them? When would their Messiah suffer? The scripture doesn't specify that, although Daniel 9:27 says that He would be cut off after 62 weeks. They were blind to this but it is logical that his sufferings would have to be while He was alive, and right before His death. Certain individuals did see it, like the old man Simeon. Look at what Simeon said in Luke 2:

> Luk 2:25 "And, behold, there was a man in Jerusalem, whose name was Simeon; and the same man was just and devout, waiting for the consolation of Israel: and **the Holy Ghost was upon him.**"

> Luk 2:26 "And **it was revealed unto him by the Holy Ghost**, that he should not see death, before he had seen the Lord's Christ."

> Luk 2:27 "And **he came by the Spirit** into the temple: and when the parents brought in the child Jesus, to do for him after the custom of the law,"

> Luk 2:28 "Then **took he him up in his arms**, and blessed God, and said,"

Luk 2:29 "Lord, now lettest thou thy servant depart in peace, according to thy word:"

Luk 2:30 "For **mine eyes have seen thy salvation**,"

Luk 2:31 "Which thou hast prepared before the face of all people;"

Luk 2:32 "**A light to lighten the Gentiles, and the glory of thy people Israel.**"

Luk 2:33 "And Joseph and his mother marvelled at those things which were spoken of him."

Luk 2:34 "And Simeon blessed them, and said unto Mary his mother, Behold, this child is set for the fall and rising again of many in Israel; and for a sign which shall be spoken against;"

Luk 2:35 "(Yea, **a sword shall pierce through thy own soul also**,) that the thoughts of many hearts may be revealed."

The RELIGIOUS leaders of Jesus day did not recognize Him, and for sure they didn't recognize Him as a baby, but Simeon knew. How did he know? Jesus had not performed one miracle. He was a baby and yet Simeon knew Him, just by seeing Him? He was led of the Holy Ghost. He knew prophecy. Are you lead of the Holy Ghost? Do you know prophecy? Simeon knew He would be a light to the Gentiles and that He would suffer, and His suffering would hurt the heart of Mary.

Basically, Israel, as a nation, missed their Messiah because they did not know their own prophetic scripture. Could history repeat itself, and Christians today be devastated because of not knowing prophecy? Absolutely. Could that be you? Absolutely. What could the results be of you not knowing prophecy? If you misunderstood the timing of His second coming like the nation of Israel misunderstood His first coming, you might think Jesus was going to rapture you out of here before the Great Persecution and Tribulation took place. Let's say it doesn't happen and you have to go through it and you're not ready for it, psychologically, physically, financially, or spiritually. What then? It could be devastating. What if all the true churches are closed down and your loved ones are tortured and killed in front of you? What then? One day you wake up and you realize you were misled about the Lord's coming. Maybe you were misled about how to be saved, also. You begin to question everything. Your whole foundation is shaken and you can't believe anything, anymore, so you give up.

Let's say you are in Jerusalem at the time of the abomination of desolation. You don't know prophecy and you don't know the city is going to be nuked in a matter of hours.

What will you do? Will you flee the city, or will you go up in a blaze of fire and smoke along with the rest of the inhabitants? Do you see how important prophecy is? The Lord is letting us know the future for a reason. If you end up suffering mercilessly, it won't be because the Lord didn't try to warn you. It will be because you refused to study prophecy when you could have. It was in the Bible all along, but the enemy wanted you to be blinded so you could be destroyed along with the rest of the sinners. It doesn't have to be that way. Please, give yourself to prophecy while you can. Remember this also. (I write this here and I will write it again later.) One of the first things Jesus said in Matthew 24 was this:

> Mat 24:4 "And Jesus answered and said unto them, **Take heed that no man deceive you.**"

Don't be misled about the future. You don't have to be. Check out this book and see if it doesn't put together a lot of verses that used to be confusing. To be saved is the most important way to be ready for the future, so make sure you are saved Biblically, and be ready for the Lord's second coming!

HOW DID PROPHECY SAVE JOSEPH AND HIS FAMILY?

Many people, in reflecting on Joseph say that his gift was that of interpreting dreams. They are right only to a certain degree. His gift had to do with interpreting dreams of the FUTURE. Think about it. Dreams can have to do with the past, present, or future. All the dreams that Joseph was involved with were dreams of the future. A major part of prophecy is laying out the future. To put it more succinctly, Joseph was a prophet. It didn't matter if he had the dream or someone else had it, the Lord always gave him the meaning of it and it always had to do with the future.

His first experience with dreams, of course, was his own dreams. He only had two. The first one was that of him and his brothers binding sheaves in the field. His sheaf arose and all the sheaves of his brothers fell down and made obeisance to his sheaf. In Joseph's second dream he saw the sun, moon, and the 11 stars making obeisance to him. A lot of Bible teachers condemn Joseph for stupidly sharing his dreams with his family. I think those comments are unfair. The dreams came for two reasons:

1. The Lord wanted Joseph to share his dreams, especially with his brothers, because in order for the dreams to come true they had to be jealous of him and hate him, and betray him (which was also true of Jesus).

2. The dreams were to give him strength and hope that eventually all his problems and troubles would melt away and give way to his exaltation. I believe in his darkest hours, his dreams danced in front of him and gave him hope of a better day.

This is a type of the church today. The Lord has said He will come back to this world and turn our troubles into joy. He will exalt us and allow us to rule and reign with Him as, eventually, Joseph ruled and reigned with Pharaoh. Paul stated that this hope would purify us. This hope would give us strength to, also, go through hard times. Knowing the future helped Joseph and it will also help us, if we study the scriptures so we know what it says about the future. It is important to study the scriptures instead of allowing our own doctrine to close our hearts to the truth of scripture.

Remember the two disciples on the road to Emmaus? WHY, WHY, WHY did Jesus tell them that they were "slow of heart to believe all the prophets"? Was it because their own doctrine betrayed them? Yes!!! They were taught something else and they believed that more than what the scripture had said. Could that be true of us today?—thus the subtitle of this book "Betrayed by My Own Doctrine". For the most part, we have been taught we are not going to have to go through the tribulation, but we are. If we know prophecy, then we will be prepared for it and know that it is only for three and a half years and then it will be over. The prophecies of His return and of us reigning with Him for a thousand years will be of great comfort to us as God's people at that time, like Joseph's dreams comforted him!

Joseph was thrown into prison and interpreted two more dreams. These were the dreams of the butler and the baker who were also thrown into prison with Joseph. The butler saw three grape vines. He squeezed the grapes into

Pharaoh's cup. Joseph said in three days you will be restored to your position. How did Joseph know that it would only be three days, instead of three weeks or three months, or three years? I don't know, but he knew and it was right and it did happen. The chief baker also had a dream of three baskets of baked goods on his head and the birds of the air ate the goods. Joseph told him that in three days his head would be cut off and Pharaoh would hang his body up for the birds to pick the flesh off his bones. The third day after this was Pharaoh's birthday and it all came to pass. I am sure that this was a great encouragement to Joseph. He saw that he had it right and if he had the dreams of those men right, his dreams would soon come to pass for himself, also.

Let's talk about when Joseph interpreted Pharaoh's (again) two dreams which got him out of prison. Pharaoh saw seven fat cows coming up out of the Nile, followed by seven starving cows. Then he saw seven fat ears of corn being eaten up by seven skinny ears. Joseph revealed that seven years of plenty were coming before seven years of famine. Since the dreams didn't tell Pharaoh what to do, Joseph took that liberty on himself. Joseph told Pharaoh to appoint a man to store up the food in the good years, so that he will have food to distribute in the time of famine. He said that God was telling Pharaoh what He was about to do in the future, and in so many words, he should ACT on it.

Again, this is very pertinent for our day. The false prophecy teachers have told us half the truth—a persecution and a tribulation are coming—then they say, "Don't worry. The rapture is going to take us out of here before the "shoe falls". The truth of the matter is we are not going to be raptured at that time. We will have to go through both the persecution and the tribulation. (The proof of that will come in a later book.) If we, the church, had prophecy right and we knew we were going to have to go through both the great persecution and the great tribulation, and we had the wisdom of Joseph we would prepare, the best we could, for it. The story of Joseph illustrates in living color HOW IMPORTANT PROPHECY is. It could save your life and the lives of your loved ones.

What did prophecy do for Joseph? What did prophecy do for Pharaoh? What did prophecy do for all of Joseph's family? Number one: because Joseph had the gift of interpreting prophetic dreams—only six in his life, and six was enough—he never lost hope in prison. It got him out of prison, and made him, probably even above Pharaoh, the most respected man in Egypt. It also brought him much wealth. Tell me prophecy doesn't benefit people. By the time the famine was over, it made Egypt one of the richest nations at that time and Pharaoh with it. It saved all of Joseph's household. They might all have died of hunger if Joseph hadn't have known the future and prepared for it. The Lord used Joseph to fulfill the prophecy that was given to Abraham that his posterity would go down to Egypt for 400 years. It was there that they grew into a mighty nation. Can you see prophecy is important and we should act on it?!

HOW DID PROPHECY SAVE DANIEL'S LIFE?

Daniel was part of the captives taken to Babylon, after Nebuchadnezzar conquered Jerusalem. Daniel was one of the wise men of Babylon. Nebuchadnezzar, the king, had a dream. (This sounds like a repeat of Joseph's life.) This story is recorded in Daniel chapter two. It appears that the king couldn't remember the dream, so he required his wise men to repeat the dream and give the interpretation. None of them could do this, so he commanded that they all be killed. Daniel gets notified that he is to be killed, and he inquires from Arioch the reason for the extermination. Arioch explains it to him, and Daniel requests an audience with the king. He is brought in and requests time to get the answer. He is granted some time. He finds his three Hebrew friends and explains it to them and they begin to seek God for the answer. When your life is at stake it has a way of building a fire underneath you. At that point you really only have two choices: either hear from God or die. They sought God and He answered. God knows how to put you in a place where you will know God's calling on your life. This set the stage for the rest of Daniel's life. After this he entered into a ministry of prophecy.

The dream, like Pharaoh's dream, was a dream of the future and God had a man there to interpret it. Prophecy was cloaked in a dream, like Joseph's dreams. Prophecy can come in more than one way. The dream was that of an image of a statue made up of four different metals: gold, silver, brass, iron, and iron mixed with clay. These represented four different world kingdoms that would come in the future, one after the other. The fourth would metamorphose into another different looking empire. After the transformation of the fourth, the Lord would come and set up a kingdom that would never pass away. Daniel repeated the dream to the king and gave the interpretation. What happened? Number one, it saved his life, but there's more. Nebuchadnezzar falls down and starts worshiping Daniel and he gives him many beautiful and wonderful gifts. The king made Daniel great. He made him ruler over the whole province of Babylon, and head governor over all the wise men.

If you were to ask Daniel, "Did understanding dreams and knowing the future benefit you?" What do you think he would say? Absolutely! If knowing prophecy benefited Joseph and Daniel, do you think that knowing prophecy would benefit you? Absolutely. It could save your life, the lives of your loved ones and could even benefit you financially. Yes, it took some work—fasting and prayer—for Daniel and his friends to hear from God, but, oh my, it was worth it. Let's give ourselves to prophecy. Keep reading this book and see if there are not some wonderful answers in it.

OBJECTION TO KNOWING THE FUTURE ANSWERED

Not long ago a Bible college classmate of mine from years gone by, and now a missionary, ministered at my church. In his field of labor he had been appointed as the prophecy teacher of their foreign Bible college. He didn't ask for the job and it wasn't his forte, if you know what I mean, and thus he told me that he introduces his class with Acts 1:6-7:

> Act 1:6 "When they therefore were come together, they asked of him, saying, Lord, wilt thou at this time restore again the kingdom to Israel?"
>
> Act 1:7 "And he said unto them, **It is not for you to know the times or the seasons, which the Father hath put in his own power.**"

A lot of people feel this way about prophecy. It is not for us to know the future so why study prophecy in the first place? It's a waste of time. Should we take these verses like that? I have a firm conviction that those who take this passage like that are taking it the wrong way, but I see how easy it would be to take it like that. At any rate, these verses need to be addressed, so let's do that. To get started then, let's look at a verse in 2 Timothy 2:

> 2 Ti 2:15 "Study to shew thyself approved unto God, a workman that needeth not to be ashamed, **rightly dividing the word of truth.**"

Yes, the word of God must be rightly divided. If the scriptures are taken incorrectly they can destroy, and even kill you. Look at Hebrews 4:

> Heb 4:12 "For **the word of God** is quick, and **powerful,** and **sharper than any twoedged sword, piercing even to the dividing asunder of soul and spirit**, and of the joints and marrow, and is a discerner of the thoughts and intents of the heart."

This verse is letting us know that the Bible is like a sword that is as sharp as a new razor blade. If a person was to take a sharp sword and start waving it around wildly, they could hurt someone, even themselves. They could cut their own leg off or even their head. This can be illustrated by a story from my mother when she worked in a small hamburger restaurant. She had a butcher knife in her hand and she was distracted for a minute and before she knew it she had jammed the knife into her leg. She was rushed to the hospital and the doctor told her, she just missed her main artery by a quarter inch. It shows what can happen when you're not careful. In like manner we must be careful and prayerful in handling the word of God. Look at 2 Peter:

> 2 Pe 3:15 "And account that the longsuffering of our Lord is salvation; even as our beloved brother Paul also according to the wisdom given unto him hath written unto you;"

> 2 Pe 3:16 "As also in all his epistles, speaking in them of these things; in which are **some things hard to**

> be understood, which they that are unlearned and unstable wrest, as they do also the other scriptures, unto their own destruction."
>
> 2 Pe 3:17 "Ye therefore, beloved, seeing ye know these things before, **beware lest ye** also, being led away with the error of the wicked, **fall from your own steadfastness.**"
>
> 2 Pe 3:18 "But **grow in** grace, and in **the knowledge** of our Lord and Saviour Jesus Christ. To him be glory both now and for ever. Amen."

Peter comes right out and tells us that if we misunderstand the word of God it can destroy us. As the Bible says, it is like a sharp sword. With that being said, are there any safe guards? Yes, there are a few. Let's look at 2 Thessalonians 2:

> 2 Th 2:10 "And with all deceivableness of unrighteousness in them that perish; because they received not **the love of the truth**, that they might be saved."
>
> 2 Th 2:11 "And **for this cause God shall send them strong delusion, that they should believe a lie:**"

2 Th 2:12 "**That they all might be damned who believed not the truth,** but had pleasure in unrighteousness."

One of the main ways to keep God from sending us strong delusion is to LOVE THE TRUTH. He didn't say KNOW the truth; He said, "LOVE the truth". The Lord wants us to throw away our biases, preconceived ideas, and crusty, generational traditions, and lean solely on the word of God for our instruction. This is not to say that we can't read the words of men, but when it comes to dividing hairs, we must make sure that it is Biblical. Another main thing is to let the Bible INTERPRET ITSELF. In that way we can be sure we have it right. Look at 2 Timothy 3:

2 Ti 3:16 "**All scripture** is given by inspiration of God, and **is profitable for doctrine, for reproof, for correction, for instruction in righteousness:**"

2 Ti 3:17 "That the **man of God may be perfect, thoroughly furnished unto all good works**."

What does this mean? How do we get the Bible to interpret itself? We get ALL the verses on one subject and put them all together and let each passage explain the other passages. Believe it or not, I would dare say most churches do not do that and largely, that is why there are so many churches and doctrines that we've embraced that have betrayed us. I must repeat what I said earlier: approach the word of God in the fear of God, respectfully, reverently, and prayerfully. Without God's help we would never get it right. With that being said, let's look at the prophecy concept of Acts 1 the same way. Let's get some more verses on prophecy to help us understand the meaning of this passage. At first glance it does appear that the Lord is saying we cannot know the future, but is He really saying that? Does He say that anywhere else in scripture? If that is the only place it is found, maybe we are misunderstanding it. How does it talk about prophecy in other places? First, let's look at another passage in Matthew 24:

> Mat 24:1 "And Jesus went out, and departed from the temple: and his disciples came to him for to shew him the buildings of the temple."

> Mat 24:2 "And Jesus said unto them, See ye not all these things? verily I say unto you, There shall not be left here one stone upon another, that shall not be thrown down."

> Mat 24:3 "And as he sat upon the mount of Olives, **the disciples came unto him privately, saying, Tell us, when shall these things be? and what shall be the sign of thy coming, and of the end of the world?**"

Mat 24:4 "And Jesus answered and said unto them, **Take heed that no man deceive you.**"

Mat 24:5 "For **many shall come in my name**, saying, I am Christ; and shall deceive many."

The disciples came to Jesus and asked in so many words, "When is the the end of the world coming?" Does Jesus say, "It is not for you to know the times or the seasons, which the Father hath put in his own power." No! What does He say? As I said earlier, He tells them to be very careful that no man deceives them and then starts giving them a list of things of how they will know when it is coming. If Jesus didn't want them or us to know the future, He wouldn't have given us all the signs to look for. In John 13:19 and again in John 14, He comes right out and tells us plainly the purpose of prophecy:

Joh 14:29 "And now **I have told you before it come to pass, that, when it is come to pass, ye might believe.**"

The Lord has told us what is going to happen in the future so that when it is come to pass our faith and trust in Him will be increased. Obviously, there is some benefit in knowing the future. This sounds very similar to the benefit of prophecy in general that Paul gives us in 1 Corinthians 14. Paul gives the purpose of prophecy in verse 3:

> 1 Co 14:3 "But he that prophesieth speaketh unto men to edification, and exhortation, and comfort."

Look at what prophecy will do. It will edify or build you up. It will exhort you or call you back to the right path. It will comfort you. Sounds pretty good to me. In this chapter Paul is teaching us that speaking in tongues when given as a message in the congregation needs to be interpreted, and when it is, is equal to prophecy. If it is not interpreted, tongues by itself compared to prophecy is not equal to it. In fact, Prophecy is better, and more beneficial. Look at verse 24:

> 1 Co 14:24 "But **if all prophesy**, and there come in one that believeth not, or one unlearned, **he is convinced of all, he is judged of all:**"

> 1 Co 14:25 **"And thus are the secrets of his heart made manifest; and so falling down on his face he will worship God, and report that God is in you of a truth."**

That sounds pretty impressive to me, but somebody will say, "That kind of prophecy is not talking about giving future events." Yes, it does include future events, but it also includes, as I said earlier, forth-telling, which is what a lot of this is talking about. Here's the deal. If the Lord does use us to give future events and they do come to pass, the people will be greatly amazed and fall down and confess that "God is in you of a truth." Not only this, but let me point out that in the first verse and in the second to the last verse Paul embellishes this even more:

> 1 Co 14:1 "Follow after charity, and desire spiritual gifts, **but rather that ye may prophesy.**"

> 1 Co 14:39 "Wherefore, brethren, **covet to prophesy**, and forbid not to speak with tongues."

Did you understand what he is saying? He said that prophecy is the BEST gift to desire and flat out that we should "covet" or GREATLY DESIRE to prophecy. This sounds like a repeat of Isaiah 45:11 which I have already talked about, but let's give it again:

> Isa 45:11 "Thus saith the LORD, the Holy One of Israel, and his Maker, **Ask me of things to come** concerning my sons, and concerning the work of my hands **command ye me**."

The Lord, over and over again is telling us how IMPORTANT prophecy is. He tells us to ask and even command to know the future. John underscores this in Revelation 1, through the inspiration of the Holy Ghost, that those who read, hear, and obey the words of prophecy will be BLESSED!

> Rev 1:3 "**Blessed is he that readeth**, and they that **hear the words of this prophecy**, and **keep those things** which are written therein: for the time is at hand."

If God says, through His apostles and prophets, that we should read, hear and obey prophecy, how can anyone say we shouldn't study prophecy? The Lord continues emphasizing this again in chapter 19:

> Rev 19:10 "And I fell at his feet to worship him. And he said unto me, See thou do it not: I am thy fellow servant, and of thy brethren that have the testimony of Jesus: worship God: for **the testimony of Jesus is the spirit of prophecy.**"

What does this mean? If you are wanting to win souls, it is very effective to give your testimony, or your account of how the Lord brought you to Himself, but there is a greater testimony than your own, and that is Jesus' testimony. Which one is that? It is the one found in prophecy and consists of prophecy. When you relate how the Lord has told the future hundreds and thousands of years in advance and then you show how it all came to pass in the smallest detail, it gets people's attention. You could say that prophecy is the most powerful and the most Biblical form of evangelism that exists today. (This is why the name of this ministry is: Endtime Survival Crusades And Prophecy Evangelism, better known as ESCAPE Ministries.)

Mark Hitchcock on page 4 of his book, THE END (published by Tyndale 2012), uses John MacArthur's figures to say that 27 percent of the Bible is prophecy (Kerby Anderson differs by 2 percent). God must think it is pretty important to include that much of it in His word. He wants us to use it to win the lost, but to use it, we must KNOW it, and to know it we must STUDY it! People say, "Nobody agrees on it. Nobody really knows what it means, anyway, so why bother?" That is all the more reason to study it. Then you will hear someone say, "It's too confusing. It is easier to study other subjects." Just because other subjects are easier, doesn't make them better. Yes, I admit that it can be difficult to know the truth about future events, but that doesn't mean we shouldn't try to know the future and decipher it. Actually, the devil doesn't want you to study or know the future because that way he can surprise you with it and lead you to destruction through your ignorance of it. Don't listen to the enemy. It appears we have a little more time to study it, so let's do that, and maybe this book will help you do that very thing!

Now, let's go back to our verse in Acts 1. What did it say?

> Act 1:7 "And he said unto them, **It is not for you to know the times or the seasons, which the Father hath put in his own power.**"

If the Lord does want us to know the future, why did He say this? Let me try and give the sense of this, because it is important that you understand it. In this setting, the apostles were no different than the whole Jewish nation. As I wrote earlier, they were taught the meaning of certain prophetic texts. These meanings were passed down from generation to generation. It had been passed down for so long that it was now part of their tradition. I am referring to the texts that specify that the Messiah would restore the kingdom to that which was like David's kingdom. It was a world class kingdom. In handing down these prophecies they conveniently left out the suffering verses, as I stated earlier. He did try to tell them that He was going to have to suffer first, but they didn't seem to grasp it. To top that off, if Jesus had of flat out told them that it was going to be 2,000 years before that prophecy was going to be fulfilled they may have got discouraged. At that moment they couldn't handle it. In other words they asked Him about the restoration of the kingdom, but He gives them a short insight; and then changes the subject to get them off the subject.

These 11 men are about to turn the world upside down after His departure. If they had of thought that it would be 2000 years before His return, they might have said to themselves, "We have plenty of time". If He discourages these men in the least, it could diffuse or postpone the fulfillment of their mission. He must not let that happen. He is the Master communicator. He knows what we need to know at the time we need to know it, and this was not their time to know it. They didn't even have the Holy Ghost yet. They were going to need that first, so He postpones giving them the information they asked for. After all, Daniel had already revealed to us that some things about the future were only meant for the end time generation. Look at Daniel chapters 8 and 12:

> Dan 8:26 "And the vision of the evening and the morning which was told is true: wherefore **shut thou up the vision; for it shall be for many days.**"

> Dan 12:8 "And I heard, but I understood not: then said I, **O my Lord, what shall be the end of these things?**"

> Dan 12:9 "And he said, Go thy way, Daniel: for **the words are closed up and sealed till the time of the end.**"

> Dan 12:10 "Many shall be purified, and made white, and tried; but the wicked shall do wickedly: and **none of the wicked shall understand; but the wise shall understand.**"

The Lord had revealed so many things to Daniel, but he did not understand everything that came to him. Actually, he didn't understand most of what he saw. In chapter 8 the Lord says for him to shut the vision up for many days. How long is that? In chapter 12 the Lord gets more specific. He says the words are closed up until the time of the END. That is probably what He was referring to in chapter 8. Guess what? THIS is the time of the END, but when the apostles asked Him about the restoration of the kingdom, that wasn't the time of the end. Those words were shut up to them, but that doesn't apply to us today, because this is the time of the end! Those words were meant for us in our time! It is now time to know "the times" and "the seasons which the Father hath put in his own power." THIS IS THE GENERATION which was designed to receive the words of Daniel and of Jesus! So now we know what Jesus meant in Acts 1:6-7. Prophecy is important, so let us arise, read, study, obey, and act upon the words of prophecy!

WHAT IS THE KEY TO KNOWING THE FUTURE?

The question is, do WE, or do YOU, really want to know what He has said? The way to unlock any door is to have the key. The key to knowing the future is DESIRE. The verse I gave above, Isaiah 45:11, is full of desire—ask, and command—speaks of desire. It is not any kind of desire. It is STRONG desire. Strong desire is the key, not only to prophecy but also eternal life. Look at Revelation 21 and Isaiah 55:

> Rev 21:6 "And he said unto me, It is done. I am Alpha and Omega, the beginning and the end. **I will give unto him that is athirst of the fountain of the water of life freely.**"

> Isa 55:1 "Ho, **every one that thirsteth,** come ye to the waters, and he that hath no money; come ye, buy, and eat; yea, come, buy wine and milk without money and without price."

Strong desire is what the Lord is looking for, not this—"give it to me if you want to"; "take it or leave it"; "makes no difference to me"; "I don't care"—kind of stuff. The same desire that will lead a person to salvation, by-passing all the deceptive paths around it, will also lead him to know and understand prophecy. Prophecy isn't for everyone, and it isn't for people who have a "ho hum" approach to it.

To say that having a strong desire is the only thing a person needs to have, to understand prophecy, is an understatement. By saying that, I am assuming a lot. I am assuming that a person is a member of God's family. Normally, God doesn't reveal a lot of His secrets to "non-family members". One needs to be SAVED and born again—now, that is really opening up a cacophony of theological thought. What I am saying is, salvation is a much debated subject. The purpose of this writing is not to delve into that to any great degree, but perhaps a few brush strokes would be in order. As stated elsewhere in this writing, I have a separate book that explains my position on New Testament salvation in minute detail. So what are we talking about? The majority believe salvation is by faith only. (Guess what? The majority is not always right.) Others include faith and repentance. Others say it is faith, repentance, and water baptism, and yet others, throw in the baptism of the Holy Ghost. Most all of them say that living a Godly life is a result of that conversion. How one defines living a Godly life is also up for grabs. Personally, in regards to salvation, I'm sticking with Peter who had the keys to the kingdom of heaven. He lays out the plan of salvation in the fewest words possible in Acts 2:

> Act 2:38 "Then Peter said unto them, **Repent**, and be **baptized** every one of you in the name of Jesus Christ for the remission of sins, and ye shall **receive the gift of the Holy Ghost**."

In a nutshell, Peter says to repent, be baptized in Jesus name, and get the Holy Ghost. I'll buy that, so being saved is first and foremost. (I'm sorry, but I have to throw this in: Peter doesn't even say you have to believe. Why? It's because it is understood. You won't do any of these things unless you do believe. These things PROVE you believe.)

Next, is having a DAILY RELATIONSHIP WITH THE LORD. This is all foundational to being qualified to perceiving the secrets of God. Daniel had a relationship with God. Look at Daniel 6:

> Dan 6:10 "Now when Daniel knew that the writing was signed, he went into his house; and his windows being open in his chamber toward Jerusalem, **he kneeled upon his knees three times a day, and**

prayed, and gave thanks before his God, as he did aforetime."

Daniel did have a relationship with God. He kept the communication lines open. In our world today it is so easy to get too busy. It is never a waste of time to pray. PRAYING is the number one vehicle to understanding prophecy and God's word in general. This was Daniel's secret. In Daniel 2 it is implied that he and his Jewish companions prayed to God for the answer. See how it says it:

> Dan 2:17 "Then Daniel went to his house, and made the thing known to Hananiah, Mishael, and Azariah, his companions:"

> Dan 2:18 "That **they would desire mercies of the God of heaven** concerning this secret; that Daniel and his fellows should not perish with the rest of the wise men of Babylon."

> Dan 2:19 "**Then was the secret revealed unto Daniel in a night vision.** Then Daniel blessed the God of heaven."

Not only did Daniel pray, but he also STUDIED the word of God like we should do. Look at Daniel 9:

> Dan 9:2 "In the first year of his reign **I Daniel understood by books the number of the years, whereof the word of the LORD came to Jeremiah the prophet**, that he would accomplish seventy years in the desolations of Jerusalem."

FASTING is another vehicle that can open up our hearts and minds to God's word. Fasting can be in many forms. It includes giving up something for God, usually food. In the Bible, only on rare occasions did fasting include both food and water, and that was for only 3 days. It is important to drink water when giving up all food. Some have heard of the Daniel's fast, just eating vegetables. Books have been written on fasting. One can fast a meal, a day, or two or three days or more and of course when joined together with prayer throws one into high gear in getting close to God. It is even more powerful when two, three or more people do it at the same time. One needs to be in good health. Be wise about it. I called a three day fast once and my grandfather-in-law was about 70 years old and he didn't want to be left out. He ended up in the hospital and guess who was to blame? Yours truly. Daniel used both fasting and prayer skillfully. It talks about it in Daniel 9 and 10:

> Dan 9:3 "And I set my face unto the Lord God, **to seek by prayer** and supplications, **with fasting**, and sackcloth, and ashes:"

Dan 10:2 "In those days **I Daniel was mourning three full weeks.**"

Dan 10:3 "**I ate no pleasant bread, neither came flesh nor wine in my mouth**, neither did I anoint myself at all, **till three whole weeks were fulfilled.**"

Mourning speaks of crying out in prayer. Getting desperate in prayer is powerful. Do you fall asleep, or half asleep when you are praying? Daniel didn't and he got results. Being in desperation really gets God's attention.

Desire can be expressed in all these ways. If you really want to know God's word, you can know it. Get saved, pray daily, and even two, three or more times a day. Fast a day, a week or more and you will hear from on High.

ONLY THE LORD CAN REVEAL SECRETS

A person can read the words of prophecy right in front of them and never see it unless the Lord quickens it to them. So, as you might suspect, this book is not for everybody, but it is for somebody. Is it for you? This is a perfect place to say, that if this book is for you, let us approach it with humility, as Daniel did and in an attitude of prayer that God will enlighten our eyes, hearts, and minds. This is a book on prophecy, so let's get this straight, I CANNOT REVEAL PROPHECY. I can put insights on paper and give the sense of the matter, but ONLY GOD can reveal it, so if anything is revealed to you while reading, studying, and praying over this material, ALL THE PRAISE goes to the Lord of Hosts! If I have any understanding of God or of prophecy, it is not because I am smart or because I am of the right lineage, or because of anything else, except that I am hungry and thirsty for truth, myself. I cannot even boast of that on my own. God Himself put that in my heart, and if He did that for me, who knows, maybe He will even do it for you! Hey, I am nobody special. The Lord will be gracious and merciful to whom He will be gracious and merciful. I have never seen the shape of the Most High, but Moses has. Look at Exodus 33 to see how God was merciful and gracious to him:

Exo 33:18 "And he said, I beseech thee, **shew me thy glory.**"

Exo 33:19 "And he said, I will make all my goodness pass before thee, and I will proclaim the name of the LORD before thee; and **will be gracious to whom I will be gracious, and will shew mercy on whom I will shew mercy.**"

Exo 33:20 "And he said, Thou canst not see my face: for there shall no man see me, and live."

Exo 33:21 "And the LORD said, Behold, there is a place by me, and thou shalt stand upon a rock:"

Exo 33:22 "And it shall come to pass, while my glory passeth by, that I will put thee in a clift of the rock, and will cover thee with my hand while I pass by:"

Exo 33:23 "And I will take away mine hand, and **thou shalt see my back parts: but my face shall not be seen.**"

God did that for Moses. Who knows what He will do for you if you seek Him with all of your heart. Look at Deuteronomy 4:

Deu 4:29 "But **if** from thence **thou shalt seek the LORD thy God, thou shalt find him, if thou seek him with all thy heart and with all thy soul.**"

And when you come to Him, you must come in full assurance that He will hear and answer your prayer. Look at Hebrews 11:

Heb 11:6 "But **without faith it is impossible to please him**: for he that cometh to God must believe that he is, and that **he is a rewarder of them that diligently seek him.**"

Serving the Lord is never dull, dry, and boring. It is action filled and alive. Let us arise, seek Him, and desire to prophesy and know the future. We will be blessed beyond measure if we will do it. Do you remember what the Lord said to Abraham in Genesis 15?

> Gen 15:1 "After these things the word of the LORD came unto Abram in a vision, saying, Fear not, Abram: **I am thy shield, and thy exceeding great reward.**"

If you and I will seek Him, He will be found of us. He is wanting to woo you and me to Himself. If we can find Him, we will find His secrets and He will definitely be our EXCEEDING GREAT REWARD. Prophecy can be the tool that will cause us to want to draw near to the Lord. Prophecy as you can see is important!

"HOW IMPORTANT IS PROPHECY?" STUDY QUESTIONS
(Open Book Quiz)

1. What does the Hebrew word "Nebuwah" mean?

2. Who was the first prophet?

3-4. God said that He would make Abraham's seed like what two things?

5. God commands His people to do what in Isaiah 45?

6. How are we to know the word which the Lord has spoken?

7-12. Fill in the blanks of the following verse found in Ecclesiastes 3:15: "That which hath ___ is ___; and that which is___ ___, hath ___ ___; and God requireth that which is past.

13-14. Why did God want Joseph to share his dreams with his brothers? Two reasons.

15. How would this help Joseph?

16. How many dreams did Joseph have in his whole life?

17-18. What two kinds of work did it take for Daniel and his friends to hear from God?

19-20. God said in II Thessalonians the He would send those that perish a strong delusion to believe a lie. Give two reasons.

Bonus Questions:

21. Finish this verse in I Corinthians 14:1: "Follow after charity, and desire spiritual gifts, but rather that ye may ___."

22. What is the key to knowing the future?

"HOW IMPORTANT IS PROPHECY?"
(Quiz Answers)

1. A prediction spoken or written

2. The Lord Himself

3-4. As the stars of heaven and as the dust of the earth.

5. Ask me of things to come concerning my sons and the work of my hands.

6. If the prophecy comes to pass it is of the Lord, and if not the prophecy is not of God.

7-12. Been, now, to be, already been

13-14. So they would be jealous of him and hate him.

15. So the dreams would come to pass

16. 2

17-18. Prayer and fasting

19-20. Because they received not the love of the truth and they did not believe the truth.

Bonus Answers:

21. Prophesy

22. Strong desire

THE IMPORTANCE OF PUNCTUATION

A mother sent a text message to her daughter after an important person in her life let her down. It read:

One comma can change the whole meaning of a sentence. The original Greek and Hebrew had no punctuation, so what punctuation is in the Bible was inserted by the translators. Therefore the best way to make sure we are understanding a verse properly is to understand it in light of every other verse in the Bible on that subject. That would be like letting the Bible interpret itself. We need to keep that in mind before making up our mind on any particular subject of doctrine or prophecy in the Bible.

Chapter Two:
THE FOUR BEASTS AND FOUR AND TWENTY ELDERS

Here are two groups of people that are not easily identified in and of themselves. There is a way to identify them and that is what we are going to do, but first let's give the scripture that reveals their existence in the book of Revelation:

> Rev 4:4 "And round about the throne *were* four and twenty seats: and upon the seats I saw **four and twenty elders** sitting, clothed in white raiment; and they had on their heads crowns of gold."

> Rev 4:5 "And out of the throne proceeded lightnings and thunderings and voices: and *there were* seven lamps of fire burning before the throne, which are the seven Spirits of God."

> Rev 4:6 "And before the throne *there was* a sea of glass like unto crystal: and in the midst of the throne, and round about the throne, *were* **four beasts** full of eyes before and behind."

Rev 4:7 "And the first beast *was* like a lion, and the second beast like a calf, and the third beast had a face as a man, and the fourth beast *was* like a flying eagle."

Rev 4:8 "And the **four beasts** had each of them six wings about *him;* and *they were* full of eyes within: and they rest not day and night, saying, Holy, holy, holy, Lord God Almighty, which was, and is, and is to come."

Rev 4:9 "And when those **beasts** give glory and honour and thanks to him that sat on the throne, who liveth for ever and ever,"

Rev 4:10 "**The four and twenty** elders fall down before him that sat on the throne, and worship him that liveth for ever and ever, and cast their crowns before the throne, saying,"

Rev 4:11 "Thou art worthy, O Lord, to receive glory and honour and power: for thou hast created all things, and for thy pleasure they are and were created."

1. THE FOUR and TWENTY ELDERS represents the Jewish leg of the CHURCH, or you could say they are the Jewish redeemed ones.

2. The FOUR BEASTS represent the Gentile leg of the CHURCH, or you could say they are the Gentile redeemed ones.

How does one know this? There are NINE ways to unmask their identity, and we will do that one at a time. When you read my chapter on the TWO WITNESSES, you will notice a similarity between these two groups of people. There is a repetition of style and mystery. The Lord has a M.O.—a mode of operation. Once you figure out his M.O. in one area, He often will repeat that M.O. in another area or in another topic. If you miss His M.O. in one area, then you will be just as much or more in the dark in another topic. That is what is going on here. The CHURCH is consistently divided into TWO groups.(That is why you see the numbers 2, 4, and 8 show up with much regularity. Again, more is discussed about that in the chapter on the TWO WITNESSES and it is illustrated here once more with these TWO groups.)

I.

The Jewish leaders in the Old and New Testament were called ELDERS. There are over 150 references referring to these leaders. In Revelation 4, it calls them "FOUR and

TWENTY" or 24. The number 12 speaks of completion and a double 12 would be double completion. You can see how the word is used in Exodus:

> Exo 3:16 "Go, and gather the **elders of Israel** together, and say unto them, The LORD God of your fathers, the God of Abraham, of Isaac, and of Jacob, appeared unto me, saying, I have surely visited you, and *seen* that which is done to you in Egypt:"

In the Old Testament in multiple places the Gentiles were depicted as animals and in Daniel 7, the Gentile ruling kingdoms were specifically named as not only BEASTS, but FOUR great BEASTS!

> Dan 7:3 "And **four** great **beasts** came up from the sea, diverse one from another."

Jesus Himself referred to the Gentiles as being animals in Matthew:

> Mat 15:22 "And, behold, **a woman of Canaan** came out of the same coasts, and cried unto him, saying, Have mercy on me, O Lord, *thou* Son of David; my daughter is grievously vexed with a devil."

> Mat 15:26 "But he answered and said, It is not meet to take the children's bread, and to cast *it* to **dogs**."

> Mat 15:27 "And she said, Truth, Lord: yet the **dogs** eat of the crumbs which fall from their masters' table."

Paul even quotes Deuteronomy 32:21 where God infers He is talking about the Gentiles and He says they are not people and if they are not people, then they must be animals, hence BEASTS. He does this in Romans 10.

> Rom 10:19 "But I say, Did not Israel know? First Moses saith, I will provoke you to jealousy by *them that are* **no people**, *and* by a foolish nation I will anger you."

Thus we have, as our first point, shown that the **24 ELDERS** refers to the Jews and the **FOUR BEASTS** refers to the Gentiles, but these are not normal Jews and Gentiles as we will see.

II.

Verses 4 and 6 tell us that both these groups are round about the throne: "And **round about the throne** were four and twenty seats: and upon the seats I saw **four and twenty elders** sitting...and in the midst of the throne, and **round about the throne**, were **four beasts** full of eyes before and behind."

Are not we the children of the Lord, Jew and Gentile, around the throne, spiritually, every day talking to the Lord? Look at Hebrews 4:

> Heb 4:16 "**Let us therefore come boldly unto the throne of grace**, that we may obtain mercy, and find grace to help in time of need."

If we are coming boldly UNTO the throne of grace, we are also AROUND IT. Revelation chapter 7 speaks even more plainly about this:

> Rev 7:9 "After this I beheld, and, lo, **a great multitude**, which no man could number, of all nations, and kindreds, and people, and tongues, **stood before the throne**, and before the Lamb, clothed with white robes, and palms in their hands;"

> Rev 7:14 "...These are they which came out of great tribulation, and have washed their robes, and made them white in the blood of the Lamb."

> Rev 7:15 "Therefore are they **before the throne of God**, and serve him day and night in his temple: and **he that sitteth on the throne shall dwell among them.**"

This great multitude is described in more detail in the chapter entitled THE 144,000, but since they've washed their garments white in the blood of the Lamb, they are the redeemed of the Lord. Where do they dwell? They are BEFORE the throne and He that sits on the throne shall "dwell AMONG" them. Therefore, they are AROUND the throne! Again, Revelation 22 speaks to this very idea:

> Rev 22:3 "And there shall be no more curse: but **the throne of God and of the Lamb shall be in it**; and his servants shall serve him:"

God's throne is in the middle of the city of God and the saints are all around it. It is clear, the 24 elders and the 4 beasts are portraying the saints of the living God—Jew and Gentile, alike.

III.

The BEASTS in Revelation 4 were not only around the throne they were IN THE MIDST OF THE THRONE. How does it read?

> Rev 4:6 "And before the throne there was a sea of glass like unto crystal: and **in the midst of the throne**, and round about the throne, were **four beasts** full of eyes before and behind."

Are the saints IN God's throne? Look at Revelation 3:

> Rev 3:21 "To him that overcometh will I grant **to sit with me in my throne**, even as I also overcame, and am set down with my Father in his throne."

Sure enough, whatever the 4 BEASTS are doing, the SAINTS are doing. Yes, it specifically references the Beasts as being in the midst of the throne and the 4 Beasts represent the Gentiles, right? Right, but the 24 Elders or saved Jews are AROUND the throne. Does that mean the saved Gentiles have a more exalted place than the saved Jews? Personally, I don't think that is what the Lord is trying to imply here. I will guarantee you that if they are around the throne, they will also be IN the throne right alongside the Gentiles up in heaven. The main idea is that the 4 Beasts and the 24 Elders are portraying the saints of the living God!

IV.

Both the 4 BEASTS and the 24 ELDERS are worshiping God.

> Rev 4:8 "And the four beasts...rest not day and night, saying, Holy, holy, holy, Lord God Almighty, which was, and is, and is to come."

> Rev 4:9 "And when those beasts give glory and honour and thanks to him that sat on the throne, who liveth for ever and ever,"

> Rev 4:10 "The four and twenty elders fall down before him that sat on the throne, and worship him that liveth for ever and ever, and cast their crowns before the throne..."

Worshiping God is one of the main activities of those who are called saints, whether they are Jews or Gentiles. Look at Psalms 95 and John 4:

> Psa 95:6 "O come, let us worship and bow down: let us kneel before the LORD our maker."

> Joh 4:23 "But the hour cometh, and now is, when the true worshippers shall **worship the Father** in spirit and in truth: for the **Father seeketh such to worship him**."

> Joh 4:24 "God is a Spirit: and they that worship him **must worship him in spirit and in** truth."

Both the 4 BEASTS and the 24 ELDERS worship God and are the SAINTS of the Living God.

V.

When the Beasts give glory, honor, and thanks to the Lord it PROVOKES the 24 ELDERS to jealousy. Read the verses again.

> Rev 4:9 "And when **those beasts give glory and honour and thanks to him that sat on the throne, who liveth for ever and ever**,"

> Rev 4:10 "The **four and twenty elders fall down before him that sat on the throne, and worship him** that liveth for ever and ever, and cast their crowns before the throne..."

Let me repeat the verse in Romans where Paul is quoting Moses in Deuteronomy 32:21 where it is prophesied that the saved Gentiles would cause jealousy among the Jews.

> Rom 10:19 "But I say, Did not Israel know? First Moses saith, **I will provoke you to jealousy by them that are no people, and by a foolish nation I will anger you.**"

> Rom 11:11 "I say then, Have they stumbled that they should fall? God forbid: but rather through their fall salvation is come unto the Gentiles, for **to provoke them** [Jews] **to jealousy.**"

Revelation 4 is describing this jealous relationship between the Jews and the Gentiles, thus showing again that this is what the scripture is talking about.

VI.

The ELDERS cast their crowns before the throne:

> Rev 4:10 "**The four and twenty elders** fall down before him that sat on the throne, and worship him that liveth for ever and ever, and **cast their crowns before the throne...**"

These ELDERS had crowns, and we know the Saints of God have crowns as I Peter reminds us:

> 1 Pe 5:4 "And when the chief Shepherd shall appear, **ye shall receive a crown of glory** that fadeth not away."

The Lord promises to His saints that are faithful to Him a "crown of Life."

> Rev 2:10 "Fear none of those things which thou shalt suffer: behold, the devil shall cast some of you into prison, that ye may be tried; and ye shall have tribulation ten days: be thou faithful unto death, and **I will give thee a crown of life.**"

> Rev 3:11 "Behold, I come quickly: hold that fast which thou hast, **that no man take thy crown.**"

Other verses include I Corinthians 9:25; II Timothy 4:8; James 1:12. The ELDERS therefore must be saints.

VII.

The ELDERS and the BEASTS prayed.

> Rev 5:8 "And when he had taken the book, **the four beasts and four and twenty elders** fell down before the Lamb, **having every one of them** harps, and **golden vials full of odours, which are the prayers of saints.**"

They possessed golden vials which were filled with the prayers that they prayed. These are not angels because angels don't pray—they worship. The scriptures never say angels pray. Saints pray. The prayers of the saints are like odors of perfume in a bottle. When the saint of God prays and cries out to the Lord, those tears go into a bottle and someday we will be able to give to our beloved Jesus a bottle of perfume made from those tears. This is what David is inferring in Psalms 56.

> Psa 56:8 "Thou tellest my wanderings: put **thou my tears into thy bottle**: are they not in thy book?"

Revelation links this bottle to a bottle of odors or perfume. As you can see saints pray and in fact they are told to pray without ceasing in I Thessalonians 5:

1Th 5:17 "**Pray without ceasing.**"

This scripture is letting us know, then, that the Elders and the Beasts are we the saints.

VIII.

I have pounded the nail into the wood, but the next verse crimps the nail on the other side, because, guess what? The Beasts and the Elders are REDEEMED! And they are redeemed from EVERY KINDRED, TONGUE, PEOPLE, and NATION:

> Rev 5:9 "And they sung a new song, saying, Thou art worthy to take the book, and to open the seals thereof: for thou wast slain, and **hast redeemed us to God** by thy blood out of **every kindred, and tongue, and people, and nation;**"

The scripture clearly tells us who has been REDEEMED. Look at I Peter 1:

> 1 Pe 1:18 "Forasmuch as ye know that **ye were not redeemed** with corruptible things, as silver and gold, from your vain conversation received by tradition from your fathers;"

> 1 Pe 1:19 "But with the precious blood of Christ, as of a lamb without blemish and without spot:"

The saints of God are the REDEEMED ones and they are divided into two groups—the Jews and the Gentiles, and thus we have the FOUR BEASTS and THE FOUR and TWENTY ELDERS. This is the exact thing we have in the TWO WITNESSES: 1. The TWO OLIVE TREES, and 2. The TWO CANDLESTICKS. It is also the same thing we have in the next point, KINGS and PRIESTS;

IX.

They are KINGS and PRIESTS:

> Rev 5:10 "And hast made **us** unto our God **kings** and **priests**: and we shall reign on the earth."

Where else is this phrase used and who is it talking about? It is used in Revelation 1:

> Rev 1:6 "And hath made **us kings and priests** unto God and his Father; to him be glory and dominion for ever and ever. Amen."

As you can see, it is the saints of the most high God who have been made KINGS and PRIESTS. This is the highest form of recognition that could be given to any individual on earth and the Lord gives it as a title to His chosen people—

the Saints of God, Jew and Gentile and these are the FOUR and TWENTY ELDERS and the FOUR BEASTS!!! The mystery is now solved. I have shown you NINE different ways to prove this.

"THE 4 BEASTS AND THE 4 AND 20 ELDERS" STUDY QUESTIONS
(*Open Book Quiz*)

1. How many ways are there to unlock their identity?

2-3. In the Old and New Testament Jewish leaders were called what and Gentiles were depicted as what?

4-5. As the saints, what two groups are "round about the throne"?

6. As the saints, the Beasts were also where else according to Revelation 4?

7. In Matthew 15 Jesus refers to the woman from Canaan as being an animal. What animal does He name in the plural sense?

8-9. In Romans 11 it says the Gentiles provoke the Jews to jealousy so therefore in Revelation 4 who provokes who to jealousy?

10. I Peter 5:4 says "ye" meaning the saints of God will receive what?

11-12. Revelation 4:10 who has crowns and what do they do with them?

13-14. In Revelation 5:8 it says the 4 Beasts and the 4 and 20 Elders both possess something. What do they possess and what does it represent?

15. In Psalms 56:8 David asked God to do something with his tears. What was it?

16-17. In I Thessalonians 5:17 the saints are told to do what and for how long?

18. In Revelation 5:9 it says that God had done what to them from every kindred, and tongue, and people, and nation?

19-20. Revelation 5:10 says that because God has made us what two things, we shall reign on the earth?

"THE 4 BEASTS AND THE 4 AND 20 ELDERS"
(Quiz Answers)

1. 9

2-3. Elders, Animals

4-5. The 4 and 20 Elders, the 4 Beasts

6. In the midst of the throne.

7. Dogs

8-9. The 4 Beasts provokes the 4 and 20 Elders to jealousy.

10. A crown of glory that fadeth not away.

11-12. The 4 and 20 Elders had crowns and they cast them before the throne.

13-14. They possess harps and golden vials full of odours, which are the prayers of the saints.

15. Put thou my tears into thy bottle.

16-17. Pray without ceasing.

18. God had REDEEMED them from every kindred, and tongue, and people, and nation.

19-20. God has made us KINGS and PRIESTS and we shall reign on the earth.

Signs are interesting. Some signs are true and some are not. I don't think this one is true because everybody is not storing their things at this one self-storage facility (even though to the owner it may "seem" that way to him or her). That can be true about prophecy teachers. They don't all agree, do they? It may "seem" true to them, but is it really? Somebody has to be wrong and it is up to the prophecy student to figure that out. This book is throwing a lot of ideas back on the table for consideration. Please, don't just brush over them and remember what Mark Twain said, "It is easier to fool people than it is to convince them they have been fooled."

Chapter Three:
WHO ARE THE TWO WITNESSES?

... REVEALING THE TRUE TIMING OF THE RAPTURE

WHO ARE THE TWO OLIVE TREES?

FOUR POSSIBLE INTERPRETATIONS

What is the identity of the TWO WITNESSES? We could talk a lot about them and this great ministry that they will have and how they will be killed, etc., but it is their identity that is the most troubling of all, and it is this that deserves the larger discussion. Since the Lord was so gracious to reveal it to me in 1996, I have anxiously been waiting since then to share it with God's people. It is my earnest desire that it will be as great a blessing to you the reader as it was to me back then and still remains to be.

The longest passage dealing with the two witnesses is found in Revelation 11 which is given to you below. The greater question is, "Are they two INDIVIDUALS?" Why even ask this question? Of course they are two individuals. Why would anybody even question that? That's the problem. Nobody even questions that, but it should be questioned. The prophecy scholars have given us their conclusions and they generally fall into THREE interpretations, but there is a fourth that few, if any, have considered that this chapter will expose.

The first theory is that they are Moses and Elijah.

There are some very valid reasons for this:

1. Moses was used in the plagues of Egypt and caused the water to be turned to blood.

2. Elijah was the prophet of fire and slew his enemies with it.

3. Moses and Elijah appeared with Jesus on the Mount of Transfiguration.

Let me say here that the impressive prophecy expert, Mark Hitchcock in his book, THE END, on page 345, makes the following statement, "…Scripture clearly identifies the two witnesses as individual people." In this statement he uses the word, "clearly". To me it is not so clearly. On page 348 he then proceeds to tell us that they are Moses and Elijah and includes my point three to verify the suggestion and adds a second point which I omitted. Malachi 4:4-5 mentions both these two men being at the end of the Old Testament. It's a good point which I failed to catch, but still isn't good enough to convince me. The problem with Elijah is that Jesus said Elijah had already come and his name was John the Baptist. If he has already come will he come again? It's possible, but not very likely. In Matthew 17:12 Jesus said that Elias was come already. He didn't at all imply or indicate he was coming again after that, so it is not very likely that Elijah will be one of the two witnesses. This, at least, lessons the possibility of this being true. It also does the same to the third view, which follows shortly.

The second theory is that they are Moses and Enoch.

In one sentence it could be said, this view is not as popular, but is held by some.

The third view is that they are Enoch and Elijah.

This, also, is very popular and if we were to take a poll, the majority would probably be divided evenly between the first and third view. Many say it is Enoch and Elijah because these are the only two men that disappeared from the earth without dying, and they say that they will have to come back to the earth and die like the rest of us. They have to be the TWO WITNESSES. Really? It seems logical, but just because it seems logical doesn't mean that is how it should be taken.

There is a fourth view! I gave the first three views in a matter of sentences, but there is a lot more to this subject than what "meets the eye". There is close to 15,000 words in this chapter that will lay out all the passages and comments that will deal with this fourth view. Since Revelation 11 contains the largest amount of verses on this subject, it would be good to start by giving those passages first. It is in those that give us the first clues of who these two witnesses might be. They are as follows:

> Rev 11:1 "And there was given me a reed like unto a rod: and the angel stood, saying, Rise, and measure the temple of God, and the altar, and them that worship therein."

> Rev 11:2 "But the court which is without the temple leave out, and measure it not; for it is given unto the Gentiles: and the holy city shall they tread under foot forty and two months."

> Rev 11:3 "And I will give power unto **my two witnesses, and they shall prophesy a thousand two hundred and threescore days, clothed in sackcloth**."

Rev 11:4 "**These are the two olive trees, and the two candlesticks standing before the God of the earth.**"

Rev 11:5 "**And if any man will hurt them, fire proceedeth out of their mouth, and devoureth their enemies: and if any man will hurt them, he must in this manner be killed.**"

Rev 11:6 "**These have power to shut heaven, that it rain not in the days of their prophecy: and have power over waters to turn them to blood, and to smite the earth with all plagues, as often as they will.**"

Rev 11:7 "**And when they shall have finished their testimony, the beast that ascendeth out of the bottomless pit shall make war against them and shall overcome them, and kill them.**"

Rev 11:8 "**And their dead bodies shall lie in the street of the great city, which spiritually is called Sodom and Egypt, where also our Lord was crucified.**"

Rev 11:9 "**And they of the people and kindreds and tongues and nations shall see their dead bodies three days and an half, and shall not suffer their dead bodies to be put in graves.**"

Rev 11:10 "**And they that dwell upon the earth shall rejoice over them, and make merry, and shall send gifts one to another; because these two prophets tormented them that dwelt on the earth.**"

Rev 11:11 "**And after three days and an half the Spirit of life from God entered into them, and they stood upon their feet; and great fear fell upon them which saw them.**"

Rev 11:12 "**And they heard a great voice from heaven saying unto them, Come up hither. And they ascended up to heaven in a cloud; and their enemies beheld them.**"

THEIR TIMING

Let's analyze this and see if we can make some sense out of it. Maybe the first thing that should be discussed is the timing, since that is the first thing that is mentioned:

> Rev 11:2 "But the court which is without the temple leave out, and measure it not; for it is given unto the Gentiles: and **the holy city shall they tread under foot forty and two months.**"

The city of Jerusalem will be under occupation for 3 1/2 years. It is during this time that the TWO WITNESSES will be given power:

> Rev 11:3 "And I will give **power** unto my **two witnesses**, and they shall **prophesy a thousand two hundred and threescore days, clothed in sackcloth.**"

Isn't it interesting that these PROPHESY and exercise their POWER for the same period of time that the occupation takes place! The length of their prophecy is also the same length of time that the Antichrist rules. They prophesy in humility. The main question is who are they?

THEIR IDENTITY, THE TWO OLIVE TREES

> Rev 11:4 "These are the **two olive trees, and the two candlesticks standing before the God of the earth.**"

To restate what the scripture is saying the TWO WITNESSES are:

1. THE TWO OLIVE TREES and

2. THE TWO CANDLESTICKS

All we have to know then is who the olive trees and the candlesticks represent. That's pretty easy right? Before we go into that, notice that it speaks of these TWO WITNESSES with no introduction. It is like we are supposed to know who they are. We do know who they are. We just don't know that we know. Ha! In fact we know them quite well. More about that later.

THEY ARE THE TWO OLIVE TREES

It says they are the olive TREES. Are there any verses that talk about TREES that could give us a hint of what it is trying to describe? Yes.

> Psa 1:1 "Blessed is **the man** that walketh not in the counsel of the ungodly, nor standeth in the way of sinners, nor sitteth in the seat of the scornful."
>
> Psa 1:2 "But his delight is in the law of the LORD; and in his law doth he meditate day and night."
>
> Psa 1:3 "And **he shall be like a tree** planted by the rivers of water, that bringeth forth his fruit in his season; his leaf also shall not wither; and whatsoever he doeth shall prosper."

In this passage we see that a very godly man is considered a TREE. This is a very strong hint of what Revelation is talking about, but is there any other place in the Bible that discusses that? Yes:

> Isa 61:1 The Spirit of the Lord GOD is upon me; because the LORD hath anointed me to preach good tidings unto the meek; he hath sent me to bind up the brokenhearted, to proclaim liberty to the captives, and the opening of the prison to them that are bound;"
>
> Isa 61:2 "To proclaim the acceptable year of the LORD, and the day of vengeance of our God; to comfort all that mourn;"
>
> Isa 61:3 "To appoint unto them that mourn in Zion, to give unto them beauty for ashes, the oil of joy for mourning, the garment of praise for the spirit of heaviness; that **they** might be called **trees of righteousness, the planting of the LORD**, that he might be glorified."

These scriptures let us know that God's chosen people are called TREES. Are there any places in scripture that refer to God's people, specifically, as OLIVE TREES? Yes:

Psa 52:8 "But **I am like a green olive tree** in the house of God: I trust in the mercy of God for ever and ever."

Hos 14:5 "I will be as the dew unto **Israel**: he shall grow as the lily, and cast forth his roots as Lebanon."

Hos 14:6 "His branches shall spread, and **his beauty** shall be **as the olive tree**, and his smell as Lebanon."

Not only are God's chosen people like a TREE but they are like the OLIVE TREE. Wow! We are getting somewhere. Let's keep going. Is there any other place in the Bible that talks about the OLIVE TREE and the CANDLESTICK in the same passage? Yes:

Zec 4:1 "And the angel that talked with me came again, and waked me, as a man that is wakened out of his sleep,"

Zec 4:2 "And said unto me, What seest thou? And I said, I have looked, and behold **a candlestick** all of gold, with a bowl upon the top of it, and his seven lamps thereon, and seven pipes to the seven lamps, which are upon the top thereof:"

Zec 4:3 "And **two olive trees** by it, one upon the right side of the bowl, and the other upon the left side thereof."

Zec 4:4 "So I answered and spake to the angel that talked with me, saying, What are these, my lord?"

Zec 4:5 "Then the angel that talked with me answered and said unto me, **Knowest thou not what these be? And I said, No, my lord.**"

Zec 4:11 "Then answered I, and said unto him, What are these **two olive trees** upon the right side of the **candlestick** and upon the left side thereof?"

Zec 4:12 "And I answered again, and said unto him, What be these two **olive** branches which through the two golden pipes empty the golden oil out of themselves?"

Zec 4:13 "And he answered me and said, **Knowest thou not what these be?** And I said, No, my lord."

Zec 4:14 "Then said he, **These are the two anointed ones, that stand by the Lord of the whole earth.**"

ZACHARIAH AND JOHN ARE SUPPOSED TO KNOW WHO THEY ARE.

Before we start in on the awesomeness of this passage let's cover a few side points. Let's look at a couple of similarities within the book of Revelation. Remember how I pointed out at the beginning of Revelation 11 it starts talking about the TWO WITNESSES with no introduction? It is like we are supposed to know who they are. The Lord does that here: "Don't you know who these are Zechariah?" (My paraphrased version). Two times He does this in verses 5 and 13. What is interesting is that He does that exact same thing in Revelation 7:13, but it's one of the elders, you might say, that he is speaking for God. (Notice that it is also verse 13 as it also takes place in Zachariah verse 13.)

> Rev 7:13 "And **one of the elders answered**, saying unto me, **What are these which are arrayed in white robes? and whence came they?**"

> Rev 7:14 "And I said unto him, Sir, thou knowest. And he said to me, **These are they which came out of great tribulation, and have washed their robes, and made them white in the blood of the Lamb.**"

> Rev 7:15 "**Therefore are they before the**

throne of God, and serve him day and night in his temple: and he that sitteth on the throne shall dwell among them."

Rev 7:16 "**They shall hunger no more, neither thirst any more; neither shall the sun light on them, nor any heat.**"

Rev 7:17 "**For the Lamb which is in the midst of the throne shall feed them, and shall lead them unto living fountains of waters: and God shall wipe away all tears from their eyes.**"

In each one of these passages the setting has to do with who? It is the elect. Most prophecy teachers by-the-way, say these saints described here are just the tribulation saints. I admit they did come out of tribulation, so they could be called that, but it could typify all of us, because I believe that all of God's people that are alive at the end of the world will eventually face some kind of tribulation. (see Acts 14:22, John 16:33). The main thing here is that it is describing His people. John, like Zechariah is expected to know who these people are? Do you know who God's people are in scripture? Maybe not. Maybe this chapter will help you, the reader, know who they are! The people described here in Revelation 7 have all the characteristics of the saints of God worldwide and through all generations.

NOW THE VERSES I LEFT OUT

Now, let's discuss the missing verses of Zechariah 4:6-10 that I left out. After the angel, in a sense, intimidates Zechariah over the identity of the candlesticks and the olive trees, he says, "this is..." and goes off into a discussion of Zerubbabel and after five verses, he takes a breath and Zechariah butts in real fast before he goes on any further and says, "What are these two olive trees ...?" The angel must have paused again, because he asked the same question the 2nd time!!! How many times have you, the reader, asked God to explain what He is talking about in scripture. Don't quit asking until you know. Zechariah must have known that the verses I omitted were just a rabbit trail and that's why Zechariah brought him back to the crux of the question. Do you get lost in a barrage of verses? Do you know when verses are inserted here and there just to get the simple off the track of what the Lord is talking about? It happens a lot in the scripture and only the deeply sincere, seeking, and hungry student of God will see the truth shrouded in the verbiage of scripture. This passage has sidetracked a multitude of Bible scholars! I have another point to make, but first let's give the verses that I skipped:

> Zec 4:6 "Then he answered and spake unto me, saying, This is the word of the LORD unto Zerubbabel, saying, Not by might, nor by power, but by my spirit, saith the LORD of hosts."

Zec 4:7 "Who art thou, O great mountain? before Zerubbabel thou shalt become a plain: and he shall bring forth the headstone thereof with shoutings, crying, Grace, grace unto it."

Zec 4:8 "Moreover the word of the LORD came unto me, saying,"

Zec 4:9 "The hands of Zerubbabel have laid the foundation of this house; his hands shall also finish it; and thou shalt know that the LORD of hosts hath sent me unto you."

Zec 4:10 "For who hath despised the day of small things? for they shall rejoice, and shall see the plummet in the hand of Zerubbabel with those seven; they are the eyes of the LORD, which run to and fro through the whole earth."

The main thought here, is why else did the Lord put these verses in there? Here is why: Not everything found in scripture is in chronological order! As soon as these words are read, the serious Bible scholar says, "I already knew that." Isaiah 61:2 is used a lot to illustrate that, but in Revelation chronology is a HUGE factor in understanding the book. Let me give you some examples. To keep this short I am not going to print out the verses. Revelation 19:1-10 describes the MARRIAGE SUPPER OF THE LAMB which happens after the Battle of Armageddon, after Mystery Babylon the Great is destroyed, and at the very beginning of the MILLENNIAL REIGN OF CHRIST. Then in the same chapter in verses 11-21, He goes back and gives events leading up to and following THE BATTLE OF ARMAGEDDON, but Armageddon is before the Marriage Supper of the Lamb not after it! You can see that this chapter is not written in chronological order.

Let me give you another example: In Revelation 9:14 it mentions the EUPHRATES RIVER which, by inference, is leading up to the Battle of Armageddon, and is part of the SIXTH TRUMPET. Seven chapters later it mentions it again, only this time as part of the SIXTH VIAL. Not exactly what I call being in chronological order.

Another example: The judgment on Mystery Babylon is mentioned several times in different places in Revelation. It is not in chronological order.

One more example: Revelation 14 is very difficult to understand. The Lord showed me that the WHOLE CHAPTER is in REVERSE ORDER!!! I will not go into great detail here about this unique chapter because I do that in other writings, but suffice it to say that it starts off with the Lord descending upon the Mount of Olives with His people, and all the rest of the chapter describes the events leading up to THAT!

I said all that to say that Zechariah chapter 4 is no different. Verses 6-10 are not part of the identity of who the two olive trees represent. He only inserts that to distract the researcher from understanding the matter.

I must be careful about making God a "deceiver". (Check out I Thessalonians 2:11-12.) God can't be ascribed as evil because He owns us and the whole universe. If our hearts are evil and we don't love the truth, we bring it on ourselves. If God hides the truth is He a deceiver? No! Gold is hidden in the ground. Very, very few will find it, but the dedicated gold miner will. The truth of God is knowledge and is much like physical gold (see Proverbs 2:2-9). When I'm preaching, often I ask, "How many here want to go to heaven?" Almost every hand is raised and then I ask, "How bad?" That is a good question to ask in regards to truth. It's not a question of, "Do you want truth?" Most would say, "yes", but the question is, "How bad do you want truth? Many say the late J. Vernon McGee put the cookies on the bottom shelf for everyone to eat or for all to understand. Sorry, God doesn't do that all the time. That is why there are ministers and those close to the Lord who can explain and reveal the hidden things of God. (See Nehemiah 8:1-8.) Remember also Daniel 12:4. Some things are "sealed" until the proper time...of the end. (It is now time for this subject to be revealed.) Only the very spiritually hungry, sincere, brave, and independent few will ever see it. That is no wonder, for this is how and why He hides many other precious truths. He wants us to search for Him and His truth with all our hearts. At any rate, He gives us the answer to the whole mystery in verse 14, which is given to us in the following section:

THE TWO ANOINTED ONES ARE THE CHURCH

> Zec 4:14 "Then said he, These are **the two anointed ones**, that stand by the Lord of the whole earth."

Is there any indication in the New Testament of who the anointed ones are? Yes, in II Corinthians and in I John:

> 2 Co 1:21 "Now he which stablisheth us with you in Christ, and hath **anointed us**, is God;"

> 1 Jn 2:27 "But **the anointing** which **ye have received** of him abideth in you, and ye need not that any man teach you: but as the same anointing teacheth you of all things, and is truth, and is no lie, and even as it hath taught you, ye shall abide in him."

Paul in II Corinthians includes himself, a Jew, along with the Gentiles in Corinth as being anointed. John in writing to the church says that they have received the ANOINTING. I dare say that the ANOINTED ONES are the church, but why does the angel say that there are TWO. We are getting to that, but first let's discuss a few similarities between the two passages of Revelation 11 and Zachariah 4.

It is obvious that Revelation 11 and this passage in Zechariah are talking about the same subject, because they are both dealing with olive trees. Let's talk about how both passages relate to each other. Zechariah does not ask about the Two Candlesticks, but he does ask about the TWO OLIVE TREES. The angel says the TWO OLIVE TREES are the TWO ANOINTED ONES that stand by the Lord of the whole earth. I have given verses in the New Testament that identifies the ANOINTED ONES as being the CHURCH, but the scripture doesn't specifically say the TWO WITNESSES ARE ANOINTED. How does that pan out? In Revelation 11 the Lord says, "And I will give POWER unto my two witnesses, and they shall PROPHESY..." Guess what? If they are going to have POWER and they are going to PROPHESY they will have to be ANOINTED! You can't have power with God and prophesy without being anointed or you will be doing it in your own ability and strength and will fall flat on your face. It can be summarized thus: The Two Olive Trees are ANOINTED and the Two Witnesses are ANOINTED. They are BOTH anointed. It is evident these passages explain each other.

The third way to prove that these two passages are talking about the same subject is to center in on the last part of the angel's answer in Zachariah: How does it read?

> Zec 4:14 says, "Then said he, These are the two anointed ones, that STAND BY THE LORD OF THE WHOLE EARTH."

Notice that Revelation 11 uses a very similar phrase:

> Rev 11:4 says: "These are the two olive trees, and the two candlesticks STANDING BEFORE THE GOD OF THE EARTH".

As you can see, the phrases, "stand by (standing before) the Lord (God) of the (whole) earth" links the anointed ones to the olive trees and the candlesticks. Therefore, they explain each other.

THE TWO OLIVE TREES ARE THE CHURCH

I have shown that the ANOINTED ONES are the church. I have already given two passages in the Old Testament that refer to Israel and David being an Olive Tree. By using New Testament scripture can I demonstrate that the OLIVE TREES are the church, as well? Is there any passage that plainly tells us who the Olive Trees are? The answer is, yes, and it is found in Romans 11:

> Rom 11:17 "And if some of the branches be broken off, and thou, being **a wild olive tree**, wert graffed in among them, and with them partakest of the root and fatness of **the olive tree**;"

Rom 11:18 "Boast not against the branches. But if thou boast, thou bearest not the root, but the root thee."

Rom 11:19 "Thou wilt say then, The branches were broken off, that I might be graffed in."

Rom 11:20 "Well; because of unbelief they were broken off, and thou standest by faith. Be not highminded, but fear:"

Rom 11:21 "For if God spared not the natural branches, take heed lest he also spare not thee."

Rom 11:22 "Behold therefore the goodness and severity of God: on them which fell, severity; but toward thee, goodness, if thou continue in his goodness: otherwise thou also shalt be cut off."

Rom 11:23 "And they also, if they abide not still in unbelief, shall be graffed in: for God is able to graff them in again."

Rom 11:24 "For **if thou wert cut out of the olive tree which is wild by nature**, and wert graffed contrary to nature into **a good olive tree**:

how much more shall these, which be the natural branches, be graffed into **their own olive tree**?"

Rom 11:25 "For I would not, brethren, that ye should be ignorant of this mystery, lest ye should be wise in your own conceits; that blindness in part is happened to Israel, until the fulness of the Gentiles be come in."

This passage unravels the meaning of Revelation 11 and Zechariah 4. It identifies the TWO OLIVE TREES:

1. The WILD OLIVE TREE is in reference to the Gentiles

2. "The Olive Tree" or "A Good Olive Tree" or "Their Own OLIVE TREE" is in reference to the saved Jewish remnant.

From this passage can you see who these represent? They are NOT individuals are they? Just in case you need a little help let me explain it in greater detail:

The Two Olive Trees represent, not two individuals, but TWO CLASSES of people: 1) The WILD OLIVE TREE represents the tree that the Gentiles were apart of at first and were cut out of it and spliced or grafted into the "good olive tree". 2) "The Olive Tree" is the same as "A Good Olive Tree", which is the same as "Their Own Olive Tree". This is the Olive Tree that the Gentiles were grafted into, and what is that? It is the born again Jewish tree—those who have accepted Jesus as their Messiah and who have accepted the plan of salvation: repented of their sins, been baptized in the name of Jesus Christ and received the Holy Ghost as declared by Peter (a saved Jew) in Acts chapters 2, 8, 10, and repeated by Paul in 19. Paul talks about unbelieving Israel that will be grafted back into their own Olive Tree—if and when they accept Jesus as their Messiah and also obey the plan of salvation as the first fruits of Israel have done. So this passage is talking about the BRIDE OF CHRIST which is comprised of BOTH:

1. The saved JEWS and

2. The saved GENTILES

This is the phenomena that Paul talks about over and over again as he talks about it here, how God could EVER have put these two opposites into one body and made them love one another is beyond comprehension—that is if you understand how deeply the hatred ran between these two classes of people for eons of time. Again, this is the saved remnant of the Jews and the saved remnant of the Gentiles. They are the Olive Trees that Psalms 1, Psalms 52:8, Isaiah 61:3, and Hosea 14:5 and 6 are referring to. As Ephesians 2 says (which I will quote later) the middle wall of partition between the Jews and the Gentiles has been broken down or removed and now they stand together in ONE BODY. They STAND—SIDE BY SIDE—(does that sound familiar? Remember Zechariah 4:3, 11, and 14) back to back guarding each other, as they witness to the masses of the great salvation offered to the world. This, my friend, is the ONE BODY called the CHURCH!

This number TWO is a big deal and we will deal more with that later, but it is just as big or bigger as the words themselves—"Olive Tree". One more thing. Remember at the beginning of this chapter, I stated that chapter 11 started out, with no introduction, talking about the Two Witnesses as though we knew who they were. See, we do know who they were or are. Again, when we went to Zechariah the Lord spoke to him as though he was supposed to know who they were. He did know who they were but he didn't know that he knew, Hah! As I said, the Lord has a sense of humor. We know who it is and who they were—it is the Remnant of God—the Body of Christ. Sometimes, we just don't know, that we know! Skip Heitzig wrote a book on Revelation and at the end of 2014 he was talking about it on his radio program. Although, I don't always agree with him, I agreed with him when he said the Book of Revelation is not only a revelation of who Jesus is, but who the Body of Christ is! The TWO WITNESSES are the Body of Christ, and wow, that is a GREAT Revelation!

THE TWO CANDLESTICKS ARE THE CHURCH

So far, we have discussed the TWO WITNESSES as being the TWO ANOINTED ONES standing before the God of the whole earth, and as being the TWO OLIVE TREES, but they are more than these two things. They are the TWO

CANDLESTICKS. Let's give the verses that deal with that in Revelation and Zechariah:

> Rev 11:4 "These are the two olive trees, and **the two candlesticks** standing before the God of the earth."
>
> Zec 4:1 "And the angel that talked with me came again, and waked me, as a man that is wakened out of his sleep,"
>
> Zec 4:2 "And said unto me, What seest thou? And I said, I have looked, and behold **a candlestick** all of gold, with a bowl upon the top of it, and his **seven lamps** thereon, and **seven pipes to the seven lamps**, which are upon the top thereof:"
>
> Zec 4:3 "And two olive trees by it, one upon the right side of the bowl, and the other upon the left side thereof."
>
> Zec 4:12 "And I answered again, and said unto him, What be these two olive branches which through the **two golden pipes** empty the golden oil out of **themselves**?"

In Revelation 11:4 the Lord tells us that the TWO WITNESSES are the TWO CANDLESTICKS, but that doesn't tell us who else they are as to their true identity. We went to the book of Romans to find the identity of the Two Olive Trees, but Paul in Romans 11 does not deal with the Two Candlesticks, so we must go to some other portion of scripture to find the meaning of them. Where do we go? Let's go back to the book of Revelation to chapter one:

> Rev 1:20 "The mystery of the seven stars which thou sawest in my right hand, and **the seven golden candlesticks**. The seven stars are the angels of the seven churches: and **the seven candlesticks** which thou sawest **are the seven churches**."

The Seven Golden Candlesticks are the Seven Churches, or you could say the Candlesticks are churches. The Seven Churches are believed by almost all theologians to be the seven main churches of Asia Minor. This same land mass is better known today as Turkey. They were in existence in the first century. Some have stated that they were not the only churches of Asia Minor but were the main ones. It sounds like there were other, smaller, less conspicuous churches. It seems symbolic, then, that by addressing each of these seven in chapters two and three of Revelation, he is really addressing all of the churches at the same time. They were in Gentile territory and were probably mainly Gentile churches, but they must have had some Jewish content, because in Revelation 2:2 some pretended to be apostles and they probably would not have made that claim unless they themselves were Jewish. Then others in Revelation 2:9

portrayed themselves as Jews. John denounced them from being TRUE Jews. He declared that they went to a synagogue alright—the synagogue of Satan. You know, Jews attend a synagogue, but "Christians" attend a "church". The implication, at any rate, is that a certain percentage of them were Jews. The rest were Gentiles. It is believed, then, he was addressing all the saved Jews and Gentiles in all the churches of Asia Minor all at the same time.

Theologians say there are two other possibilities of the meaning of the Seven Churches. 1) The seven churches represents seven major church periods in history from 95 A.D. up to the present day. 2) They represent all individual churches in all eras of time, including those in existence today.

No matter how you divide it up or which interpretation you want to take, the scripture is plain! The Candlesticks are CHURCHES, and the churches are made up of Jews and Gentiles. That is why Revelation 11:4 says there are TWO Candlesticks, because basically there are two main kinds of believers: JEWS and GENTILES. The word given to Zechariah has the same idea, but expresses it differently. He does not say there are seven candlesticks. There are SEVEN LAMPS on ONE CANDLESTICK. In other words there are "SEVEN CHURCHES", but they all make up ONE CHURCH. The seven lamps represent ALL the churches that are true churches of God. There is no way to give a number representing all churches because that number is constantly growing—so, seven represents them all! In a sense we could say that there are not TWO CANDLESTICKS as Jew and Gentile, there is only ONE Candlestick, and both Jew and Gentile are in that one candlestick. That is the idea that Zechariah lays out, so that when you take both sets of scriptures the whole gamete is covered, but, as I mentioned above, there are TWO CANDLESTICKS—one for the saved Jews and one for the saved Gentiles and they are both represented in the BODY OF CHRIST. They are the TWO WITNESSES, and they are the TWO CANDLESTICKS! As you can see, they are not two individuals, but two GROUPS of people! There is more to be said on this. Let's go back to Revelation 11.

THE SAVED JEW AND GENTILE ARE ALSO THE TEMPLE

> Rev 11:1 "And there was given me a reed like unto a rod: and the angel stood, saying, Rise, and **measure the temple of God**, and the **altar**, and **them that worship therein.**"

> Rev 11:2 "But **the court** which is without **the temple** leave out, and measure it not; for it is **given unto the Gentiles**: and the holy city shall they tread under foot forty and two months."

John was told to take the reed that was given to him and measure:

1. The TEMPLE

2. The ALTAR and

3. THEM THAT WORSHIP therein.

Notice that NOTHING was ever done with whatever measurements he took. Why? Why even record the fact that he was asked to measure it in the first place? Here is the answer: It is meant to get our attention so that what is to follow is to be measured in light of the TEMPLE and the COURT being divided into TWO DIVISIONS. We know that only the JEWS were allowed to WORSHIP in the TEMPLE (notice #3 has to do with measuring those who are worshiping in the Temple—they were supposed to be Jews). There is a "flip flop" in all this because at this time in John's life (around 95 A.D.) he is on the Isle of Patmos and Titus has already destroyed Jerusalem, including the TEMPLE! So, what temple was he to measure? Could it be the one in heaven or the one that was in the future. Could it be one in which the Gentiles would be permitted as much access as the Jews? In the old temple it had TWO main divisions and each division was divided into TWO parts: first, you had the COURT that was divided into the inner and outer court. Secondly, you had the HOLY PLACES that was divided into the Holy Place and the Most Holy Place. The Gentiles were permitted in the outer court, but not the inner court. The

Levites and priests were permitted in the Holy Place every day, but only the High Priest was allowed in the Most Holy Place and that only once a year. As you can see you have this repeating theme of TWO.

I have said all that to say, at the beginning of this chapter the Lord is inspiring us to remember these divisions and to bring our attention to the TWO GROUPS of people here: JEWS and GENTILES. We know there WAS just ONE TEMPLE and when Jesus died the veil in the Temple was rent from top to bottom, allowing everybody access into the Most Holy Place, even the Gentiles. Today, one could say, both Jews and Gentiles are allowed into God's temple. When I say temple I am talking about His temple of SALVATION. In fact, you could say, WE are the temple, or the BRIDE is the temple. The temple is the CHURCH. The building is not the church. The people are the church, or the temple, and which people am I referring to? I am referring to the saved JEWS and the saved GENTILES of course! This is verified in Ephesians 2:

> Eph 2:11 "Wherefore remember, that ye being in time past **Gentiles** in the flesh, who are called Uncircumcision by that which is called the Circumcision in the flesh made by hands;"

> Eph 2:12 "That at that time ye were without Christ, being aliens from the commonwealth of **Israel**, and

strangers from the covenants of promise, having no hope, and without God in the world:"

Eph 2:13 "But now in Christ Jesus ye who sometimes were far off are **made nigh by the blood of Christ**."

Eph 2:14 "For he is our peace, who hath made **both one**, and hath broken down the middle wall of partition between us;"

Eph 2:15 "Having abolished in his flesh the enmity, even the law of commandments contained in ordinances; for to make in himself **of twain one new man**, so making peace;"

Eph 2:16 "And that he might **reconcile both unto God in one body** by the cross, having slain the enmity thereby:"

Eph 2:17 "And came and preached peace to you which were afar off, and to them that were nigh."

Eph 2:18 "For through him we **both have access** by one Spirit unto the Father."

Eph 2:19 "Now therefore ye are no more strangers and

foreigners, but fellowcitizens with the saints, and of the household of God;"

Eph 2:20 "And are built upon the foundation of the apostles and prophets, Jesus Christ himself being the chief corner stone;"

Eph 2:21 "In whom all the building fitly framed together groweth unto an **holy temple** in the Lord:"

Eph 2:22 "In whom **ye also** are builded together for **an habitation of God** through the Spirit."

It is quite plain to see that we are His TEMPLE in a spiritual sense and the Jew and Gentile SAVED person makes up the TWO CANDLESTICKS. Where are the Candlesticks placed, or where are they standing? They are in the Temple. And that is why 11:4 says they are, "STANDING BEFORE THE GOD OF THE EARTH". And Zechariah says in 4:14 they "...STAND BY THE LORD OF THE WHOLE EARTH". That is why John is told in 11:1 to measure "THEM THAT WORSHIP THEREIN", because He is emphasizing that the TWO WITNESSES are the saved JEW and GENTILE! And by the way, if Jesus can be both the sacrificial lamb and the High Priest that offers the lamb at the same time, then so can we saved Jew and Gentile be both the Candlestick in the Temple and the Temple itself, at the same time.

THE JEW AND GENTILE ARE CALLED WITNESSES

To continue our proof, are the Jewish people of God called witnesses and how about the Gentile people of God? And why all this fuss over witnesses in the first place? Are witnesses important? Yes, they are. Let's go to Numbers and Deuteronomy to answer the last question first:

> Num 35:30 "Whoso killeth any person, the murderer shall be put to death by the mouth of **witnesses**: but **one witness** shall **not** testify against any person to cause him to die."

> Deu 19:15 "**One witness** shall not rise up against a man for any iniquity, or for any sin, in any sin that he sinneth: at the mouth of **two witnesses**, or at the mouth of three witnesses, shall the matter be established."

Therefore to establish the guilt of any person there was a minimum requirement of TWO WITNESSES. Even in the New Testament, witnesses were important. Let's go to Matthew and First Timothy:

> Mat 18:16 "But if he will not hear thee, then take with thee **one or two more**, that in the mouth of **two or three witnesses** every word may be established."

> 1Ti 5:19 "Against an elder receive not an accusation, but before **two or three witnesses**."

I want to mention something right here, since we are discussing, two or THREE witnesses. Our whole emphasis in this chapter is to zero in on the Two Witnesses, but three of these verses say two or THREE witnesses. (Three verses say THREE witnesses. That is interesting.) Since the scripture identifies who the Two Witnesses are, is it possible that there could be a passage or set of passages that might identify who the THIRD witness might be in a spiritual parallel? Let me rephrase that: since there is a spiritual parallel for the Two Witnesses, could there be one for the THIRD witness? I don't want to take away too much attention from the Two Witnesses, but let me just mention a quick word about who the THIRD witness might be, if there is one, and I believe there is. The THIRD witness is the SAMARITANS: half Jew and half Gentile. Get this. Peter had the keys to the kingdom of heaven as they were given to him by our Lord. He used them to open the door of salvation to the Jews in Acts 2. All of Acts chapter 10 is devoted to Peter opening the door of salvation to the Gentiles. (These are our Two Witnesses.) But the Lord allows Luke to use up to the greater part of chapter 8 to describe how Peter (and John) opened up the door of salvation to (guess who?) the SAMARITANS. They could be considered the THIRD witness. Remember what Jesus said before he ascended:

> Act 1:8 "But ye shall receive power, after that the Holy Ghost is come upon you: and ye shall be witnesses unto me both in Jerusalem, and in all Judaea, and in SAMARIA, and unto the uttermost part of the earth."

It says Jerusalem and Judea first, Samaria second, and "the uttermost part of the earth" third, which was referring to the Gentiles. Isn't it interesting that it's the exact order found in the book of Acts: chapter 2, the Jews, chapter 8, the Samaritans, and chapter 10, the Gentiles—all in proper order. The Samaritans could be considered the third witness, but they are so few in number that it is barely worth mentioning. (Skip Heitzig on a broadcast aired December 17, 2014 on 107.1 FM in Albuquerque over KNKZ stated:

> ...there are only 700 Samaritans left as a race of people. Wikipedia verified this with a quote by Matti Freidman from: ISRAEL, SIGNS FOR HER ESTRANGED PEOPLE, "Today there are precisely 705 Samaritans, according to the sect's own talley...") The majority of the world, then, is divided between TWO major groups of people, the Jew and the Gentile, so back to our main point.

Next, it is important to establish the fact that the JEWS, OLD and NEW Testament alike, are literally considered to be witnesses. Let's go to Isaiah, Hebrews, Luke, and Acts:

Isa 44:8 "Fear ye not, neither be afraid: have not I told thee from that time, and have declared it? **ye** *are* even **my witnesses**. Is there a God beside me? yea, *there is* no God; I know not *any*."

Heb 10:28 "He that despised Moses' law died without mercy under **two or three witnesses**:"

Heb 12:1 "Wherefore seeing we also are compassed about with so great a cloud of **witnesses**, let us lay aside every weight, and the sin which doth so easily beset *us,* and let us run with patience the race that is set before us,"

Luk 24:47 "And that repentance and remission of sins should be preached in his name among all nations, beginning at Jerusalem."

Luk 24:48 "And **ye are witnesses** of these things."

Act 1:8 "But ye shall receive power, after that the Holy Ghost is come upon you: and **ye** shall be **witnesses** unto me both in Jerusalem, and in all Judaea, and in Samaria, and unto the uttermost part of the earth."

Act 2:32 "This Jesus hath God raised up, whereof **we all are witnesses**."

Act 3:15 "And killed the Prince of life, whom God hath raised from the dead; whereof **we are witnesses.**"

The Gentiles who are saved and in the church are witnesses, also. That can be seen in I Thessalonians:

1 Th 2:10 "**Ye are witnesses**, and God *also*, how holily and justly and unblameably we behaved ourselves among you that believe:"

So, therefore THE SAVED JEW AND GENTILE are BOTH WITNESSES as we have seen in scripture and the TWO WITNESSES of Revelation 11:3 are the BODY OF CHRIST and are divided into JEW and GENTILE.

THE NUMBER TWO IS A BIG DEAL

The number **TWO** is a big thing as I mentioned earlier. It reoccurs many times in scripture and it occurs by itself as 2 and in multiples of 2 as 4, 8 and in other formats. I don't always agree with the late J. Vernon McGee, but I agreed with him when in January or February 2012 over KKIM 1000 A.M. on the radio dial he stated that TWO is the number of witness. I want to mention quite a few passages that center in on this "TWO" thing, which is only a partial list. In Genesis **2:24** "Therefore shall a man…cleave unto his wife and they (TWO) shall be one flesh." In Genesis **4** the first children of Adam and Eve were TWO sons, Cain and Able. At the beginning of this paper I said there were

TWO men who left this world without dying: Enoch in Genesis 5:**24** and Elijah in **II** Kings **2:11** (double one).

In Genesis **12:4** "So Abram departed...and Lot went with him", so it was the TWO of them that departed. Abraham at first had TWO seed: Ishmael of the Egyptian Hagar and Isaac of Sarah. Abraham could not bring peace to His family, (and by the way, neither can the United Nations today) but God did it when He created the CHURCH. He united Jew and Gentile (and I might add, Arabs, including the Palestinians) in ONE BODY, the church. Ishmael may have been a mistake in the mind of Sarah and Abraham, but not in the mind of God. He used them to be a type of the TWO WITNESSES, Jew and Gentile in the church. Not only that, but He promised Abraham that he would be the father of many nations and they both became a nation (and the Ishmaelites, or Arabs into many nations). When the Lord appeared unto Abraham in the plains of Mamre, how many angels did He have with Him in Genesis 18:**2**? TWO! When the Lord was about to judge Sodom and Gomorrah (TWO cities) in Genesis 19, how many angels did He send? TWO! In Genesis **22** (notice TWO, TWO) when Abraham was asked to sacrifice his son, how many of his young men did he take in verse 3? TWO! Again a type of the TWO WITNESSES. Joseph dreamed two dreams about his family, interpreted two dreams in prison, and interpreted two of Pharaoh's dreams. The kingdom of Israel was divided into how many kingdoms? TWO, the south (Judah and Benjamin—2) and the north (the other 10 tribes). In the Old Testament in Leviticus 23 it talks about an holy day that

TWO loaves of bread are waved before the Lord along with TWO lambs of the first year. Here is the passage:

> Lev **23**:17 "Ye shall bring out of your habitations **two wave loaves** of **two** tenth deals: they shall be of fine flour; they shall be baken with leaven; they are the **firstfruits** unto the LORD."

> Lev **23**:18 "And ye shall offer with the bread seven lambs without blemish of the first year, and one young bullock, and **two** rams: they shall be for a burnt offering unto the LORD, with their meat offering, and their drink offerings, even an offering made by fire, of sweet savour unto the LORD."

> Lev **23**:19 "Then ye shall sacrifice one kid of the goats for a sin offering, and **two** lambs of the first year for a sacrifice of peace offerings."

> Lev **23**:20 "And the priest shall **wave** them with the bread of the **firstfruits for a wave offering** before the LORD, with the **two** lambs: they shall be holy to the LORD for the priest."

> Lev **23**:21 "And ye shall proclaim on the selfsame day, that it may be an holy convocation unto you: ye shall do

no servile work therein: it shall be a statute for ever in all your dwellings throughout your generations."

Did you notice how many times the word TWO was used here? It was used **4** times. What do these TWO loaves represent? Elihu Ben David with Tsyon Ministries, says they are the two houses of Israel. They might represent them to some degree, but more importantly, they represent the TWO Witnesses, the TWO Olive Trees, the TWO Candlesticks, and the TWO parts of the One body of Christ made up of Jew and Gentile. The bread is baked with leaven, a type of sin. We, His body, are all sinful creatures saved by the blood of Christ and the Lord says they are the firstfruits unto the Lord. Who are the firstfruits? James and Revelation tell us:

> Jas 1:**18** "Of his own will begat he us with the word of truth, that **we** should be a kind of **firstfruits** of his creatures."

> Rev **14:4** "These are they which were not defiled with women; for they are virgins. These are they which follow the Lamb whithersoever he goeth. **These were redeemed** from among men, being the **firstfruits** unto God and to the Lamb."

WE are the firstfruits that follow the lamb wherever He leads, that are not defiled by women and have been redeemed by His blood. (Now we go back to Leviticus 23.) Notice the symbols of salvation all around the TWO loaves:

1. A sin offering was made representing repentance

2. A drink offering was present representing water baptism.

3. Receiving the Holy Ghost is illustrated in three ways:

    a. It was a wave offering or waved in the air creating wind—a type of the Spirit as in Acts 2.

    b. The offering was made by fire and that reminds us that ye shall receive the Holy Ghost and fire.

    c. They were to rest. The rest as in Isaiah 28:11-12 and Hebrews 3 and 4 is a type of the Holy Ghost rest.

I have highlighted the verse references. Have you noticed the number 4 showing up alongside the number 2? **4 is a double 2**. In Revelation 4 there is introduced to us **2** groups: ELDERS and BEASTS. Notice the number of elders: **4** and **20** or **24**. Notice the number of beasts: **4**, and did you notice it is found in chapter **4**. In Revelation 13 we see the BEAST and he is to reign **40** and **2** months or **42**. In the same chapter we see another beast, so now there are TWO of them, and the SECOND one has TWO horns. The devil mimics God. The devil has his TWO WITNESSES as you can see.

Let's go back to Daniel 7 since the number 4 keeps showing up with the number 2. In this chapter there are a lot of 4's: There are **4** winds and **4** beasts. The leopard has **4** wings on his back and **4** heads. The strangest of all the beasts is the **4th** beast and he becomes the antichrist. In chapter **8** the ram has **2** horns. The goat with a notable horn finds that when it is broken, **4** notable ones pop up toward the **4** winds, which were actually **4** kingdoms. And in Daniel 11:**2** it says that there will be **4** kingdoms that stand up in Persia.

Isn't it interesting in Luke **24:4** after Jesus arose from the dead, a group went to the sepulcher and TWO men stood by them. In Galatians **4:24** (a reverse of Luke **24:4**) there were TWO covenants. He taketh away the first that He may establish the SECOND (Hebrews 10:9). There are TWO Testaments Old and New. All of earth's time is divided into TWO eras B.C., Before Christ and A.D. which comes from the Latin "anno domini" meaning "in the year of our Lord" (In modern times, historians trying to get away from Jesus being the center of history, have gone to BCE, before the common era and CE, the common era.) In relationship to the deity of God, it was the SECOND manifestation—the Son—who in Revelation 1:5 was called The Faithful **WITNESS!** There are two things (death and hell) cast into the lake of fire. There are 2 deaths, 2 resurrections, and 2 (and only 2, not 3) comings of Christ. And how long has the Lord tarried so the CHURCH can witness to the world? TWO thousand years. The 2 thousand years separates the 2 comings of Christ. Remember what Hosea said:

> Hosea **6:2** "After TWO days will he revive us: in the third day he will raise us up, and we shall live in his sight."

When the Lord ascended up into heaven, how many angels stood by the disciples in Acts 1:10? TWO! And on what mountain were they standing when that happened? Mount Olivet. And on what mountain will Jesus touch down when He returns? It is the same Mt. Olivet, and why there? Olive trees are there (and maybe some of the very ones are still there that were there when Jesus was there the first time.) And what do olive trees represent? They represent His body made up of Jew and Gentile. What happens to that mountain when His feet touch it? It splits into TWO parts in Zechariah **14:4**, half to the south and half to the north. Why? Besides offering an escape route for those fleeing for protection, it is symbolic of the olive tree (or olive mountain) consisting of TWO parts, Jew and Gentile. There were also two mountains mentioned in Deuteronomy 27, Mount Ebal and Mount Gerizim.

The world is filled with two's. There have been times, yes, when even the tilt of the earth has been at 22%! The family has two heads over it, husband and wife. There are two realms of this world, spiritual and physical. There are two kinds of micro particles that circulate around the nucleus, electrons and protons. There were two structures for meeting with God, the tabernacle and the temple. There were two parts of these, the inner court and the outer court. There were two parts of the inner court, the Holy Place and the Most Holy Place. There were two lamp stands. There were two pillars in the front of the temple. There are two parts of being born again of water and Spirit. There are two parts of water baptism, the mode (how it's done) and the formula (what is said). In Numbers 11 (two ones) there were two men that were part of the 70 outside the camp, Eldad and Medad that the Spirit of God fell on. There are two places of eternity, heaven or hell (including the lake of fire. The human body is an illustration of two: two vessels, veins and arteries; two eyes, ears, arms, hands, legs, feet, lungs, kidneys, adenoids, brain lobes, thighs, nostrils, kinds of intestines, and two kinds of reproductive members, testicles, and ovaries. There are two kinds of elimination, solids and liquids. There are two kinds of humans, male and female, and I could go on and on. Oh, the depth of the knowledge, and wisdom of God! As I said, TWO is the number of witness, and the Two Witnesses represent His BODY THE CHURCH!!

WHY DOES GOD NEED TWO WITNESSES?

One might ask, "Why does God need TWO witnesses?" Wouldn't one be enough? That is a good question, but in a sense, we have already answered that. It really does have to do with the END of time and the tribulation, and this is the first part of the main point. Let's go back to Hebrews:

> Heb 10:28 "He that despised Moses' law died without mercy under **two or three witnesses**:"
>
> Heb 10:29 "Of how much **sorer punishment**, suppose ye, shall he be thought worthy, who hath trodden under foot the Son of God, and hath counted the blood of the covenant, wherewith he was sanctified, an unholy thing, and hath done despite unto the Spirit of grace?"

During the tribulation at the end of the world, God is going to judge the world. God talks about this in the book of Revelation in regards to the seals, trumpets, and vials. When you read about these you will know that many people are going to die, or be killed with armies from governments, from pestilences, and "natural" disasters, etc. Chuck Missler quotes a bumper sticker which read, "Jesus is coming back and boy is He MAD!" Yes, He's mad and many are going to die. Why will the Lord let this happen?

This world has trodden underfoot the blood of the Son of God and has poured out and will pour out the blood of millions of people who are the very children of the living God. For this the people of this world will be judged and destroyed, but not without TWO WITNESSES, the body of Christ, Jew and Gentile scattered over the face of the whole world to WITNESS this destruction. If you are saved, that my friend is you and that is me. Remember Numbers 35:30?

None could be put to death except by the word of two or three witnesses. Now let's go to Revelation 11:3 and 4:

> Rev 11:3 "And I will give *power* unto **my two witnesses**, and they shall prophesy a thousand two hundred *and* threescore days, clothed in sackcloth."

> Rev 11:4 "These are the **two** olive trees, and the **two** candlesticks **standing before the God of the earth.**"

THE JEWS AS A NATION WILL BE GRAFTED BACK INTO THEIR TREE.

The second part of the main point is this: If the TWO WITNESSES are TWO groups of people, the saved Jews and the Gentiles, when the Lord returns, is He coming back to take one half of the TWO WITNESSES—the saved Gentiles—to heaven for three and a half or seven years and then come back after the Marriage Supper to get the other half of the TWO WITNESSES—the saved Jews? I don't think so. In other words, by knowing who the TWO WITNESSES are, helps us realize that there is not going to be a secret pre-tribulation rapture. He is not coming two times (even though I love the word two) to get His people. He is coming one time (notice the word "coming" is not plural, but singular.) at the end of the world to get His people, saved Jew and Gentile. He came once to give His life a ransom for many and will come again, ONCE (this would be the second time) in the end of the world to get His people, which makes a total of TWO times. That is it. He is not coming twice to get His people—not even in two phases. (To say He is coming in two phases separated by three and a half or seven years apart is a redefinition of a singular coming event, and is not, in my opinion, being intellectually honest.)

Let's say it another way: the Lord is coming back to get His people which, in Romans 11, is typified by the olive tree. In this chapter it discusses TWO olive trees, a good one and a wild one. It says the wild one is grafted into the natural or good olive tree thus making how many olive trees? Not two, but ONE, just like there is not TWO bodies, but ONE body of Christ. So, when the Lord returns does He come down from heaven as a chariot of fire like when he snatched Elijah and slice the olive tree down the middle and whisk half of it to heaven and then return three and a half or seven years later to get the rest of the olive tree? Not hardly! To understand this process, we must ask the question, "Who is grafted into whose tree?" The answer is, we Gentiles are grafted into the Jewish blessing, and not the other way around. Folks, we are not going until they go. And, guess what? The Jewish saved tree is not going until all the Jews that are going to get saved are saved, and that will not happen until right before the Lord comes, at the end of the tribulation. To add credence to this point, look at this verse:

> Rom 11:15 "For if the casting away of them be the reconciling of the world, what shall **the receiving of them be, but life from the dead?**"

It sounds like there is going to be a revival among the Jews. A great remnant will come to life and salvation in Jesus and Paul says when that happens the resurrection will occur — the coming of Christ!

> Rom 11:17 "And if some of the branches be broken off, and **thou**, being a wild olive tree, wert graffed in among them, and with them **partakest of the root and fatness of the olive tree**;"

> Rom 11:18 "Boast not against the branches. But if thou boast, **thou bearest not the root, but the root thee**."

See what this is saying, "…thou bearest not the root, but the root thee"? As I stated earlier, we Gentiles are in their tree and we are not going until they go. They are not ready yet. God is going to graft them back into their tree as the following verses testify:

> Rom 11:23 "And they also, **if they abide not still in unbelief, shall be graffed in**: for God is able to graff them in again."

> Rom 11:24 "For if thou wert cut out of the olive tree which is wild by nature, and wert graffed contrary to nature into a good olive tree: how much more shall these, which be **the natural branches, be**

graffed into their own olive tree?"

Rom 11:25 "For I would not, brethren, that ye should be ignorant of this mystery, lest ye should be wise in your own conceits; that **blindness in part is happened to Israel, until the fulness of the Gentiles be come in.**"

Rom 11:26 "And so **all Israel shall be saved:** as it is written, There shall come out of Sion the Deliverer, and shall turn away ungodliness from Jacob:"

Rom 11:27 "For **this is my covenant unto them, when I shall take away their sins.**"

In my next upcoming book I take a whole chapter to explain the timing of the resurrection in regards to the tribulation and I describe this at length in other chapters, so I am not going to expound on this now. Again, not many prophecy teachers, are discussing this, but I want to make some limited comments. As it states in the previous verses, blindness has been upon Israel until the bulk of the Gentiles that are going to be saved are saved, then the Lord will turn back to Israel and the scripture that follows says they will "**all**" be saved. Look at it this way. If everybody that is saved is taken to heaven, then you could say the whole tree is in heaven. How is the Lord going to graft the Jewish nation (the saved remnant) into a tree that is not there—its already been taken to heaven??? But, the scripture says they will ALL be saved. What does that mean? Will every last one of them be saved? Maybe that is an idiom for most of them. This could be referring to the saved remnant. All the remnant will be saved. It appears that this great in-gathering of the Jews will take place during and at the end of the The Great Tribulation which is the same period of time the Two Witnesses minister, and that is why the Lord will not come until the end. He is not going to come down and take the olive tree to heaven or even half of it and come back later to get a newly started olive tree or the other half of it later.

Let me help you further see how ludicrous this concept is by a simple illustrative question: Is the Lord going to be celebrating the Marriage Super of the Lamb with half His people (mostly Gentiles), looking over the balcony of heaven, seeing thousands (mostly Jews) slaughtered in cold blood, and saying, "pass me another steak I'm still hungry. I'm sorry about those Jews being killed down there, but my appetite is still good"? I don't think so. He is going to come and get the whole tree all at one time and the Marriage Super will be celebrated with ALL His people at the same time. This is the ministry of the TWO WITNESSES, THE CHURCH, to take the gospel that the nation of Israel rejected back to them. If everybody that is saved is in heaven, who will take the gospel back to them? Who will the preachers be? Will it be the sinners? Not hardly. Do you see it doesn't make scriptural sense. It is at the end when the Lord will return to take the WHOLE Olive Tree, His Body, the CHURCH, saved Jew and Gentile, to be with Him and reign with Him a thousand years and beyond.

Stop for a minute. What did I say? I don't think you grasped what I said. Let me say it again only a little clearer. The saved Jew and Gentile, as the TWO WITNESSES, will come ALIVE and will start ministering to the nation of Israel in a greater fashion than ever before to complete the olive tree, the body of Christ for His name's sake. This has been prophesied forever. I am referring to what Paul said in Romans 11:

> Rom 11:26 "And **so all Israel shall be saved**: as it is written, There shall come out of Sion the Deliverer, and shall turn away ungodliness from Jacob:"

> Rom 11:27 "For this is **my covenant unto them, when I shall take away their sins**."

What was Paul referring to? He was referring to verses all through the Old Testament prophets, as I stated, like in Jeremiah and Joel:

> Jer 31:33 "But this shall be the covenant that I will make with the house of Israel; After those days, saith the LORD, I will put my law in their inward parts, and write it in their hearts; and will be their God, and they shall be my people."

Jer 31:34 "And they shall teach no more every man his neighbour, and every man his brother, saying, Know the LORD: for they shall all know me, from the least of them unto the greatest of them, saith the LORD: for **I will forgive their iniquity, and I will remember their sin no more**."

Jer 33:6 "Behold, I will bring it health and cure, and I will cure them, and will reveal unto them the abundance of peace and truth."

Jer 33:7 "And I will cause the captivity of Judah and the captivity of Israel to return, and will build them, as at the first."

Jer 33:8 "And I will **cleanse them from all their iniquity, whereby they have sinned against me; and I will pardon all their iniquities, whereby they have sinned, and whereby they have transgressed against me**."

Joe 2:28 "And it shall come to pass afterward, that I will **pour out my spirit upon all flesh**; and **your** sons and **your** daughters shall prophesy, **your** old men shall dream dreams, **your** young men shall see visions:"

Joe 2:29 "And also upon the servants and upon the handmaids in those days will I **pour out my spirit**."

Joe 2:30 "And I will shew wonders in the heavens and in the earth, blood, and fire, and pillars of smoke."

Joe 2:31 "The sun shall be turned into darkness, and the moon into blood, before the great and the terrible day of the LORD come."

Joe 2:32 "And it shall come to pass, that **whosoever shall call on the name of the LORD shall be delivered: for in mount Zion and in Jerusalem shall be deliverance**, as the LORD hath said, and in the **remnant** whom the LORD shall call."

God will return to the Jewish nation and will circumcise the flesh of unbelief from their mind and heart and graft them, as they should be, back into their TREE of blessing and truth! Yes, some Jews have been saved, but "you haven't seen nothing yet, baby". You talk about MIRACLES and SIGNS, and WONDERS…great REVIVAL—a tidal wave of power and glory—is coming to Israel. "Hold on to your hat." Those who will try and kill these evangelists, fire will come out of their mouths and devour their persecutors. Plagues will be dispatched at their word. This is just a smattering of examples of what will be on display. The door of salvation to the Gentiles will soon slowly close as the religion of the Antichrist slowly engulfs each and every nation. Multitudes of superficial Christians will give up their faith. This could be the great falling away or part of it referred to in II Thessalonians 2. At the very same time the door of salvation to the Jewish nation will open wider and wider. Will there just be TWO literal people used of God to bring about this great revival? Will it be a Jew and a Gentile? Will it be the 144,000? No! The next chapter will reveal it is the same group of people. It is a repeating theme throughout the book of Revelation. As I stated earlier, I believe the scripture is saying it will not just be TWO people. It will be the CHURCH, comprised of both Jew and Gentile that God is going to use to accomplish this great work.

Where are the Jews? They are scattered around the world, but no matter where they are at, they are still a part of the nation of Israel. It's already happening and God will continue to open their hearts and minds wherever they are at. God will use chosen vessels all over the world to reach this fractured nation. Don't get me wrong. It will be centered in the very nation of Israel itself, but will go around the world, just like it did for the Gentiles and just like it started in Jerusalem at the beginning. Great signs and wonders will be performed, as I said, in the sight of the whole world. Okay, Body of Christ, get ready. Be prayed up, fasted up, consecrated up. Be clean and white. Be sure you know the true salvation of God, because God is going to transform a physical Jewish nation into a Jewish SPIRITUAL nation! There will be some Jews that still will resist and not accept this message, but God is going to use somebody, and I dare say a lot of somebodies. Will it be you? Will it be me? Twelve apostles were used to take the gospel the first time to Israel, but on this second go-around He is going to use a lot more than that—be ready for anything.

ARE YOU ONE OF THE ELECT?

If, while reading this, you realize you are not part of the church or are unsure about it, you can be a part of the TWO WITNESSES and know, that you know, that you know, you are saved. To be properly saved, obey the words of Peter in Acts 2:38. He had the keys (Matt. 16:19) to the kingdom of heaven: 1) Repent. 2) Be baptized in water in the name of Jesus Christ for the forgiveness of your sins and 3) You will receive the gift of the Holy Ghost just like they got it in Acts 2, 8, 10, and 19. I have a whole book, not yet published, that explains this in minute detail to be released in the future.

WHY SO LONG?

Some may ask the question: "If this chapter declares the truth why has it taken so long for this message to get out? Why hasn't anyone else seen this or wrote about it?" I will try to answer that right now. Christendom for a hundred years or more in popular writings and in the modern social media venues has embraced the erroneous pre-tribulation rapture teaching and this teaching would restrict such an interpretation of these scriptures. Sadly, on the surface, it seems like everybody believes this pre-trib dogma. "If you don't believe in the pre-tribulation rapture theory then you are out of the main stream. Man, you are just plain out of it." When you circulate around a lot of pastors and different organizations, as I have, it does appear to be just about like that. Here's the deal, though. According to that teaching, the church will not be present on the earth during the reign of the Antichrist, and this has blindfolded and restricted the Christian masses from being able to put the kind of verses that are in this chapter together to come up with this kind of conclusion. Yes, I know that I am in the minority, but since when was the majority always right? Somebody's got to stand up and be willing to speak the truth in the face of being labeled a false teacher, and it might as well be me. Hey, they said it of Paul. I'm in good company.

Even after saying this I must confess there are some rumblings going on. What I said above is how it has been for a long time, but something's happening. The blindfolds are coming off and the truth is coming out. There are a growing number of teachers and preachers who are seeing that there is only one coming of the Lord at the end of time, and this is paving the way for them to be able to put the pieces of the puzzle together and give them the insights into the deep secrets of prophecy. I mean it. More and more preachers are stepping out to declare the rapture takes place at the end of the tribulation, right before the millennial reign of Christ. However, this issue of when the rapture takes place is not the main purpose of this chapter. My purpose right now is simply to reveal the truth of who the two witnesses are, etc., but for myself, I have seen it since I was 17 years old. That was back in 1968, 50 years ago. As you can see, I have studied it for years and ended up writing a book (as yet unpublished) that can prove it by approaching the subject from twelve different angles. R. C. Sproul said at one place, "I have put my cards on the table", and that is what I have done here. You know where I stand on the issue. I know I have set myself up to be shot at and to be labeled, "not main stream", by the religious majority. But what about you? Jesus was willing to be rejected by His own people. Are you?

I admit that it is not very likely that this one chapter, by itself, is going to change anybody's eschatology. On the other hand, if the true student or teacher of prophecy is hungry enough for the truth on the matter, I am quite confident this chapter will help lead them to take another scrupulous look at the subject. If that is all this chapter does, it will have accomplished a major feat, in addition to answering one of the greatest mysteries of prophecy in our day. For the true lover of scripture it is not a matter of personal taste. This kind of person would never say, "I don't want to go through the Great Tribulation, so I am going to rearrange the prophetic text to reflect my bias." So, who would say that? Probably none, and the only ones who would, are those who are not in love with the scripture. We all know that you can make the scriptures say whatever you want it to say, but who would ever admit to that? Again, probably none, but yet it does happen. Again, who does it?

Not the lover of scripture. People all have reasons for doing what they do. Whatever the reasons are, they are not good reasons, and yet, it happens. The Lord is watching to see who we let influence us.

Reader, let me encourage you. Only believe what the Bible says "point blank". Don't build your doctrine on inferences. Build it on solid verses of scripture. Newton has given us the law of motion: "an object set in motion, tends to stay in motion until acted upon by some outside force." For instance, it is hard to stop a freight train, but it can be done with a little time and space. And once a false doctrine gets into prominence, it is hard to derail it. Look at the large body of prophecy authors, like Tim LaHaye, Jerry Jenkins, David Jeremiah, Chuck Missler, David Hocking, Hal Lindsey, Jack Van Impy, Dwight Pentecost and others. They have millions of dollars in books, CD's, and DVD's. Do you think if they ever saw prophecy differently, they would have the "where with all" to change their stand and pull all their literature off the shelf and suffer the loss, and start all over? I'm not saying one or two of them wouldn't, but it's pretty doubtful! They have made a PUBLIC confession of "faith" as it were, and it is hard, very hard, to turn around and go another direction. Who could do that? Mighty few — hopefully some, but probably none! So, in a nutshell, the majority is proclaiming a pre-tribulation rapture message and that is what you are going to see in the religious, social media networks. That is another reason why this chapter is so valuable. It is different and unique. It is not likely you will find another book or chapter like this anywhere. The main thought here is that if this chapter is true, which it is because it is built solidly on a proper interpretation of God's word, then the Lord will HAVE TO come back for His people AFTER the Great Tribulation, and this changes the whole "game".

Arthur Schopenhauer has said it beautifully and been quoted by many and goes something like, "truth has a way of passing through three stages. It is first ridiculed, then it is violently opposed, and then accepted as self-evident". Post tribulation has been going through this process. This chapter may lead you to make a decision. You will either continue to hold the popular, weak, antiquated, foundless and false pre-tribulation doctrine and reject this answer of who the Two Witnesses are or accept the challenge to dig into God's word and see if this isn't the answer to one of the greatest mysteries of prophecy in God's word. One thing is for certain. You cannot do both. I know most of the chapters in this book do not support the "status quo", and for that reason they may face a lot of opposition, but it doesn't mean they are wrong or incorrect. They are only wrong or incorrect if they violate the true word of God, and this book, thankfully, does NOT do that. It may violate the "perceived" word of God in the minds of some, but not the true word of God. I feel so strongly about that, that I would be willing to debate this issue with anybody.

Contrary to those who are not hungry for the true word of God, there are many who are. It is becoming more evident that there are more and more children of God who hunger for truth at any cost. It is refreshing to see a mass of people emerging and growing in number, as I stated earlier. They just want to know what God is saying even if it counters how they were taught or what "tradition" has dictated to them in the past. Friend, if this describes you, this book is for you.

IN REVIEW

From this chapter we have seen several things.

1. In Revelation 11 the TWO WITNESSES are the TWO OLIVE TREES.

2. In the Old Testament God's people are called OLIVE TREES.

3. In Zechariah the OLIVE TREES are the TWO ANOINTED ONES, and in the New Testament the CHURCH is the ANOINTED ONES. Therefore the TWO OLIVE TREES are the CHURCH.

4. In Romans 11 the TWO OLIVE TREES are also the CHURCH made up of Jew and Gentile.

5. In Revelation 11 the TWO WITNESSES are also the TWO CANDLESTICKS.

6. In Revelation 1 the CANDLESTICKS are the CHURCH.

7. The CANDLESTICKS stand Before the God of the Whole Earth and at the same time are standing in the Temple, and since the Temple is the CHURCH made up of Jew and Gentile, the TWO CANDLESTICKS are the CHURCH!

8. Jews in the Old Testament and Gentiles in the New Testament are both called WITNESSES. This witnesses to the fact that they are the TWO WITNESSES.

9. TWO is a big thing from Genesis to Revelation, and by the way, so is the CHURCH.

10. The TWO WITNESSES (the CHURCH) will be on the earth, when the wicked are judged.

11. Great revival will come to Israel during and at the end of the Great Tribulation.

12. If the TWO WITNESSES are the church, then the rapture, which is the first resurrection, will not happen until after the Great Tribulation.

OBJECTIONS ANSWERED

There will be those who question how the TWO WITNESSES could be the CHURCH if they are killed and their bodies lie in the streets for 3 1/2 days? Let's read the verses in Revelation 11:

Rev 11:7 "And when they shall have finished their testimony, the beast that ascendeth out of the bottomless pit shall **make war against them, and shall overcome them, and kill them.**"

Rev 11:8 "And **their dead bodies shall lie in the street of the great city, which spiritually is called Sodom and Egypt, where also our Lord was crucified.**"

Rev 11:9 "And they of the people and kindreds and tongues and nations shall see their dead bodies three days and an half, and shall not suffer their dead bodies to be put in graves."

Rev 11:10 "And they that dwell upon the earth shall rejoice over them, and make merry, and shall send gifts one to another; because these two prophets tormented them that dwelt on the earth."

Rev 11:11 "And **after three days and an half the Spirit of life from God entered into them**, and they stood upon their feet; and great fear fell upon them which saw them."

> Rev 11:12 "And they heard a great voice from heaven saying unto them, **Come up hither. And they ascended up to heaven in a cloud; and their enemies beheld them.**"

Mark Hitchcock tells us on page 346 in his book that Zechariah "mentioned two great witnesses in his day—Joshua...and Zerubbabel". He quotes David Jeremiah and John Walvoord to verify that the wording in Revelation 11:4 "alludes" to the fact that these two witnesses are two literal people. This section in Hitchcock's book has a lot of problems and they start right here. Number one, Zechariah doesn't MENTION or even call Joshua or Zerubbabel witnesses. Number two, the word witnesses isn't even used. Third, alluding to ideas doesn't make for good doctrine. Let's get verses on the subject to give meaning to ideas as I do earlier in this chapter. The scripture calls them the two olive trees and the two candlesticks, but then says their bodies do this and that. In one sense I agree it does sound like they are two individuals, but just because something sounds like it doesn't make it true. I have laid out my argument through this whole chapter that they are the church and few to none have given this side of the story so it is up to the reader to choose what is most Biblical.

In the foregoing verses I have highlighted the critical parts of the passage with enlarged, bold face type. The very same thing that is said of the TWO WITNESSES is said of the CHURCH. There will be a great persecution launched against the TWO WITNESSES which is the CHURCH. They will kill the saints and let them lie in the streets of Jerusalem and, by the way, in cities around the world and they will rejoice over their deaths. The TWO WITNESSES or the CHURCH will testify for three and a half years (a day for a year as it is used in Daniel 9). After three and a half years the Lord will come at the end of the Great Tribulation and will cause His saints to rise up on their feet in the sight of all their enemies and from there they will slowly ascend into heaven to the chagrin of all those who hated them and killed them. Someone will say, "The Bible says that we shall be changed in the twinkling of an eye. This doesn't seem to fit with this." Don't be confused. Our bodies are changed in the twinkling of an eye, but our ascent will happen just like Jesus' ascent into heaven. He slowly ascended into heaven showing us how we will also rise. This is the RAPTURE! It is at the end when everything is wrapped up as verse 15 of this chapter verifies:

> Rev 11:15 "And the seventh angel sounded; and there were great voices in heaven, saying, **The kingdoms of this world are become the kingdoms of our Lord, and of his Christ; and he shall reign for ever and ever.**"

As you can see, this is when the millennial reign begins. It is all about the CHURCH. The TWO WITNESSES are the Church and if you're not one of them, you can be!

"WHO ARE THE TWO WITNESSES?" STUDY QUESTIONS
(*Open Book Quiz*)

1-3. Give the three most popular names who prophecy experts say might be the Two Witnesses.

4. Power will be given to the Two Witnesses to prophesy how long?

5-6. Revelation 11:4 tells us who the Two Witnesses are by giving two sets of two. What are they?

7. Why did God imply, both to Zachariah and John, that they knew who the Two Witnesses were?

8. The verses in Zachariah 4:6-10 didn't deal with the Two Witnesses. Why?

9. What almost exact phrase links the Anointed Ones to the Olive Trees and the Candlesticks?

10. What chapter in the New Testament tells us who the Two Olive Trees are?

11-12. What two classes of people do the Two Olive Trees represent?

13. What verse in Revelation tells us who the Two Candlesticks are?

14. What building in the Bible does the saved Jew and Gentile represent?

15-16. Who are called witnesses in the Old and New Testament?

17. What is the number of witness?

18-20. How was the number two represented in Joseph's life as to his dreams and interpretations?

19. Why does God need two witnesses in the end of time?

20. What according to Paul will cause the resurrection, or life from the dead?

21. What group of people is graffed into the saved Jewish tree?

22. According to Romans 11 what is the covenant of God to Israel?

23. What verse in the book of Acts tells the Jews how to be saved?

"WHO ARE THE TWO WITNESSES?"
(Quiz Answers)

1-3. Moses, Elijah, Enoch

4. 1260 days

5-6. The two Olive Trees and the two candlesticks

7. Because they were God's people and they knew God's people.

8. Because not everything is in chronological order.

9. "...that stand by the Lord of the whole earth" or "...standing before the God of the earth"

10. Romans 11

11-12. The saved Jews and the saved Gentiles

13. Revelation 1:20

14. The temple

15-16. The saved Jews and the saved Gentiles

17. Two

18-20. He had two dreams about himself. He interpreted two from the two prisoners, and two from Pharaoh.

19. Because in the end of time many will die and according to the law of Moses the Lord would not allow the death of anyone without two or three witnesses.

20. The receiving of the Jews, as a nation, back into the favor and the salvation of God
21. The saved Gentiles
22. God has covenanted to save Israel and in so doing, take away their sins.
23. Acts 2:38

I was driving down the road one day behind a vehicle with a bumper sticker as pictured here:

Is it really true that, "on time is when I get there"? Not really, at least, in our American busy life style.

Some might accuse me of being guilty of that, but it's interesting how we change the definition of things to agree with our own life style. Without realizing it, I think many of us do that with the word of God. Maybe we shouldn't, huh? What should we do? As much as possible, find the definition of whatever we're looking up in God's word. How does that apply to prophecy? For example, how about the word, "rapture"? We use this word to refer to our hope, but since the word is not found in scripture in the King James Version of the Bible, what word or phrase does the Bible use to describe our hope? The answer is: the most common words are, "coming", "appearing", or "revelation" of our Lord.

Chapter Four:
WHO ARE THE 144,000?

(IS THE CHURCH FOUND IN REVELATION 5-18?)

This question seems to always arise after someone reads the first 5 verses of Revelation 14, and it's a good question. It's a natural result of reading the chapter. I have asked that question for a very long time. After the Lord revealed to me who the Two Witnesses, the Four Beasts, and the Four and Twenty Elders were, He began speaking to me about the 144,000. I want to share with you what He showed me, and then you can determine whether it was God or not.

Many have tried to answer the question, but few agree on the subject. Wayne Jackson writes for the Christian Courier and gives us an interesting survey of different views. He says the Jehovah Witness's Watchtower publication, LET GOD BE TRUE, pg. 113 says: "the final number of the heavenly church will be 144,000 according to God's decree". I take that to mean that they feel this is a literal number of how many will be in the true church. To me that sounds too restrictive. What do you think? Jackson continues, "It should be noted that the term 'thousand' is used nineteen times in the Book of Revelation, but not once is it employed literally in this document." I think Jackson is trying to say that since the term "thousand" is used so many times in a figurative way it is not likely that the "cousin" term "144,000" is a literal number as well. The statement is quite insightful and I would agree with him. Jackson continues, "There are some minor differences among Bible scholars. John T. Hinds has argued that it represents the saved of the physical nation of Israel. J. W. Roberts believes this company is spiritual Israel, that is the church, while others believe that this is the group of martyrs who have given up their lives for Christ." I think Jackson has captured in as few words as possible the consensus of main stream Christianity, but which is it? Is it spiritual Israel, physical Israel, or the martyrs? Could it possibly be all three combined?

Again, "Who are the 144,000?" is a frequently asked question. Before I can give my take on the issue, I must bring up the second question, which really should be answered first. The main reason I bring up the second question is because many, or should I say, most modern day prophecy buffs tell us emphatically that the rapture took place in the first verse of chapter 4. If that is true then, of course, the church would not be found in chapters 5-18, and that would give us a partial answer of who the 144,000 are by knowing who they aren't. But is this truly the case? If the rapture didn't happen in 4:1, then maybe the church is found in Revelation 5-18. Maybe, just maybe, if it's a symbolic number, the 144,000 could, at least include the church. So, let's deal with the first of these three questions.

DOES THE RAPTURE TAKE PLACE IN REVELATION 4:1?

As I said, the most popular prophecy teachers tell us that Revelation 4:1 is the rapture and that the church is not found again in the book of Revelation until the 19th chapter. Let's give the verse, so we can see what it's saying:

> Rev 4:1 "After this I looked, and, behold, a door was opened in heaven: and the first voice which I heard was as it were of a trumpet talking with me; which said, **Come up hither**, and I will shew thee things which must be hereafter."

I have some problems agreeing that this is the rapture, for some very apparent reasons. My opponents say the word "church" is not used in chapters 5-18, so therefore God's people are not on the earth during this time period. If those same proponents are forced to use their same kind of interpretation to this verse, then they have not a leg to stand on, because the word "church" is not used in this verse nor is it even used in chapter 19 either! Hey, in this verse 4:1 it isn't the church, it's John. This is a case where "sound Bible expositors" are twisting the Word to fit their own preconceived Bible notions. They want to prove their Bible doctrine so they have to put a round peg in a square hole. I'm sorry, it doesn't work that way. If we are going to use proper hermeneutics and interpret this correctly, we need to admit that this is simply John being carried away in the Spirit to hear what God has to say about future events.

The phrase, "come up hither", might be construed to mean what they say, but what are we going to do with the same phrase in Revelation 11:12. Is that the rapture too and what about other similar phrases like "come hither" that are given to us in chapters 17 and 21? Are those two other raptures? Look at:

> Rev 17:1 "And there came one of the seven angels which had the seven vials, and talked with me, saying unto me, **Come hither**; I will shew unto thee the judgment of the great whore..."

> Rev 21:9 "And there came unto me one of the seven angels which had the seven vials full of the seven last plagues, and talked with me, saying, **Come hither**, I will shew thee the bride, the Lamb's wife."

There isn't a lot of difference between "come up hither" and "come hither", except who it's spoken to. The second "come up hither" is spoken to the two witnesses or the church and that is the "rapture" and is simply a snap shot event in the middle of the book, but the other three phrases are spoken to John, so are there three more raptures? No. The Lord is simply taking John three different times in the Spirit to show him prophetic events. With that in mind, I think most will agree with me, that 4:1 isn't the rapture and neither is

17:1 or 21:9, and that can be further verified by 16:15, and 18:4:

> Rev 16:15 "Behold, **I come as a thief**. Blessed is he that watcheth, and keepeth his garments, lest he walk naked, and they see his shame."

> Rev 18:4 "And I heard another voice from heaven, saying, **Come out of her, my people**, that ye be not partakers of her sins, and that ye receive not of her plagues."

I think you will agree with me that if Jesus is going to "come as a thief", that means He hasn't come yet, and if the Lord's people are still in Mystery Babylon, and He is telling them to "come out of her", then they weren't in heaven, and the rapture hasn't happened until that point. This concept can be further strengthened by simply considering who the book is written to.

TO WHOM WAS THE BOOK OF REVELATION ADDRESSED?

To whom was the book of Revelation addressed? The answer is found in chapter 1, verses 4 and 11:

> Rev 1:4 "John **to the seven churches** which are in Asia: Grace be unto you, and peace..."

> Rev 1:11 "Saying, I am Alpha and Omega, the first and the last: and, What thou seest, write in **a book**, and send it unto the **seven churches** which are in Asia..."

John wraps up his letter in the last chapter by quoting Jesus and again mentions who he is writing to:

> Rev 22:16 "I Jesus have sent mine angel to testify unto you these things **in the churches**. I am the root and the offspring of David, and the bright and morning star."

The book was addressed to the seven churches of Asia or you could say to the church in general. It was not written to the Sabbath keeping, backslidden Israelites, as a class of people, but to the church. There were probably some Jews among them but largely, the church was made up of Gentiles. It was written for whoever was in the church throughout the ages, whether Jew, Gentile, or Samaritan—it is a timeless book. To assume that because the word "church" is not found in 14 chapters of the book and to even imply that those chapters are not for the church (because the church is not there) is a GROSS misinterpretation of scripture. Again, let me say, the whole book was and is for the whole church throughout the church age. It bothers me because the enemy has come against this book and mislead many, many believers.

I have shared two points so far. 1) the rapture did not take place in Revelation 4:1. 2) The whole book of Revelation, including chapters 5-18, is for the whole church and it is implied that it is for the church, because the church will be on the earth when it all unfolds. The third point will have to do with the word "church" not being used in 14 chapters of Revelation. I will go over that and then we will be ready to discover the true meaning of, "Who are the 144,000?"

THE WORD "CHURCH" IS NOT USED IN REVELATION 5-18

Noah Hutchings in 2013 did a whole program on the Southwest Radio Church, Watchman on the Wall broadcast and talked about a book that he wrote that "proves" that the church is not on the earth during the tribulation. He does this by showing the word "church" is not used in the book of Revelation when it talks about the tribulation being poured out. His opinion represents that of many prophecy students and teachers alike. I must respond to this assertion. I think it is a weak argument. God's people are referred to as the church in the epistles 31 times, but as servants 20 times and as saints 42 times (taken from the Strong's Concordance). Just from that alone, you can see that God refers to His people more by the word "saint" than even by the word "church". If God chooses to call His people by a name other than "church", does that mean that those people are not part of the church? I hardly think so. Is God sovereign, or are we going to tell Him how to write His Book? These seem like stupid questions, yet they beg to be asked because of the outlandish statements made by prophecy teachers who are bent on bending the Word of God to prove their erroneous interpretations of prophecy. The fact that the word saint is used, in no way detracts from the fact that these same individuals are not part of the church. **Just because the Lord does not refer to His people as "the church" in the book of Revelation between chapters 5 and 18 doesn't mean the church isn't there!** That is not solid evidence. Let's look at those chapters to see if God's church is there by using other names.

Revelation Chapter 5:8-10 has four key phrases that let us know that this is the church:

> Rev 5:8 "And when he had taken the book, the four beasts and four and twenty elders fell down before the Lamb, having every one of them harps, and golden vials full of odours, which are **the prayers of saints.**"

> Rev 5:9 "And they sung a new song, saying, Thou art worthy to take the book, and to open the seals thereof: for thou wast slain, and hast **redeemed us to God** by thy blood out of every kindred, and tongue, and people, and nation;"

> Rev 5:10 "And hast **made us unto our God**

kings and priests: and **we shall reign on the earth.**"

If these four phrases don't describe the church, then I don't know what does. Those in the church pray, they are redeemed, they are made kings and priests, and they will reign with Christ on the earth.

Revelation Chapter 6 tells us what happens after he opens the fifth seal:

> Rev 6:9 "And when he had opened the fifth seal, I saw under the altar the souls of them that were **slain for the word of God, and for the testimony which they held:**"

> Rev 6:10 "And they cried with a loud voice, saying, How long, O Lord, holy and true, dost thou not judge and avenge our blood on them that dwell on the earth?"

> Rev 6:11 "And **white robes were given unto every one of them**; and it was said unto them, that they should rest yet for a little season, **until their fellow servants also and their brethren, that should be killed as they were, should be fulfilled.**"

Who is this being slain for the Word of God and for the testimony which they held? Sounds like the church to me. Hey, white robes were given to every one of them and they were supposed to wait until the end of the Great Persecution until others would be killed as they were. They are getting what the saints get: white robes. Doesn't sound like the rapture has happened yet. The dead in Christ are still waiting. I smell a skunk. Somebody is lying to us, or is grossly ignorant of the truth and is going around, misleading (on purpose or not) a lot of people. If you have ears, hear the truth!

Revelation Chapter 7: The first descriptive phrase in verse 3 is, "…till we have sealed the servants of our God in their foreheads." I mentioned it above, but let me repeat it, if those in the church are not the servants of the Lord who are they? I will come back to this chapter, and prove that the phrases describing the great multitude are also describing the church.

Revelation Chapter 8 verse 3 lets us know that this chapter also is talking about the church:

> Rev 8:3 "And another angel came and stood at the altar, having a golden censer; and there was given unto him much incense, that he should offer it **with the prayers of all saints** upon the golden altar which was before the throne."

Revelation Chapter 9 has only an inference to the church in verse 4:

> Rev 9:4 "And it was commanded them that they should not hurt the grass of the earth, neither any green thing, neither any tree; but only those **men which have not the seal of God in their foreheads.**"

If there are men there that do NOT have the seal of God in their foreheads, then there are men there that DO, and who are they? They are those in the church.

Revelation Chapter 11 is the next mention of the people of God. I have already written extensively in 28 pages that those mentioned in this chapter are truly the church of the living God, so I don't intend to repeat all of that here, except to summarize briefly how the church is mentioned there. For a more detailed look, see my chapter entitled "The Two Witnesses":

> Rev 11:3 "And I will give power unto **my two witnesses**, and they shall **prophesy** a thousand two hundred and threescore days, clothed in sackcloth."

Here in chapter 11 we see God has "two" witnesses. Is this the church? Yes. In Luke 24:48, Acts 1:8, 2:32, Acts 3:15, and I Thessalonians 2:10, the church is described as being His witnesses. (We could call them Jesus' Witnesses—this is a different group from what is known today as the Jehovah Witnesses, ha.) It says these prophesy. I deal with the idea of prophesying when we get to verse 11, because this idea is repeated there. Now, please look at verse 4:

> Rev 11:4 "These are the two **olive trees**, and the **two candlesticks** standing before the God of the earth."

Who are the two OLIVE trees? Romans 11 lets us know that it is the church made up of Jews and Gentiles. Who are the two CANDLESTICKS? Revelation 1:20 tells us plainly that the seven candlesticks are the churches, so what do we have here? We have the church "smack dab" in the middle of the book of Revelation—chapter 11—contrary to what others might say. Look at verse 7:

> Rev 11:7 "And when they shall have finished **their testimony**, the beast that ascendeth out of the bottomless pit **shall make war against them**, and shall overcome them, and kill them."

Who is it that testifies and has a testimony? In Acts 13:22, 14:3, and 22:18 we see it is Paul and those in the church. I will discuss making war against them when we get to chapter 13. Look at verse 10:

> Rev 11:10 "And they that dwell upon the earth shall rejoice over them, and make merry, and shall send

gifts one to another; because these two **prophets** tormented them that dwelt on the earth."

In verse 3 it says they prophesy, and this verse calls them prophets. Who is it that prophesies and are called prophets in the New Testament? Acts 21:10; I Corinthians 12:28, 14:29,37; and Ephesians 4:11 lets us know that prophets are in the church and they prophesy. Look at verse 12:

Rev 11:12 "And they heard a great voice from heaven saying unto them, Come up hither. And they ascended up to heaven in a cloud; and their enemies beheld them."

WHAT IS THIS? This passage is actually describing the rapture. The timing is not totally logged in here, but it is a snap shot of the rapture that is to come, right in the middle of the book of Revelation. It is further verified starting in verse 15:

Rev 11:15 "And the seventh angel sounded; and there were great voices in heaven, saying, **The kingdoms of this world are become the kingdoms of our Lord, and of his Christ; and he shall reign for ever and ever.**"

Rev 11:16 "And the four and twenty elders, which sat before God on their seats, fell upon their faces, and worshipped God,"

Rev 11:17 "Saying, We give thee thanks, O Lord God Almighty, which art, and wast, and art to come; because thou hast taken to thee thy great power, and **hast reigned.**"

Rev 11:18 "And the nations were angry, and thy wrath is come, and **the time of the dead**, that they should be judged, and that **thou shouldest give reward unto thy servants the prophets, and to the saints, and them that fear thy name, small and great**; and shouldest destroy them which destroy the earth."

At and after the coming of the Lord, Jesus is going to reward His people. According to most people, the rapture would have already taken place long before this, so why is it describing it here? It is because the rapture didn't happen before the tribulation. It happens AFTER the tribulation. Someone might ask, "But this is the middle of the book of Revelation and not the end of the book. If what you are saying is true, then it should be describing it at the end of the book, not in the middle of the book." The answer is, if you are going to understand the book of Revelation, you must always keep in mind that the events of this book are like scenarios. It covers one scenario or train of thought to the end, then it backs up, starts at the beginning or middle and gives another scenario to the end, then backs up and starts over and gives another scenario to the end, so the end is REPEATED SEVERAL TIMES throughout the book! Can you see that? Just UNDERSTANDING THIS ONE PRINCIPLE of the book will help you tremendously to put the pieces together, and that is what is happening here!

Revelation Chapter 12 also mentions the people of God. Somebody might say, "Ah, ha, this woman clothed with the sun and the moon under her feet is the nation of Israel." No, you are only partially right. In the New Testament you will see over and over again that the people of God are united into one body. The Lord, here, doesn't split them into two separate groups anymore. They are all conglomerated into one, as you will see, shortly, but I agree with you, that it sounds like the nation of Israel at first, but look at her descriptions further down:

1. She is referred to as the "woman", and the church is the bride of Christ which if you hadn't noticed is a woman.

    > verse 4 "the dragon stood before the woman..."
    > verse 6 "and the woman fled into the wilderness..."

2. In verse 10, she now takes on the male side of the equation

    > "...for the accuser of **our brethren** is cast down..."

3. Verse 11 confirms it further.

> "And they overcame him by the blood of the Lamb and by the word of their testimony: and they loved not their lives unto the death." There are three phrases here and they describe God's people, the church. The church overcomes by the blood of the Lamb. The church has the word of testimony. The church is subjected to being killed. Can you see it? Israel is no longer segregated by itself. It is incorporated into the church and has become one with the Gentile part of the people of God. When I return back to chapter 7, you will see it again, and chapter 14 is also the same theme continued, and that is what is happening in this chapter, also. All through Revelation you see the people of God, Israelite and Gentile, in one body.

4. Verses 13-17 returns back to talking about the woman, and remember this is the bride:

> Verse 13 "...he persecuted the woman which brought forth the man child."
> Verse 14 "And to the woman were given two wings of a great eagle..."
> Verse 15 "And the serpent cast out of his mouth water as a flood after the woman..."

> Verse 16 "And the earth helped the woman, and the earth opened her mouth..."
>
> Verse 17 "And the dragon was wroth with the woman, and went to make war..."

5. Verse 17, the last half of this verse verifies that this woman is the church because it says:

   > "...which keep the commandments of God, and have the testimony of Jesus Christ."

The old Jewish nation has refused to walk in the new light of God and keep the new salvation part of the commandments of God, whereas the redeemed part of the Jewish nation along with the Gentiles which make up the church, DO KEEP the commandments of God, and DO HAVE the testimony of Jesus Christ. The backslidden Jewish nation surely does not have that testimony.

Revelation Chapter 13 continues mentioning the church right alongside the beast, or Antichrist. Let's look at verses 6-8:

> Rev 13:6 "And he opened his mouth in blasphemy against God, to blaspheme his name, and **his tabernacle, and them that dwell in heaven.**"

Rev 13:7 "And it was given unto him **to make war with the saints**, and to overcome them: and power was given him over all kindreds, and tongues, and nations."

Rev 13:8 "And all that dwell upon the earth shall worship him, **whose names are not written in the book of life of the Lamb slain from the foundation of the world.**"

This beast opens his mouth and speaks against what and whom? He speaks against God and His "tabernacle". Is that the Old Testament tabernacle in the wilderness? No! That's God's way of saying that the CHURCH is God's present day tabernacle. The beast is speaking against the church! Who is "them that dwell in heaven"? I deal with this in other places in this book, but let me repeat that this is not talking about the saints of God that have already died and gone to heaven, but it is saying the beast is blaspheming the living saints on earth. I am saying then, that at the same time we as saints of God who walk on the earth, are at the same time sitting in heavenly places, as this verse indicates. You might say, "Where did you get that?" It comes from Ephesians 2:

Eph 2:5 "Even when we were dead in sins, hath quickened us together with Christ, (by grace ye are saved;)"

Eph 2:6 "And hath raised us up together, and made us **sit together in heavenly places in Christ Jesus:**"

Paul was addressing the living saints on earth in the above verse, 13:6, and was telling them that at the same time they were on earth, they were sitting in heavenly places, that is heaven. Hopefully you can see it. The beast is blaspheming the church and them that are in it and it is confirmed by the following verse, that is 13:7 when it plainly says he makes war with the saints. He is not making war on the saints in heaven that have already been raptured. No, because the saints haven't been raptured yet. These saints are alive on earth. You can't make war with corpses. Some try to tell us that these are the tribulation saints. They must have just gotten saved, because the rapture, supposedly, already happened, and miraculously they have just got saved and are mature enough to lay their lives down for the Lord. I would respond, "How did they get saved without a preacher, because all the saved preachers were also, supposedly taken to heaven? How can they hear without a preacher as Romans 10:14 says?" Then they retort, "Oh, these were saved by the "two witnesses". I respond, "If the two witnesses (or prophets) were right with God and had a close relationship with Jesus, why didn't they get taken to heaven in the rapture that supposedly just happened? The rapture is supposed to take everybody that is right with God and is saved, to heaven to enjoy the marriage supper of the Lamb. How come these two preachers had to miss out on the great banquet in heaven?" They say the Holy Ghost has been taken off the earth, but yet they talk about people being saved on the earth to make up the tribulation saints. I have news for them. No one can get saved without the Holy Ghost being on earth to convict and save them. It doesn't make sense. That's not the only complication. As I asked before, "when do these who are dying in the Lord get raised up, because according to them, the dead in Christ have already been raised? Jesus said, there is only one resurrection of the just. Wooh...Too many unanswered questions.

An improper understanding of prophecy, will mess up everything. The church has not been raptured. It is still here on earth and the beast is trying to kill every church person he can find. It is going to take a mature saint of God who has been preparing for a while to be able to go through this period of time. Do you think a new born child of God is going to be able to do that? Even present day saints who have been serving God for years might not be able to make it through this time of persecution, at least, not without some kind of teaching, training, and warning. That is what this chapter and book is all about. That is what God has called me to do: "warn the church." Wake up. Let's get close to God, now. The time is coming when you won't even be able to go to church, even if you wanted to. Jesus said the night cometh when no man can work. They will have closed all the churches down. We must prepare ourselves, emotionally, psychologically, spiritually, and physically. Someone said Corrie Ten Boom warned that the church in China told their people that God would spare them from the tribulation and many fell away because they weren't ready to suffer. Can't you see, the pretribulation rapture theory is the devil's trap. It makes people think they are going to miss tribulation, persecution, and wrath, so why prepare. The devil wants to catch the church unprepared, so he can damn their soul. Don't let him do that to you and your family. Keep reading this book and GET READY. We do not have much time left!

Revelation 13:7 says he makes "war with the saints..." Remember Revelation 11:7 said, "And when they shall have finished their testimony, the beast that ascendeth out of the bottomless pit **shall make war against them**, and shall overcome them, and kill them. Chapter 12:17 said, "And the dragon was wroth with the woman, and **went to make war with the remnant of her seed**, which keep the commandments of God, and have the testimony of Jesus Christ." When we discussed the woman in chapter 12, I said it was the church, and you can see here in chapter 13 that what happens to the woman—made war against her—also happens to the saints. This is another indication that the woman of Revelation 12 is the same as the saints in chapter 13. You see, the Lord repeats Himself over and over again using different words saying, "War is coming against the church, the saints, God's people, and the woman." Chapter 13 of Revelation is also quite clear that war is coming against the saints and they will be killed. The book of Daniel already forewarned us that this was going to happen. Let's jump over to Daniel and compare the description he gives us in his book with what John gives us in chapter 13. You will see it verifies everything. It starts off in Daniel 7:

> Dan 7:21 "I beheld, and **the same horn made war with the saints**, and prevailed against them;"

> Dan 7:25 "And he shall speak great words against the most High, and **shall wear out the saints of the most High**, and think to change times and laws: and they shall be given into his hand until a time and times and the dividing of time."

> Dan 8:24 "And his power shall be mighty...and **shall destroy the mighty and the holy people**."

> Dan 11:33 "And **they that understand among the people** shall instruct many: yet they **shall fall by the sword, and by flame, by captivity, and by spoil, many days**."

> Dan 11:34 "Now when **they shall fall**, they shall be holpen with a little help: but many shall cleave to them with flatteries."

> Dan 11:35 "And **some of them of understanding shall fall**, to try them, and to purge, and to make them white, even to the time of the

end: because it is yet for a time appointed."

Dan 12:7 "And I heard the man clothed in linen, which was upon the waters of the river, when he held up his right hand and his left hand unto heaven, and sware by him that liveth for ever that it shall be for a time, times, and an half; and when he shall have accomplished **to scatter the power of the holy people**, all these things shall be finished."

You can see that Daniel verifies Revelation 13 that the saints of God, which is the church, will be persecuted. At the end of this section I will list the different phrases used in Revelation and Daniel describing God's people. This list will demonstrate in one view that truly these descriptions are describing the church in both the book of Daniel and the book of Revelation.

Now, look at verse 10 of chapter 13 and you will see again that it mentions the saints: "…Here is the patience and the faith of the saints." Yes, this is the church.

Revelation Chapter 14: We will come back to this chapter to answer, "Who are the 144,000?".

Revelation Chapter 15 starts off in verses two and three:

Rev 15:2 "And I saw as it were a sea of glass mingled

with fire: and **them that had gotten the victory over the beast, and over his image, and over his mark, and over the number of his name, stand on the sea of glass, having the harps of God.**"

Rev 15:3 "And **they sing the song of Moses** the servant of God, and **the song of the Lamb**,"

Who is this group that got the victory over the beast, his image, his mark, and the number of his name? Revelation 20:4-5 answers that:

Rev 20:4 "And I saw thrones, and they sat upon them, and judgment was given unto them: and I saw the souls of them that were beheaded for the witness of Jesus, and for the word of God, and which had **not** worshipped **the beast,** neither **his image,** neither had received **his mark** upon their **foreheads,** or in their **hands; **and they **lived** and **reigned with Christ a thousand years.**"

Rev 20:5 "But the rest of the dead lived not again until the thousand years were finished. **This is the first resurrection.**"

The RAPTURE and the FIRST RESURRECTION are synonymous events. We see the ones who were caught up in the first resurrection are the same ones who got the victory over the beast, his image, his mark, and the number of his name by NOT TAKING IT. (So if you're singing the song, "We're Going Up in the First Resurrection", you need to understand what you're singing. You're admitting that we are going up AFTER the Great Tribulation.) They were on the earth when the Antichrist was there and they refused the mark of the beast and were beheaded for it. Who is this group? It is the CHURCH! I can verify it again by asking who is this in Revelation 15:2 and 3 that has the "harps of God"? (Many tell jokes about the saints being up in heaven sitting on clouds playing harps, and singing for all eternity. Actually, there's some truth to that.) Please recall, we discovered the answer to that in Revelation 5:

> Rev 5:8 "And when he had taken the book, the four beasts and four and twenty elders fell down before the Lamb, **having every one of them harps**, and golden vials full of odours, which are **the prayers of saints**."

> Rev 5:9 "And **they sung a new song**, saying, Thou art worthy to take the book, and to open the seals thereof: for thou wast slain, and **hast redeemed us to God** by thy blood out of every kindred, and tongue, and people, and nation;"

Rev 5:10 "And hast **made us unto our God kings and priests: and we shall reign on the earth.**"

Here we know it's the church because it says of this group it is the "prayers of saints". They are singing a new song, "…thou wast slain, and hast REDEEMED US to God…; and hast made us unto our God kings and priests: and we shall reign on the earth." These things are all typical of the church and chapter 15 is telling us that they are singing again. This time they are singing two songs: the song of Moses, and the song of the Lamb. Why? It is underscoring the fact, again, that this group is made up of two parts: saved Jews (Israelites) who sing the song of Moses and saved Gentiles who sing the song of the Lamb. (Actually, the Gentiles sing the song of Moses too, and the Jews sing the song of the Lamb, as well.) At any rate, this group in chapter 15 is the same group that was mentioned in chapter 5. They have gone through the tribulation, refused to worship the beast, his image, refused his mark, the number of his name, and are being resurrected, because this is the CHURCH!

(I cannot resist to throw in here how in verse 6 the angels are to start pouring out the seven plagues of the wrath of God and no one was permitted to enter the temple, (or heaven) until AFTER they were finished being poured out. Sorry, there's no room for a pre-wrath rapture scenario here.)

Chapter 16: Is there any reference to the church in this chapter? Yes. The first 6 vials of the wrath of God are poured out and then in verse 15 it lets us know that the church is still on the earth and whoever is still keeping their garments white are blessed:

> Rev 16:15 "Behold, **I come as a thief**. Blessed is he that watcheth, and **keepeth his garments**, lest he walk naked, and they see his shame."

Also, the Lord is saying, "I come as a thief." He hasn't come yet! The rapture hasn't happened. Wow! That's as plain as day. Remember, Paul talked about the Lord's coming as a thief in the night, in I Thessalonians 5. Let's get the exact words:

> 1 Th 5:1 "But of the times and the seasons, brethren, ye have no need that I write unto you."

> 1 Th 5:2 "For yourselves know perfectly that **the day of the Lord so cometh as a thief in the night**."

> 1 Th 5:3 "For when they shall say, Peace and safety; then sudden destruction cometh upon them, as travail upon a woman with child; and they shall not escape."

1 Th 5:4 "But **ye, brethren**, are not in darkness, that **that day should overtake you as a thief**."

The "day of the Lord" that most prophecy scholars say is the tribulation is here referred to as the rapture and Paul says it will not overtake the believers as a thief. In Revelation 16:15, after the 6th vial is poured out, as I said earlier, he still hasn't come for His church, yet. Isn't that interesting. Let's go to the next chapter.

Revelation Chapter 17 has one verse which lets us know that the church is still there.

Rev 17:6 "And I saw the woman drunken with **the blood of the saints**, and with **the blood of the martyrs of Jesus**: and when I saw her, I wondered with great admiration."

How is the woman going to drink the blood of the saints, and the blood of the martyrs of Jesus if they aren't there? (The phrase, "drink their blood" means they are being killed.) According to the bulk of the prophecy scholars they are in heaven at this time. If that is the case, then the woman wouldn't be able to "drink their blood", but she does do this, and the only way she can is because they are still on the earth. Notice again, we see God's people divided into two camps: 1) the saints, and 2) the martyrs of Jesus. (Notice it is not "saints" and "tribulation saints". More about that later.) What's the difference between these two groups? Probably not very much, so why does it say it like that? It is an often repeated theme throughout the New Testament. It is found, also, in chapter 7 as we will see shortly. The Lord is just trying to drive home this point that His people are made up of two groups: Jews and Gentiles, but all in one body. How many times does the Lord have to do this before we get the point?

Revelation Chapter 18 lets us know the church is still on the earth because of verse 4:

> Rev 18:4 "And I heard another voice from heaven, saying, **Come out of her, my people**, that ye be not partakers of her sins, and that ye receive not of her plagues."

Why would the voice from heaven be saying, "come out" of Babylon my people, if the people of God were already in heaven, being taken there by means of the rapture? That is not very likely. The voice was "from heaven", as though whoever was speaking was in heaven, so if this was an angel, he would know if they were there or not. His command to come out of Mystery Babylon would be irrelevant, wouldn't it? The point is, they are still on the earth. The rapture, still hasn't happened yet. This is verified by the last verse:

> Rev 18:24 "And in her was found **the blood of prophets**, and **of saints**, and of all that were slain upon the earth."

Besides "all that were slain upon the earth", here we find two groups, again: 1) the blood of prophets, and 2) the blood of saints...same old story—two groups—but this tells us plainly, "God's people are on the earth." They are not in heaven, yet.

Revelation Chapter 19 sort of culminates everything. Verses 1-10 gives us a snapshot view of God's people in heaven (but remember it doesn't use the word church to describe them.) and tells us:

> Rev 19:7 "Let us be glad and rejoice, and give honour to him: for the marriage of the Lamb is come and his wife hath made herself ready."

How this chapter is constructed is mysterious, because God's people are definitely in heaven, but it bypasses how they got there. This is not a chronological statement of events. These are snap shots of end time events. Actually chapters 11:11-12 and 14:1-5 should fit right before verse 1. The rest of the chapter is not in chronological order either. Again, without telling us how they got there, the chapter, further down, fills in a detail how the Lord returned to the earth to get the victory over the beast, his army, and the false prophet (again, before He raptured His people). Many prophecy teachers say this chapter is in chronological order, and that's why they have us in heaven for seven years before the Lord and His army return on white horses. Not so. The order of events has to be pieced together by other passages (not by false ideas). Please, do not get mixed up by this. It is a trap for the unsuspecting.

At this juncture, even Dr. Noah Hutchings admits that 19:1-10 is undoubtedly the church in heaven (or where ever the Lord is—He is actually on the earth) enjoying the marriage supper of the Lamb. This is what's amazing. He admits this, even though the word "church" is NOT even used in this chapter! I agree with him, though. This is the church and this is the same body of people that has been described all through Revelation, as I have shown you.

Let me summarize this by saying that I have been showing you how the church is mentioned and talked about in Revelation 5-18 by many names. Since the book is addressed to the church, it doesn't have to keep using the word "church" throughout the book. Without including all the references in chapter 7 and 14, it uses 33 different names and descriptions that all apply to the church, and they are:

1.	It is in the church that believers are called	SAINTS: 5:8; 8:3-4; 11:18; 13:7,10; 17:6
2.	You can only get into the church by being	REDEEMED: 5:9
3.	In the church you will reign on the earth	AS KINGS AND PRIESTS: 5:10
4.	In the church believers in Jesus are	SLAIN FOR THE WORD OF GOD: 6:9; 11:7; 17:6

5.	Only in the church do they have a	TESTIMONY THAT THEY HOLD: 6:9; 11:7
6.	It is those in the church that have	WHITE ROBES GIVEN TO THEM: 6:11
7.	Those in the church are called	FELLOW SERVANTS: 6:11
8.	Those in the church are called	BRETHREN: 6:11; 12:10
9.	It is those in the church that are	SEALED: 7:3; 9:4
10.	Those in the church are called	THE SERVANTS OF OUR GOD: 7:3
11.	Those in the church are called	WITNESSES: 11:3
12.	It is those in the church that	PROPHESY: 11:3
13.	The church is called the	OLIVE TREES: 11:4
14.	The church is called the	CANDLESTICKS: 1:20; 11:4
15.	Select ones in the church are called	PROPHETS: 11:10
16.	At the time of the rapture the church will	COME UP HITHER: 11:12

17.	At the time of the rapture the church will	ASCEND UP TO HEAVEN: 11:12
18.	After this the church will be rewarded as	"THY" SERVANTS THE PROPHETS: 11:18
19.	The church is comprised of	THEM THAT FEAR THY NAME, SMALL AND GREAT: 11:18
20.	The church is called	THE WOMAN: 12:1, 4, 6, 13-17
21.	Those in the church overcome	BY THE BLOOD OF THE LAMB: 12:11
22.	Those in the church overcome	BY THE WORD OF THEIR TESTIMONY: 12:11
23.	Those in the church	LOVE NOT THEIR LIVES UNTO THE DEATH: 12:11
24.	The church is made up of	THE REMNANT OF HER (THE WOMAN'S) SEED: 12:1
25.	The church is made up of those that	KEEP THE COMMANDMENTS OF GOD: 12:17
26.	The church is comprised of those that	HAVE THE TESTIMONY OF JESUS CHRIST: 12:17

27.	The church is made up of them	THAT DWELL IN HEAVEN 13:6
28.	Those in the church get the victory over	THE BEAST, HIS IMAGE, MARK, AND NAME 15:2
29.	Those in the church	STAND ON THE SEA OF GLASS 15:2
30.	Those in the church	HAVE THE HARPS OF GOD 5:8; 15:2
31.	Those in the church sing a new song and	THE SONG OF MOSES, AND THE LAMB 5:9; 15:3
32.	Those in the church are told to watch and	KEEP THEIR GARMENTS (WHITE) 16:15
33.	The church is told to come out of mystery	BABYLON THE GREAT AS "MY PEOPLE" 18:4

The book of Daniel is similar. It uses the following names and phrases that, also apply to the church:

1. saints, 7:21
2. saints of the most high, 7:25
3. the mighty and the holy people, 8:24
4. they that understand among the people, 11:33
5. some of them of understanding, 11:35
6. the holy people, 12:7

I have thus answered the second question of this section and covered the third point: Is the Church found in Revelation

5-18? I have shown the answer to be, yes. This prepares me to make my fourth point and answer the third and main question:

WHO ARE THE 144,000?

The passage that brings up the question more often than not is the passage found in Revelation 14, so before I go any further, I want to give those verses:

> Rev 14:1 "And I looked, and, lo, a Lamb stood on the mount Sion, and with him **an hundred forty and four thousand**, having his Father's name written in their foreheads."

> Rev 14:2 "And I heard a voice from heaven, as the voice of many waters, and as the voice of a great thunder: and I heard the voice of harpers harping with their harps:"

> Rev 14:3 "And they sung as it were a new song before the throne, and before the four beasts, and the elders: and no man could learn that song but **the hundred and forty and four thousand**, which were redeemed from the earth."

> Rev 14:4 "These are they which were not defiled with

women; for they are virgins. These are they which follow the Lamb whithersoever he goeth. These were redeemed from among men, being the firstfruits unto God and to the Lamb."

Rev 14:5 "And in their mouth was found no guile: for they are without fault before the throne of God."

The first step in understanding who they are would be to enumerate all their characteristics from this passage. This will be the biggest key in revealing their identity.

1. 144,000 stood with the Lamb on Mount Sion.

2. They had their Father's name written in their foreheads.

3. Their voice was from heaven as the voice of many waters.

4. Their voice was as the voice of a great thunder.

5. Their voice was as the voice of harpers, harping with their harps.

6. They sung a new song before the throne, the four beasts, and the elders and no man could learn that song but the 144,000.

7. They were redeemed from the earth and from among men.

8. They were not defiled by women because they were virgins.

9. They followed the Lamb whithersoever He went.

10. They were the firstfruits unto God and to the Lamb.

11. There was no guile found in their mouth.

12. They are without fault before the throne of God.

It is interesting that there are 12 characteristic descriptions. It appears that all of these are typical descriptions of the church or saints in general, except one, and that is the first. Most Bible scholars have concluded that since the first characteristic of this group is given as the 144,000 (and this group seems to match that group mentioned in Revelation chapter 7, which I will give shortly) it seems justifiable to assume that they are 12,000 Jews from every tribe of Israel who are saved during the tribulation. I admit, it does specifically say that in chapter 7, but the question I have is, why does it not repeat that in this 14th chapter? This passage, after saying they are the 144,000, lists 11 other characteristics, but not one time does it repeat the fact that they are Jews that come from the 12 tribes of Israel. If the Lord would have made that one of the 11 characteristics it would have settled the issue for ever and there would not be any more question, but it doesn't say that, so it throws it open for debate. There are only two places in the whole Bible that talk about the 144,000, so the answer of who they are must come from them. To round out our understanding then, we must examine the companion passage found in Revelation 7:

> Rev 7:1 "And after these things I saw four angels standing on the four corners of the earth, holding the four winds of the earth, that the wind should not blow on the earth, nor on the sea, nor on any tree."
>
> Rev 7:2 "And I saw another angel ascending from the east, having the seal of the living God: and he cried with a loud voice to the four angels, to whom it was given to hurt the earth and the sea,"
>
> Rev 7:3 "Saying, Hurt not the earth, neither the sea, nor the trees, till we have sealed the servants of our God in their foreheads."
>
> Rev 7:4 "And I heard the number of them which were sealed: and there were sealed **an hundred and forty and four thousand** of **all the tribes of the children of Israel.**"

Rev 7:5 "Of the tribe of **Juda** were sealed twelve thousand. Of the tribe of **Reuben** were sealed twelve thousand. Of the tribe of **Gad** were sealed twelve thousand."

Rev 7:6 "Of the tribe of **Aser** were sealed twelve thousand. Of the tribe of **Nepthalim** were sealed twelve thousand. Of the tribe of **Manasses** were sealed twelve thousand."

Rev 7:7 "Of the tribe of **Simeon** were sealed twelve thousand. Of the tribe of **Levi** were sealed twelve thousand. Of the tribe of **Issachar** were sealed twelve thousand."

Rev 7:8 "Of the tribe of **Zabulon** were sealed twelve thousand. Of the tribe of **Joseph** were sealed twelve thousand. Of the tribe of **Benjamin** were sealed twelve thousand."

Remember this is the first mention of this group and it appears to be in the middle of the tribulation. Four angels are sent out to hurt the earth and they are forbidden to do that until "THE SERVANTS OF OUR GOD" are SEALED. The passage then goes into how the 144,000 number was derived, that is 12,000 from each tribe. I want you to make a mental note of two things before I progress. 1) This group has a second name: "the servants of our God", and 2) they were "sealed". I want you to be sensitive to these phrases, because it will go a long way in helping us understand who they are, but this is it. There is no more information here, about this group until we get to chapter 14. There is another point that is very interesting, that has a bearing on who these are. Without any introduction it goes from verse 8 to verse 9 and it starts talking about another group of people. Does this second group affect, modify, change, or incorporate the first group? Maybe it does. Let's give those verses:

ANOTHER GROUP: A GREAT MULTITUDE

> Rev 7:9 "After this I beheld, and, lo, a great multitude, which no man could number, of all nations, and kindreds, and people, and tongues, stood before the throne, and before the Lamb, clothed with white robes, and palms in their hands;"

> Rev 7:10 "And cried with a loud voice, saying, Salvation to our God which sitteth upon the throne, and unto the Lamb."

> Rev 7:11 "And all the angels stood round about the throne, and about the elders and the four beasts, and fell before the throne on their faces, and worshipped God,"

Rev 7:12 "Saying, Amen: Blessing, and glory, and wisdom, and thanksgiving, and honour, and power, and might, be unto our God for ever and ever. Amen."

Rev 7:13 "And one of the elders answered, saying unto me, **What are these which are arrayed in white robes? and whence came they?**"

Rev 7:14 "And I said unto him, Sir, thou knowest. And he said to me, These are they which came out of great tribulation, and have washed their robes, and made them white in the blood of the Lamb."

Rev 7:15 "Therefore are they before the throne of God, and serve him day and night in his temple: and he that sitteth on the throne shall dwell among them."

Rev 7:16 "They shall hunger no more, neither thirst any more; neither shall the sun light on them, nor any heat."

Rev 7:17 "For the Lamb which is in the midst of the throne shall feed them, and shall lead them unto living fountains of waters: and God shall wipe away all tears from their eyes."

Here we are trying to figure out who this second group is, and John may have felt the same way—you know, scratching his head— and one of the elders asks him, "What are these which are arrayed in white robes? and whence came they?" Doesn't this sound vaguely familiar? In my chapter on the Two Witnesses, under the heading ***Zachariah And John Are Supposed To Know Who They Are***, Zachariah is shown two candlesticks and two olive trees and he is asked in so many words to identify them. Well, the angel acts like Zachariah is supposed to know who they are and the angel asks him twice. It is in Zechariah 4:

> Zec 4:5 "Then the angel that talked with me answered and said unto me, Knowest thou not what these be? And I said, No, my lord."

> Zec 4:13 "And he answered me and said, Knowest thou not what these be? And I said, No, my lord."

> Zec 4:14 "Then said he, These are the two anointed ones, that stand by the Lord of the whole earth."

CHAPTER 7 IS A REPEAT. In the chapter on the Two Witnesses, we found that it had to do with an identity problem. What does this great multitude have to do with? An Identity problem. Who comprises the church? Who comprises the body of Christ? It is comprised of Jew and Gentile in one body. Is that what this 7th chapter in Revelation is causing us to deal with???? YES, YES, YES!!!

Do you see it? We have TWO groups of people here—one seems to be Jews and the other...? It's probably the Gentiles. That is exactly what the angel was wanting Zachariah to understand.

Chapter 14 (7 chapters later) brings up the 144,000 again, but conveniently leaves out the fact that it is not, this time, only the Jewish nation. It is an amalgamation of BOTH in the same body. It is a common theme in God's word—ONE BODY, but two main parts. Why does the scripture keep going over and over this? It is because He wants us to get this if we don't get anything else. This is the Mystery of Christ! Paul talks about it in Colossians chapter one and mentions it again in chapter 4:

> Col 1:21 "And **you**, that were **sometime alienated** and **enemies** in your mind by wicked works, yet now hath he reconciled"

> Col 1:25 "Whereof I am made a minister, according to the dispensation of God which is given to me for you, to fulfil the word of God;"

> Col 1:26 "Even **the mystery** which hath been hid from ages and from generations, but **now is made manifest to his saints**:"

> Col 1:27 "To whom God would make known what is the

riches of the glory of **this mystery among the Gentiles; which is Christ in you, the hope of glory:"**

Col 4:3 "Withal praying also for us, that God would open unto us a door of utterance, to speak the **mystery of Christ**, for which I am also in bonds:"

Paul was in prison because he took the gospel to the Gentiles and ushered them into the kingdom of God. Remember when he was in the temple, the Jews were infuriated at him because they thought he let Gentiles into the sanctuary? This happened because his ministry was to the Gentiles, and it was a mystery how the Gentiles could be reborn into a body made up of Jews. James, the superintendent of the fledgling church came face to face with this truth that the Gentiles should be among their number in Acts 15 at the first Christian council. It was there that James said:

Act 15:14 "Simeon hath declared how **God at the first did visit the Gentiles, to take out of them a people for his name.**"

Act 15:15 "And to this **agree the words of the prophets**; as it is written..."

Act 15:17 "That the residue of men might seek after

the Lord, and **all the Gentiles, upon whom my name is called**, saith the Lord, who doeth all these things."

I bring this up about the "mystery of Christ" and the council at Jerusalem because it was a "big deal" back then and it is still a "big deal" today. It is that the Gentiles should be together with the Jews in one body, thus making peace. This is why Revelation keeps making this point over and over again, and it is made here in this 7th chapter, that there are TWO groups of people and if you are not careful you'll miss that they are in the same body. To finish our illustration and help answer our main question, then let me list the characteristics of this great multitude, and you tell me if it isn't describing the SAME body of people that chapter 14 is describing:

1. They are a great multitude, which no man could number, of all nations, and kindreds, and people and tongues.

2. They stood before the throne and before the Lamb.

3. They were clothed with white robes, and had palms in their hands.

4. They cried with a loud voice, saying, Salvation to our God which sitteth upon the throne, and unto the Lamb.

5. They came out of great tribulation.

6. They washed their robes, and made them white in the blood of the Lamb. They are before the throne of God, and serve him day and night IN HIS TEMPLE; and he that sitteth on the throne shall dwell among them.

7. They shall hunger no more.

8. They shall thirst no more.

9. The sun shall not light on them, nor any heat.

10. The Lamb which is in the midst of the throne shall feed them, and shall lead them unto living fountains of waters:

11. God shall wipe away all tears from their eyes.

How interesting! Twelve descriptions are given which are also typical of the Bride of Christ! Twelve descriptions were given of the 144,000 in chapter 14 also, and the 144,000 were just mentioned in the verses preceding this portion of scripture. In other words they are tied together in the SAME chapter with hardly a breath in between their descriptions. One group seems to be the Jews while the other group seems to be the Gentiles. Both groups seem to be involved in the same things: persecutions, trials, and death. The descriptions of each put them both as the body of Christ and are thus a part of the heavenly saved.

THE TWO GROUPS OF REVELATION 7: SEALED AND ARRAYED

As I was saying the TWO groups of people in chapter 7 are linked together in another way. I will give you the verses on this shortly, but you will see one group is SEALED and the other was ARRAYED. This is both typical of the body of Christ, the church. This is going to illustrate what I said above. A pattern has emerged from the pages of the book of Revelation. Whenever we find the FOUR BEASTS we find the FOUR AND TWENTY ELDERS. Whenever we find the TRUE olive tree we find the WILD olive tree. Whenever we find the ONE witness we find the SECOND witness represented as the TWO WITNESSES, which Zechariah 4:14 calls the TWO ANOINTED ONES. And now we are about to see those who are SEALED and those who are ARRAYED. They have their distinctions, but they are actually two parts of one group. It is much like a husband and wife. They are two distinct persons and yet the scripture says they are ONE FLESH! When you find the saved Jew, you will find the saved Gentile. The middle wall of partition is broken down between the two groups and the Lord keeps singing the same song. In Revelation 7 it is the same, as I said, one group is sealed and the other is arrayed. Look at chapter 7 again:

> Rev 7:2 "And I saw another angel ascending from the east, having **the seal** of the living God: and he cried with a loud voice to the four angels, to whom it was given to hurt the earth and the sea,"

Rev 7:3 "Saying, Hurt not the earth, neither the sea, nor the trees, till we have **sealed** the servants of our God in their foreheads."

Rev 7:4 "And I heard the number of them which were **sealed**: and there were **sealed** an hundred and forty and four thousand of all the tribes of the children of Israel."

Rev 7:5 "Of the tribe of Juda were **sealed** twelve thousand. Of the tribe of Reuben were **sealed** twelve thousand. Of the tribe of Gad were **sealed** twelve thousand."

Rev 7:6 "Of the tribe of Aser were **sealed** twelve thousand. Of the tribe of Nepthalim were **sealed** twelve thousand. Of the tribe of Manasses were **sealed** twelve thousand."

Rev 7:7 "Of the tribe of Simeon were **sealed** twelve thousand. Of the tribe of Levi were **sealed** twelve thousand. Of the tribe of Issachar were **sealed** twelve thousand."

Rev 7:8 "Of the tribe of Zabulon were **sealed** twelve thousand. Of the tribe of Joseph were **sealed** twelve thousand. Of the tribe of Benjamin were **sealed** twelve thousand."

Yes, I know this just described 12,000 from each of the twelve tribes of Israel, but does the New Testament talk about the CHURCH being **sealed**? Yes! Look at Ephesians 1 and 4:

Eph 1:13 "In whom ye also trusted, after that ye heard the word of truth, the gospel of your salvation: in whom also after that ye believed, ye were **sealed** with that holy Spirit of promise,"

Eph 4:30 "And grieve not the holy Spirit of God, whereby ye are **sealed** unto the day of redemption."

This is talking about how the Gentiles were saved and placed in the church being filled with the Holy Ghost, and thus being SEALED or preserved until the day of His coming. Notice the Jews are sealed as it is mentioned in Revelation 7, but so are the Gentiles sealed as is stated in the two verses in Ephesians. Isn't that interesting? As you can see, I have touched on the fact that both Jew and Gentile alike have been sealed, and now let's turn our attention to the great multitude, which doesn't say they were sealed, but they were "arrayed":

Rev 7:13 "And one of the elders answered, saying unto me, What are these which are **arrayed** in **white**

robes? and whence came they?" Rev 7:14 "And I said unto him, Sir, thou knowest. And he said to me, These are they which came out of great tribulation, and have **washed their robes**, and **made them white** in the blood of the Lamb."

This great multitude was saved and arrayed in white robes. Guess what? The bride of Christ, the church, according to Revelation 19 was arrayed in white linen which is the righteousness of saints:

Rev 19:7 "Let us be glad and rejoice, and give honour to him: for the **marriage of the Lamb** is come, and **his wife** hath made herself ready."

Rev 19:8 "And **to her was granted** that she should be **arrayed in fine linen**, clean and **white**: for the fine linen is the righteousness of saints."

There's not a whole lot of difference between "white robes" and "white linen". Beloved, it is quite clear that this great multitude is the church or more correctly, a part of the church, but so are the Jews that were sealed by the Holy Ghost—two groups in one body. That is why when you leave Revelation 7 and go 7 more chapters to chapter 14, not one of the 12 characteristics of that group says they are Jews. They are made up of BOTH Jew and Gentile!

SEALED "FROM" OR "BEFORE" TRIBULATION

Some believe the sealing of the Jews has to do with being preserved FROM tribulation, and the other group, the great multitude, is not sealed from tribulation. They believe that this adds credence to their view that they are two definite and distinct groups of people that are NOT inseparably tied together in one body. They believe one is the Jewish remnant that is protected during the tribulation and the other is called "tribulation saints" who are Gentiles, who are not protected during the great tribulation, but is this really the case? No it isn't. (Remember as I stated earlier, there has been no clear indication of a rapture so there can't be any "tribulation saints", just "saints".) Look again at 7:2 and 3.

> Rev 7:2 "And I saw another angel ascending from the east, having the seal of the living God: and he cried with a loud voice to the four angels, to whom it was given to hurt the earth and the sea,"
>
> Rev 7:3 "Saying, Hurt not the earth, neither the sea, nor the trees, **till we have sealed** the servants of our God in their foreheads."

Notice these verses do not say He is sealing them FROM great tribulation, as by a pre-trib rapture. He is sealing them BEFORE He pours out hurt on the earth, sea, and trees! There is a big difference between sealing FROM tribulation and sealing them BEFORE tribulation. Therefore, we must be careful not to believe this misrepresentation, because if we do then it makes the difference between these two groups of people greater than what it should be and ruins the symmetry between all the other illustrations of two in one and this one. The 144,000 are not sealed FROM tribulation as some would have us believe, because it doesn't say they are, and two, I can show you that both groups are persecuted during the great tribulation. It is well accepted that since it says the great multitude, came OUT OF great tribulation, it means they went through it, but it is not accepted widely that the 144,000 had to endure the same persecution and death during that same tribulation period. (When I use the term 144,000, I use it as many people believe it is, only the saved portion of the Jewish nation.)

Is it possible the great multitude AND the 144,000 could be two parts of one body? I believe it is. If it is, though, it will have to be shown that both groups are persecuted during the great tribulation. If that can be done, it will at least, take away the main distinguishing factor separating these two groups of people. It is well accepted that the "great multitude" suffered persecution, so the only thing that has to be shown, to start with, is that the 144,000 also suffered their own share of persecution and death.

To start with, it could be stated that the 144,000 were not sealed FROM tribulation in the beginning days of the church and neither will they be sealed FROM the great tribulation at the end of days.

When I say "sealed" I am referring to being totally shielded from it. Let us pick it up at the words of Jesus when He spoke to His disciples laying a foundation for the church which was at that time totally Jewish, and besides that Jesus mentions that He's talking about the cities of Israel. Matthew 10:21-23:

> Mat 10:21 "And the brother shall deliver up the brother **to death**, and the father the child: and the children shall rise up against their parents, and cause them to be **put to death**."
>
> Mat 10:22 "And ye shall **be hated of all men for my name's sake**: but he that endureth to the end shall be saved."
>
> Mat 10:23 "But when they **persecute you** in this city, flee ye into another: for verily I say unto you, Ye shall not have gone over **the cities of Israel**, till the Son of man be come."

The **Jewish disciples** He was talking to were NOT going to be sealed FROM persecution and death. Let us jump over to the book of Acts at a time when the church was still, almost totally, Jewish. Acts 8:1-2:

> Act 8:1 "And Saul was consenting unto his death. And at that time there was a great persecution against the

church which was at Jerusalem; and they were all scattered abroad throughout the regions of Judaea and Samaria, except the apostles."

Act 8:2 "And devout men carried Stephen to his burial, and made great lamentation over him."

The church under the tutelage of the apostles was NOT free of persecution and death, either. Let us now go into the book of Revelation to a passage that most Bible scholars believe the church was still on the earth. Revelation 2:10:

Rev 2:10 "Fear none of those things which thou shalt suffer: behold, the devil shall cast some of you into prison, that ye may be tried; and ye shall have tribulation ten days: be thou faithful unto death, and I will give thee a crown of life."

It does not sound like the Lord is giving John any indication of any change of a situation yet. Tribulation and death are still a possibility for His people at that time. Let us go a little farther into the future to when the two witnesses prophecy or witness on the earth. Most scholars believe they are totally Jewish. I believe they are both Jews and Gentiles, but let us use their views here in Revelation 11:7:

Rev 11:7 "And when they shall have finished their testimony, the beast that ascendeth out of the bottomless pit shall **make war against them**, and shall **overcome them**, and **kill them**."

Still, these are NOT sealed from tribulation, persecution, and death! Now, let us go to Revelation chapter 12 to the chapter that talks about the woman who gave birth to the man child that most scholars believe is the nation of Israel and that this portion of scripture says was carried into the wilderness where she was NOURISHED for a time, and times, and half a time, from the face of the serpent. Even though she was nourished it still says the following about her in 12:13 and 17:

> Rev 12:13 "And when the dragon saw that he was cast unto the earth, **he persecuted the woman** which brought forth the man child."
>
> Rev 12:17 "And the dragon was wroth with the woman, and went to **make war** with the remnant of her seed, which keep the commandments of God, and have the testimony of Jesus Christ."

Here we see that the "Jewish" remnant is still facing persecution and war which evidently includes death also. So, these were NOT sealed from it, either! Let us go deeper into Revelation where it is talking about the Antichrist at a time, again, when most Bible scholars believe there are only Jewish believers on the earth. Revelation 13:7, 15:

Rev 13:7 "And it was given unto him to **make war with the saints**, and to **overcome them**: and power was given him over all kindreds, and tongues, and nations."

Rev 13:15 "And he had power to give life unto the image of the beast, that the image of the beast should both speak, and cause that as many as would not worship the image of the beast **should be killed**."

These were NOT sealed from tribulation, war and death either. Let us go deeper, yet to the very chapter 14 where we read about the 144,000 in the first place. Please, do not be confused with the order of events in this chapter which seem to be in reverse order, but at any rate, supposedly it is still a Jewish church. Revelation 14:12-13:

Rev 14:12 "Here is the patience of **the saints**: here are they that keep the commandments of God, and the faith of Jesus."

Rev 14:13 "And I heard a voice from heaven saying unto me, Write, Blessed are **the dead which die** in the Lord from henceforth: Yea, saith the Spirit, that they may rest from their labours; and their works do follow them."

From the sounds of this verse, they ARE dying from persecution because they know the Lord. They, evidently were NOT sealed from it. Look further at Revelation 15:2-3:

> Rev 15:2 "And I saw as it were a sea of glass mingled with fire: and them **that had gotten the victory over the beast**, and **over his image**, and **over his mark**, and **over the number of his name**, stand on the sea of glass, having the harps of God."
>
> Rev 15:3 "And **they sing the song of Moses** the servant of God, and the song of the Lamb, saying, Great and marvellous are thy works, Lord God Almighty; just and true are thy ways, thou King of saints."

These had gotten the VICTORY over the Antichrist. What does that mean? They were killed for their faith in the Lord. They did not capitulate. They did not give up. They kept their faith to the end. There is more about this in Revelation 18:24:

> Rev 18:24 "And in her was found **the blood** of **prophets**, and of **saints**, and of **all that were slain** upon the earth."

When Mystery Babylon will be destroyed (which I identify in my third book, yet to be published) it will be discovered that many prophets and saints were killed in her. This happens at the end of the last seven years of tribulation, and evidently, these were NOT sealed from tribulation and death. Let us jump over to Daniel and look at chapter 7 and verses 21, 22, and 25

> Dan 7:21 "I beheld, and the same horn **made war with the saints**, and prevailed against them;"

> Dan 7:22 "Until the Ancient of days came, and judgment was given to the saints of the most High; and the time came that the saints possessed the kingdom."

> Dan 7:25 "And he shall speak great words against the most High, and shall **wear out the saints** of the most High, and think to change times and laws: and **they shall be given into his hand** until a time and times and the dividing of time."

Again, most Bible scholars say these are Jews. If they are, they are being killed for the witness of Jesus as it is depicted also in chapter 8:10, 24:

> Dan 8:10 "And it waxed great, even to the host of heaven; and it **cast down** some of the host and of the stars to the ground, and **stamped upon them**."

> Dan 8:24 "And his power shall be mighty, but not by his own power: and he shall destroy wonderfully, and shall prosper, and practise, and shall **destroy the mighty and the holy people.**"

The holy people, we all agree, at least, includes the Jews, and are DESTROYED or killed as is also depicted in Daniel 11:33-35:

> Dan 11:33 "And they that understand among the people shall instruct many: yet they shall **fall by the sword**, and **by flame**, by **captivity**, and by spoil, many days."

> Dan 11:34 "Now when they shall fall, they shall be holpen with a little help: but many shall cleave to them with flatteries."

> Dan 11:35 "And some of them of understanding **shall fall**, to try them, and to purge, and to make them white, even to the time of the end: because it is yet for a time appointed."

This is pretty plain. Most scholars believe these are Jews that are falling here. They evidently were not sealed from tribulation and death. I think you can agree that it has been demonstrated that the 144,000 were NOT sealed FROM tribulation! As you can see; they definitely had their share of it. They were sealed BEFORE the hurt was poured out upon the earth, sea, and trees. The 144,000 have gone through the same tribulation that the GREAT MULTITUDE of all nations, and kindreds, and people, and tongues have gone through. This helps prove that these two groups are inseparably tied together, because both groups are thrown into persecution and tribulation. Does this persecution and tribulation occur at two different and distinct ages or "periods" of time? No, it takes place at the same time. This demonstrates one more time that what we have here is two parts of the one body of Christ.

What have we established so far?

1. I emphasized that the book was addressed to the seven churches of Asia, letting us know that it was written more to the Gentiles than to the Jews, although it included them. I brought this up because to insinuate that the majority of the book isn't even written to the Gentiles is ludicrous. To say that they are not part of 144,000 that appear with the Lord on Mount Zion could be classified the same.

2. We showed that the rapture didn't happen in chapter 4:1.

3. We found out that just because the word CHURCH does not appear in chapters 5-18 doesn't mean the church was raptured or is absent from those chapters. The Lord simply identifies His body, the church, Jew AND Gentile, by using 33 other descriptive phrases. If

the church is all through those chapters then perhaps the church (including the Gentiles) is found, covertly, in the 144,000.

4. This idea is supported in chapter 7 because it lists two groups of people that seem to be inseparably tied together. Some were sealed and some were arrayed.

5. Some (as the Jews) were sealed before tribulation but still went through it just like the Great Multitude, as the Gentiles, had to go through it, thus underscoring the fact that, indeed these are the two parts of the one body of Christ. We found out that it is the Mystery of Christ, how the Gentiles could be a part of the body of Christ which started out being almost exclusively Jews.

6. We briefly laid out the 12 descriptive phrases of the 144,000, and then flew back to Revelation 7 to lay out the 12 descriptive phrases of the Great Multitude and found them to be much the same.If the Great Multitude is speaking of the Gentiles, then the Lord is telling us that the 144,000 includes the Gentile part of the church! Can you see how many times this is being hinted at? How many times did the Lord say in chapters 2 and 3 of Revelation, "He that hath ears, let Him hear"? As we saw in the parables, the Lord doesn't always come out and say things directly. He spoke in parables because everything isn't for everybody. Some things are reserved only for those with open ears and open hearts. How open is your ears? How open is your heart?

144,000: THE NUMBER OF THE CITY

Where do we go from here? We will now turn our eyes specifically, to the 144,000 and discuss why the Lord has chosen to use this number. We do know one reason why He chose this number—it comes from 12,000 from the 12 tribes of Israel (multiplied together equals 144,000). There might be more than one reason why the Lord chose that number. In looking at this number we will find that it is used because it encompasses more than just a concept of the saved portion of the nation of Israel! If we can show that, then this will be the **seventh way** of demonstrating that the 144,000 includes not only the Jews, but the Gentile portion of the Bride also! We will be seeing shortly that there is a lot to this one theme. Understand that the city that is to be the home of God's people is made up of multiples of 12. Let us read some verses from Revelation 21:

> Rev 21:10 "And he carried me away in the spirit to a great and high mountain, and shewed me that great city, **the holy Jerusalem**, descending out of heaven from God,"

> Rev 21:11 "Having the glory of God: and her light was like unto a stone most precious, even like a jasper stone, clear as crystal;"

> Rev 21:12 "And had a wall great and high, and had **twelve** gates, and at the gates **twelve** angels, and

names written thereon, which are the names of the **twelve** tribes of the children of Israel:"

Rev 21:13 "On the east three gates; on the north three gates; on the south three gates; and on the west three gates."

Rev 21:14 "And the wall of the city had **twelve** foundations, and in them the names of the **twelve** apostles of the Lamb."

Rev 21:15 "And he that talked with me had a golden reed to measure the city, and the gates thereof, and the wall thereof."

Rev 21:16 "And the city lieth foursquare, and the length is as large as the breadth: and he measured the city with the reed, **twelve** thousand furlongs. The length and the breadth and the height of it are equal."

Rev 21:17 "And he measured the wall thereof, **an hundred and forty and four cubits**, according to the measure of a man, that is, of the angel."

Why is the Lord wanting to emphasize the number 12? He uses it 6 times. In THEOMATICS, discussed at the end of this chapter, it means chosen or elect. In the Old Testament, the number 12 first appears in the book of Genesis, the book of beginnings, in chapter 35 when Rachel bore Jacob his twelfth son. There it mentions he had twelve sons and they soon became the chosen twelve tribes. **Twelve then became the symbolic number of Israel**. The names of the 12 tribes of Israel were written on the twelve gates, but the names of the 12 apostles were written on the twelve foundations. SO! It is NOT just about the nation of Israel! It is also about the **church**, for the 12 Apostles were chosen and represent the church, so the city is about BOTH the nation of Israel, or the Jews, and the **church**, which pulls in the Gentiles. The Gentiles were and are a part of the **church**, so we could simplify it more by saying that the city is for BOTH Jew and Gentile. We could state it another way: 12 stands for the 12 tribes AND the 12 apostles and therefore the city encompasses ISRAEL and the CHURCH, both Jew AND Gentile alike.

We have talked about the number twelve being used 6 times, but what about the other numbers? There are 6 other numbers that are used here making a total of 12. Is there significance to these other numbers? I think so. There were 3 GATES pointing the 4 DIRECTIONS of the earth; that is, pointing to the 4 CORNERS of the earth: EAST, NORTH, SOUTH, and WEST. Why? I am convinced it is to welcome people and saints from all parts of the earth ($3 \times 4 = 12$, or 3 gates x 4 directions = 12 or completion). God is inferring in this that though the city has a strong Jewish element and was built for the Jews, IT IS NOT JUST FOR THE JEWS!! It is for the Gentiles also!

There is another number that is used: TWELVE THOUSAND FURLONGS. In other words, 12,000 not only represents the 12,000 from each tribe, it represents something that is generic—furlongs. Furlongs have nothing to do with the nation of Israel per se, but just happens to be the largest city in the universe—1,500 miles long, wide and high. In other words, how big is the city? It is big enough to include something that isn't just Jewish—it includes the Gentiles! Wow!

THE WALL OF AN HUNDRED AND FORTY AND FOUR CUBITS

There is one more number that is used in this passage of scripture: AN HUNDRED AND FORTY AND FOUR CUBITS. It is not mentioned how this number was derived. Of course, if you multiply 12 x 12 you get 144, so where do we get the two 12s. We get it from the 12 tribes and the 12 apostles. You multiply the nation of Israel by the church you come up with a lot of people that will dwell together in one city surrounded by a wall whose height of 144 cubits designates who dwells there, Jew and Gentile. You see 144 is figurative, and so is the number 144,000. Don't get hung up on the numbers. Get hung up on the MEANING of the numbers.

144 and 144,000 are in different forms, but they are look-a-like numbers. What am I saying? I am saying the meanings of both numbers are similar. When we found the 144,000 in Revelation chapter 7 seemingly they were from the 12 tribes

of Israel, but following hard on their heels was this great multitude that no man could number. This group appeared to be the Gentiles, and they were in the same chapter without an explanation between the two groups. When you see the one, guess what, you see the other. When you get to chapter 14, you see the number 144,000 again and this time the scripture doesn't say how the number was derived as it was explained in chapter 7. For sure it doesn't say they are Jews, but they are solely described as the body of Christ. By the time you get to chapter 21 you see the look-a-like number 144 without the three zero's and what does it mean? It means the same thing. It's significant of the body of Christ made up of Jews and Gentiles! (Notice the first mention of the 144,000 is in chapter 7. The next mention of the 144,000 is in (2 x 7) chapter 14. Notice the correlation between chapter 14 and 144,000. Interesting. Do you think it was by accident? I don't think so. God specializes in anomalies, and the meaning of the group intensifies—in other words it doesn't say they are just Jews. The next mention of the "144" format is found in (3 x 7) chapter 21, and the implication of this number explodes, as you will see.), but in chapter 21 we could come up with the 144,000 by multiplying 12 apostles by the 12,000 furlongs. Just as 12 is the symbolic number for the nation of Israel so it appears that **144,000 is the symbolic number of the city**. I will talk more about that later.

Watch this. I am going to get a little deeper. If the Lord meant for us to think of this body of people that was with the Lord on Mt. Zion to be just Jews, He would have depicted them some other way. You know. He would have chosen a number that was picturesque of the number 12 by itself. You know, like 12, 1200, 12,000, 120,000, or 1200,000 (twelve hundred thousand). The Lord instead chose a number that was a multiple of 12, meaning that the Lord was not just going to add to them, but was going to MULTIPLY them! He was going to throw the whole realm of the Gentiles into the mix to be their suckling babies. There was not going to be any way to calculate their offspring because there would be so many of them. Remember what God told Abram before his name was changed in Genesis 15?

> Gen 15:1 "After these things the word of the LORD came unto Abram in a vision, saying, Fear not, Abram: I am thy shield, and **thy exceeding great reward.**"

> Gen 15:2 "And Abram said, Lord GOD, what wilt thou give me, seeing **I go childless**, and the steward of my house is this Eliezer of Damascus?"

> Gen 15:3 "And Abram said, Behold, **to me thou hast given no seed**: and, lo, one born in my house is mine heir."

> Gen 15:4 "And, behold, the word of the LORD came unto him, saying, This shall not be thine heir; but he that shall come forth out of thine own bowels shall be thine heir."

Gen 15:5 "And he brought him forth abroad, and said, **Look now toward heaven, and tell the stars, if thou be able to number them: and he said unto him, So shall thy seed be.**"

Gen 15:6 "And he believed in the LORD; and he counted it to him for righteousness."

What did the Lord mean by 15:5? He was going to give him a spiritual seed so numerous that they could not be counted, but the Lord didn't explain much about that until way down the line when Isaiah prophesied in chapter 54:

Isa 54:1 "Sing, **O barren**, thou that didst not bear; break forth into singing, and cry aloud, thou that didst not travail with child: for **more are the children of the desolate** than the children of the married wife, saith the LORD."

Isa 54:2 "Enlarge the place of thy tent, and let them stretch forth the curtains of thine habitations: spare not, lengthen thy cords, and strengthen thy stakes;"

Isa 54:3 "For thou shalt break forth on the right hand and on the left; and **thy seed shall inherit the Gentiles,** and make the desolate cities to be inhabited."

Isa 54:4 "Fear not; **for thou shalt not be ashamed**: neither be thou confounded; for thou shalt not be put to shame: for thou shalt forget the shame of thy youth, and shalt not remember the reproach of thy **widowhood** any more."

Isa 54:5 "For thy Maker is thine husband; the LORD of hosts is his name; and thy Redeemer the Holy One of Israel; The God of the whole earth shall he be called."

Isa 54:6 "For the LORD hath called thee as **a woman forsaken** and grieved in spirit, and a wife of youth, when thou wast refused, saith thy God."

The Lord revealed that "thy seed shall inherit the Gentiles". It was all prophesied to happen. James the superintendent of the church at Jerusalem confirmed that when the Gentiles were coming into the church this prophecy was being fulfilled. That is found in Acts 15:

Act 15:13 "And after they had held their peace, **James answered**, saying, Men and brethren, hearken unto me:"

Act 15:14 "Simeon hath declared how God at the first did **visit the Gentiles**, to take out of them a people for his name."

Act 15:15 "And to this agree **the words of the prophets**; as it is written,"

Act 15:16 "After this I will return, and will build again the tabernacle of David, which is fallen down; and I will build again the ruins thereof, and I will set it up:"

Act 15:17 "That the residue of men might seek after the Lord, and **all the Gentiles**, upon whom my name is called, saith the Lord, who doeth all these things."

Act 15:18 "Known unto God are all his works from the beginning of the world."

Act 15:19 "Wherefore my sentence is, that we trouble not them, which **from among the Gentiles are turned to God**:"

When was this to happen, what Isaiah prophesied? Of course it was starting when the church was starting, but time factors are hinted at further down in Isaiah 54:

Isa 54:10 "For **the mountains shall depart**, and the **hills be removed**; but my kindness shall not depart from thee, neither shall the covenant of my peace be removed, saith the LORD that hath mercy on thee."

Isa 54:11 "O thou afflicted, tossed with tempest, and not comforted, behold, **I will lay thy stones with fair colours, and lay thy foundations with sapphires**."

Isa 54:12 "And I will make **thy windows of agates, and thy gates of carbuncles, and all thy borders of pleasant stones**."

Isa 54:13 And **all thy children shall be taught of the LORD; and great shall be the peace of thy children**."

Isa 54:14 "**In righteousness shalt thou be established**: thou shalt be far from oppression; for thou shalt not fear: and from terror; for it shall not come near thee."

It sounds like the Lord is hinting to His wrath in regards to the mountains and the hills departing which refers to the end of time. Then He describes all the windows, gates, and borders of pleasant stones. Sounds like the foundations of the New Jerusalem, and it is confirmed by being established in righteousness and being far from terror, like when the Lord wipes away all our tears when we enter His kingdom and city. The Jewish people are MULTIPLIED by the Gentiles. Isaiah gets more graphic in chapter 60:

Isa 60:14 "The **sons also of them that afflicted thee shall come bending unto thee**; and all they that despised thee **shall bow themselves down at the soles of thy feet**; and they shall call thee, **The city of the LORD, The Zion** of the Holy One of Israel."

Isa 60:15 "Whereas thou hast been forsaken and hated, so that no man went through thee, **I will make thee an eternal excellency, a joy of many generations.**"

Isa 60:16 "Thou shalt also **suck the milk of the Gentiles**, and shalt **suck the breast of kings**: and thou shalt know that I the LORD am thy Saviour and thy Redeemer, the mighty One of Jacob."

Isa 60:17 "For brass I will bring gold, and for iron I will bring silver, and for wood brass, and for stones iron: I will also make **thy officers peace**, and thine **exactors righteousness.**"

Isa 60:18 "**Violence shall no more be heard in thy land**, wasting nor destruction within thy borders; but thou shalt call **thy walls Salvation, and thy gates Praise.**"

Isa 60:19 "**The sun shall be no more thy light by day**; neither for brightness shall the moon give light unto thee: but **the LORD shall be unto thee an everlasting light**, and thy God thy glory."

Isa 60:20 "Thy sun shall no more go down; neither shall thy moon withdraw itself: for **the LORD shall be thine everlasting light**, and the days of **thy mourning shall be ended**."

Israel will inherit the Gentiles and dwell with them in the city of God in a day when the Lamb shall be the light. This is talking about the millennium. Her walls are called salvation and they are 144 cubits high, representing protection around those who are saved, Jew and Gentile. Yes, the Old Testament witnesses to this fact and thankfully the New Testament verifies this very thing also. Look at Ephesians 2 and into chapter 3:

Eph 2:11 "Wherefore remember, that ye being in time past **Gentiles in the flesh**, who are called Uncircumcision by that which is called the Circumcision in the flesh made by hands;"

Eph 2:12 "That at that time ye were without Christ, **being aliens from the commonwealth of Israel**, and strangers from the covenants of promise, having no hope, and without God in the world:"

Eph 2:13 "But **now in Christ Jesus ye who sometimes were far off are made nigh by the blood of Christ.**"

Eph 2:14 "For he is our peace, who hath **made both one**, and hath **broken down the middle wall of partition between us;**"

Eph 2:15 "Having **abolished in his flesh the enmity**, even the law of commandments contained in ordinances; for to make in himself **of twain one new man, so making peace;**"

Eph 2:16 "And that he might reconcile **both unto God in one body by the cross, having slain the enmity thereby:**"

Eph 2:17 "And came and preached peace to **you which were afar off**, and to **them that were nigh.**"

Eph 2:18 "For through him **we both have access by one Spirit unto the Father.**"

Eph 2:19 "Now therefore **ye are no more strangers and foreigners**, but **fellow citizens with the saints**, and of **the household of God;**"

Eph 2:20 "And **are built upon the foundation of the apostles and prophets**, Jesus Christ himself being the chief corner stone;"

Eph 2:21 "In whom all the building fitly framed together groweth unto **an holy temple** in the Lord:"

Eph 2:22 "In whom ye also are builded together for **an habitation of God through the Spirit**."

Eph 3:4 "Whereby, when ye read, ye may understand my knowledge in the **mystery of Christ**."

Eph 3:5 "Which in other ages was not made known unto the sons of men, as it is now revealed unto his holy apostles and prophets by the Spirit;"

Eph 3:6 "**That the Gentiles should be fellow heirs, and of the same body**, and partakers of his promise **in Christ by the gospel**:"

Folks, we who are Gentiles were castaways and aliens from Israel, but now through Christ and His cross we have become "fellow heirs and of the same body". Romans 11 witnesses of the same:

Rom 11:17 "And if some of the branches be broken off, and **thou, being a wild olive tree, wert graffed in among them, and with them partakest of the root and fatness of the olive tree;"**

Rom 11:18 "Boast not against the branches. But if thou boast, **thou bearest not the root, but the root thee."**

As the Gentiles, we were a wild olive tree, and as such were grafted into the Jewish blessing. Truthfully, this is their blessing and New Jerusalem is their city, but guess what? We are grafted into and made a part of the 144,000. We take on their label because of the promise to Abram who became Abraham—the Father of MANY nations—the Gentile nations.

While I am on the subject of Romans 11, the resurrection or rapture which I mention in other chapters, will happen, not before the tribulation, but after. Why? It is because we are in THEIR tree. They are not in our tree, and they won't be ready until after the tribulation. We're NOT going up without them. We will only go up when they are ready. Remember we are in their tree, not vice versa. Romans 11 witnesses to this fact:

Rom 11:12 "Now **if the fall of them be the riches of the world, and the diminishing of** them the riches of the Gentiles; how much more their fulness?"

If that wasn't enough, he repeats himself two verses later, only more emphatically:

Rom 11:15 "For **if the casting away of them be the reconciling of the world, what shall the receiving of them be, but life from the dead?**"

When the nation of Israel rejected their Messiah, it was bad, but because of it, the Gentile world was reconciled to Christ. Something good came out of something bad. Now, if that is the case what would happen if something good happened to Israel, where they accepted their Messiah—it would bring on something super, super good—the resurrection from the dead, or what we would call the rapture. As I said, we are not going to be raptured until they are raptured. It's all about them. We are in their tree and in their blessing. This is a continuation of the point I have been making, that the Jews and the Gentiles are in one body and the 144 cubit wall is a witness to that fact, but let's get more specific about that wall. Look again at that verse in Revelation 21:

Rev 21:17 "And he measured the wall thereof, an hundred and forty and four cubits, **according to the measure of a man**, that is, of the angel."

It is interesting that the measurement has to do with the measure of a man. Is it possible that God is giving to us a hint that this wall truly is a symbol of the men and women who dwell there around which the wall surrounds. As I stated earlier, it is 12 x 12, the Jewish nation multiplied by the church, that gives us a whole lot of Jews and Gentiles inside that wall. In regards to walls relating to men, I am reminded of the scripture in Isaiah 49:

> Isa 49:13 "Sing, O heavens; and be joyful, O earth; and break forth into singing, O mountains: for the LORD hath comforted his people, and will have mercy upon his afflicted."
>
> Isa 49:14 "But Zion said, The LORD hath forsaken me, and my Lord hath forgotten me."
>
> Isa 49:15 "Can a woman forget her sucking child, that she should not have compassion on the son of her womb? yea, they may forget, **yet will I not forget thee**."
>
> Isa 49:16 "Behold, **I have graven thee upon the palms of my hands; thy walls are continually before me.**"

The Lord typifies His people as WALLS. Isn't that interesting? That is why in Revelation 21:17 the 144 cubits IS a type of the people who dwell there. He keeps telling these afflicted people to be joyful, and break forth into singing. Why? He will not forget them. They are like walls before Him and He is going to make up for their fewness of number. I am going to repeat it again because it is so powerful and magnificent! He is going to MULTIPLY them by GIVING them the Gentiles to share their inheritance and their city! In this very chapter, down a few verses He restates the reason for them to rejoice:

Isa 49:20 "**The children which thou shalt have, after thou hast lost the other**, shall say again in thine ears, The place is too strait for me: give place to me that I may dwell."

Isa 49:21 "Then shalt thou say in thine heart, **Who hath begotten me these, seeing I have lost my children**, and am desolate, a captive, and removing to and fro? and who hath brought up these? Behold, I was left alone; **these, where had they been?**"

Isa 49:22 "Thus saith the Lord GOD, Behold, **I will lift up mine hand to the Gentiles**, and set up my standard to the people: and **they shall bring thy sons in their arms**, and **thy daughters** shall be carried upon their shoulders."

Isa 49:23 "And **kings shall be thy nursing fathers**, and **their queens thy nursing mothers**: they shall bow down to thee with their **face toward the earth, and lick up the dust of thy feet**; and thou shalt know that I am the LORD: for **they shall not be ashamed that wait for me.**"

You see, it is the Gentiles that bring this to pass. The emotion is captured here, but it is stated above in Isaiah 54:3 that thy seed would INHERIT the Gentiles. The Lord will multiply them by the Gentiles who will dwell with them in that great city. You see, it was to the church that He promised to prepare a "place" for them in John 14:

Joh 14:1 "Let not your heart be troubled: ye believe in God, believe also in me."

Joh 14:2 "**In my Father's house are many mansions**: if it were not so, I would have told you. **I go to prepare a place for you.**"

Joh 14:3 "And if I go and **prepare a place for you**, I will come again, and receive you unto myself; **that where I am, there ye may be also.**"

The place He is preparing is the city of New Jerusalem, but the Lord promised that same city to the Jewish nation through the inheritance of Abraham. Look at Hebrews 11:

Heb 11:8 "**By faith Abraham**, when he was called to go out into a place which he should after receive for an inheritance, obeyed; and he went out, not knowing whither he went."

Heb 11:9 "By faith he sojourned in the land of promise, as in a strange country, dwelling in tabernacles with Isaac and Jacob, the heirs with him of the same promise:"

Heb 11:10 "**For he looked for a city which hath foundations, whose builder and maker is God.**"

The city is what Jesus was talking about to His apostles, meaning that it was a promise to His church. This is also the city that John describes in Revelation 21, a book that was written to the Gentile church, but this was the same city that Abraham was looking for. Can you see how the 144 cubits is reinforcing this concept. It is figurative and powerful, and so repetitive through scripture to prove its importance that that city will be shared by both Jew and Gentile.

IF THE 144,000 IS LITERAL IT'S TOO RESTRICTIVE

I pointed out earlier that Revelation 7 tells us that 12,000 from each of the 12 tribes of Israel make up the 144,000. I do not believe the Lord is giving this to us as a literal number because it is too restrictive. Remember verse 9 of that chapter said, "After this I beheld, and, lo, **a great multitude**, which **no man could number**, of all nations, and kindreds, and people, and tongues, stood before the throne, and before the Lamb, clothed with white robes, and palms in their hands;" Most believe this verse is referring to the Gentiles who go through the tribulation. With that being said, is the Lord saying He is going to save an innumerable amount of Gentiles but only a 144,000 Jews? I believe there will probably be more Gentiles saved than Jews because of the humongous number of Gentiles populating the globe, but to relegate a literal mere 144,000 to be saved out of the millions of Jews that are upon the face of the earth? I do not believe that for a moment. It is diametrically opposed to other scripture, such as the following verse found in Romans 11:26:

> Rom 11:26 "And so **all Israel shall be saved**: as it is written, There shall come out of Sion the Deliverer, and shall turn away ungodliness from Jacob:"

There are more in Israel than 12,000 in each tribe, and there are more than 12,000 from each tribe who are going to be saved, because it says, ALL ISRAEL will be saved. The

12,000 from each tribe that is mentioned in Revelation 7 has to be FIGURATIVE!!

There is another reason that this number has to be figurative. There are two tribes that are not even mentioned in this Revelation 7 passage. Who are these two tribes? They are: Dan and Ephraim (Some might say, "The tribe of Joseph is representing Ephraim." Even if it is and it might be, the tribe of Dan is still left out.) Does that mean none from the tribe of Dan and possibly Ephraim will be saved? Absolutely not. As we discussed earlier, the Lord is only showing us how He is coming up with the numbers 12 and 12,000. The Lord had to have some number to multiply 12 by to come up with 144,000. That number just happens to be 12,000. E.W. Bullinger in his book, Number in Scripture, published in 1967, on page 253 talks about the tribes of Israel, "Though actually thirteen in number, there are never more than twelve named in any one list. There are about 18 enumerations altogether, but in each list one or other is omitted." If we are able to get to the place where we can say that it is figurative of the 12 tribes of Israel and of the amount from each tribe; then it is but another small step to also say that the 144,000 includes all of the saved Gentiles found in the church as well. The 144,000 represents all the saved people of God from ages past to ages future as it is more fully revealed in chapter 14. It is not so vitally important how He came up with the number 144,000. The main idea is that He uses the number to represent the completeness of all completeness, or the whole and complete BODY OF CHRIST!

What I am saying then, is that the number 144,000 is the symbolic number for the city of New Jerusalem, and as such, is the number that depicts His body, the church. It could also be considered a label for the city and a label for His body. That is why the Lord says in chapter 14 when the Lamb appeared on Mount Zion, His body (the church) was with Him, and thus calls them the 144,000. The city and the people of God are, in some way, synonymous. You could say the city is the people of God, or the people of God is the city or we could stretch a little farther and say whatever is the number of the city is the number of the people of God. The city and the people of God are linked together as chapter 21 testifies:

> Rev 21:9 " there came unto me one of the seven angels which had the seven vials full of the seven last plagues, and talked with me, saying, Come hither, **I will shew thee the bride, the Lamb's wife.**"

> Rev 21:10 "And he carried me away in the spirit to a great and high mountain, **and shewed me that great city, the holy Jerusalem**, descending out of heaven from God,"

Did you understand what that said? The angel said, "I will show you the BRIDE, THE LAMB'S WIFE," and then he did not show John a group of people. He showed him THE HOLY CITY, NEW JERUSALEM! The Holy City represented the complete body of Christ! But that is what the (144,000) number of the city represented—the complete body of Christ! Verse two reflects the same idea:

> Rev 21:2 "And **I John saw the holy city, new Jerusalem**, coming down from God out of heaven, prepared **as a bride** adorned for her husband."

John saw the city and it was as a bride, or as the body of Christ. Actually, this same idea was shared with us earlier in chapter 3:

> Rev 3:12 "Him that overcometh **will I make a pillar in the temple of my God**, and he shall go no more out: and I will **write upon him the name of my God**, and the **name of the city of my God**, which is new Jerusalem, which cometh down out of heaven from my God: and I will **write upon him my new name**."

WOW! What did that say? He will make you a pillar in the TEMPLE of my God! What did Ephesians chapter 2 say? "…groweth unto an HOLY TEMPLE in the Lord: In whom ye also are builded together for an HABITATION OF GOD through the Spirit." Here the Lord is speaking to the angel of the church of Philadelphia. This is to, largely, a Gentile church. They will be made a "part" of the temple, no, they will be the temple, no, they will be "an habitation of God" or (one more leap) they will be the city of God. How will they be the city of God? They will be the city of God by means of the Spirit of God or the Holy Ghost. What does He say to this church? If you overcome I will write upon you three things:

1. The name of my God
2. The name of the city of my God
3. My new name

Number one: HOW do you get the name of God on you according to God's word? It is by water baptism in His name JESUS! When you are baptized in that name, it is "stamped on your forehead". Number two: These Gentile believers will have the name of the city of New Jerusalem written on them. Why? Because they will be there. They will be part and parcel of that city. And number three: Jesus is the new name of God, and where will that name be written? It will not be on their feet, nor on their back, nor on their stomach. It will be written on their foreheads! That means He could be saying that those in Revelation 14:1 are the same as those in Revelation 3:12. How could that be? Let's put the pieces together. What did Jesus say in John 5?

> Joh 5:43 "**I am come in my Father's name,** and ye receive me not: if another shall come in his own name, him ye will receive."

Jesus is saying He came in His father's name. So, what was His Father's name? If we can believe the verse and I know we can, His Father's name was JESUS! It was Jesus because

He said He came in it. Is this verified other places? Yes. Look at John 17:

> Joh 17:6 "I have **manifested THY name** unto the men which thou gavest me out of the world: thine they were, and thou gavest them me; and they have kept thy word."

> Joh 17:26 "And I have **declared unto them THY name**, and will declare it: that the love wherewith thou hast loved me may be in them, and I in them."

How did Jesus manifest and declare His Father's name? Did He ever address His Father by any other title than God or Father? No, never, so then how did He manifest it and declare it? He did it by coming in it! Wow! So, when He said He was going to write the name of His God and write His NEW name on those who were overcomers, what was He saying? He was saying to these Gentiles of Philadelphia, in so many words, that when they got baptized in His NAME they had the name of God and His new name written on them, and that name was JESUS. And where was that name written? That name as I said earlier, was on their foreheads. With the pieces of this puzzle put together can you see that the 144,000 of Revelation 14:1 includes all these Gentile believers who also had the NAME of their God in their foreheads! It's another witness that the number 144,000 is symbolic. It has to be, but there is one more witness found in Revelation 22:

Rev 22:3 "And there shall be no more curse: but the throne of God and of the Lamb shall be in it; and **his servants** shall serve him:"

Rev 22:4 "And they shall see his face; and **his NAME shall be in their foreheads.**"

This describes, does it not, the same group of people that chapter 14 describes! What is interesting is that it does not call them the 144,000. These are called generically, "HIS SERVANTS". It does not say they are just Jews or for that matter, just Gentiles. What is it describing? It is describing the RIVER OF WATER OF LIFE which proceeds out of the throne of God. This description in chapter 22 follows the description of the city of God in chapter 21. It is inferring that those who inhabit the city of New Jerusalem and those that inherit eternal life and drink of the water of life are called THE SERVANTS OF GOD. They are no longer referred to as Jews and Gentiles. The middle wall of partition between them has been broken down (see Chapter 3, *The Jew And Gentile Are Called Witnesses*) and they have their FATHER'S NAME written in their foreheads. We know that this portion of scripture is describing the saved Jews and the Gentiles and we know that the scripture in Revelation 3:12 was written to the Gentiles but of course it includes the Jews. So then, what about Revelation 14:1? Is this group separate and distinct from those mentioned in 3:12, and 22:3 and 4? If you will take all the information in this chapter and absorb it, keeping in mind that there is one and only one coming of the Lord, that being the one resurrection of the just, and accept the fact that the middle wall of partition has been broken down between the Jew and the Gentile, then there is only one conclusion: the 144,000 is symbolic of all the people of God, from ages past to the present time, Jew and Gentile who will enter the CITY OF GOD, NEW JERUSALEM!

There is another way to verify that what has been stated in this chapter is very true. It is by means of an absolutely independent source, through a book called THEOMATICS, God's Best Kept Secret Revealed, written by Jerry Lucas and Del Washburn, published in 1979, a Scarborough Book, published by Stein and Day, NY. Without going into too much detail, this book reveals God's arithmetic in every letter of His book. Every Hebrew and Greek letter has a numeric value. Letters make words and words make sentences and the total values of those can be added up and divided by a number that shows us that God had an underlying theme when He penned them. (By itself this book will powerfully convince agnostics that God wrote the Bible.) If you remember, the number 12 means "chosen" or "elect" and is found on page 204 of THEOMATICS. The twelve disciples Christ chose "symbolize all of us" and it "is the number of the elect" and "typifies those who belong to Christ." So what is 144? It is 12 x 12. "So 144 is simply an amplification of that number…Now here is the key that unlocks the whole thing. In the original Greek…the number is not '144,000,…' Instead, it is the '144 thousands.' The Greek word for thousands…is not singular but plural. It is a symbolic number of all the redeemed, the elect,...the body of Christ..." The words: saints, witness, believers, body of Christ, the temple, New Jerusalem, house of Israel, my people Israel, and even the name Abraham itself, all have the numeric value of 144! So the 144,000 represents all the body of Christ, saved Jews and Gentiles, and the church.

CONCLUSION

In this chapter:

1. I emphasized that the book was addressed to the seven churches of Asia, letting us know that it was written more to the Gentiles than to the Jews, although it included them. I brought this up because to insinuate that the majority of the book (chapters 5-18) isn't even for them (the Gentiles) is ludicrous. To say that they are not part of 144,000 that appeared with the Lord on Mount Zion could be classified the same.

2. I showed that the rapture didn't happen in chapter 4:1.

3. We found out that just because the word CHURCH does not appear in chapters 5-18 doesn't mean the church was raptured or is absent from those chapters. The Lord simply identifies His body, the church, Jew AND Gentile, by using 33 other descriptive phrases. If the church is all through those chapters then perhaps the church, including the Gentiles, is found, covertly, in

the 144,000. Yes, I am saying, then the 144,000 is a symbolic number, including the Gentiles.

4. This idea is supported in chapter 7 because it lists two groups of people that seem to be inseparably tied together. Some were sealed and some were arrayed.

5. Some, as the Jews, were sealed before the tribulation but still went through it just like the Great Multitude, the Gentiles, had to go through it, thus underscoring the fact that, indeed, these are the two parts of the one body of Christ. We found out that it is the Mystery of Christ, how the Gentiles could be a part of the body of Christ which started out being almost exclusively Jews.

6. We briefly laid out the 12 descriptive phrases of the 144,000, and found them similar to the 12 descriptive phrases of the Great Multitude. If the Great Multitude is speaking of the Gentiles, then you have it—the Lord is telling us that the 144,000 includes the Gentile part of the church! This same conclusion was reached when we discussed how the 144,000 number was derived— not only 12 tribes times 12,000 from each tribe, but 12 apostles times 12,000 furlongs. The 3 gates pointing 4 directions also speaks of the Gentiles being part of the city and part of the 144,000. The 144 cubit high walls, we found, spoke dramatically of the Jews (12 tribes) being multiplied by the Gentiles (found in the church, being represented by the 12 apostles). If the 144,000 were literal, it would be far too restrictive. We found it

must be, has to be, symbolic or else it wouldn't make sense. In this chapter we have looked at almost every possible angle in regards to the 144,000 and in regards to the numbers used in the city of the New Jerusalem. Hopefully, I have given enough proof to substantiate taking the number in a symbolic fashion. Therefore the 144,000 is the whole body of Christ from ages past to ages future, Jews, partial Jews, and Gentiles saved by the blood of Christ, born again of the water and the Spirit!

"WHO ARE THE 144,000?"
STUDY QUESTIONS
(*Open Book Quiz*)

1-2. "...come up hither..." appears in Revelation 4:1, but "...come hither..." appears in two other places. Name the chapters where they are found.

3. To whom was the Book of Revelation addressed?

4. How do we know the "people of God" were still on the earth up to Revelation 15 during the reign of the Antichrist (AC)?

5. Why Doesn't Revelation chapters 5-18 have to use the word "church" in referring to God's people?

6. How many different phrases are used for God's people in Revelation 5-18, all of which would be true of the church?

7. How many different characteristics are used to describe the 144,000 in chapter 14, all of which, would be true of the church?

8. The "Mystery of Christ" is a very important topic in the New Testament, but what does it mean in a nut shell?

9-10. What two apostles stood up in the first Christian conference in Acts 15 and confirmed that the Gentiles should be a part of the Jewish body of believers and have God's name called over them?

11. How many of the characteristics of the "Great Multitude" in Revelation 7 would be true of the Church?

12-13. In Revelation 7 which group was sealed in their foreheads and which group was arrayed in white robes?

14. Fill in the blank: "...hurt not the earth, neither the sea, nor the trees, till we have sealed the ___ of our God in their foreheads." Revelation 7:3

15. In regards to the previous question, how do we know that God is not sealing the Jews from the tribulation?

16. What is the number of the city of New Jerusalem?

17. What is the number of Israel?

18. What is the number of the apostles?

19. According to Ephesians 2, why was the "middle wall of partition" broken down?

20. What would be the biggest problem with the 144,000 being literal?

Bonus Question:

21. Why would God choose two numbers to be multiplied instead of choosing two numbers to be subtracted, divided, or added? (Hint: the answer is based on Isaiah 49 and 54.)

"WHO ARE THE 144,000?"
(Quiz Answers)

1-2. Chapters 17 and 21

3. To the seven churches of Asia (mostly Gentiles churches) or you could just say it was written to the church.

4. Because John saw them who had gotten the victory over the beast, his image, his mark and over the number of his name. They couldn't have gotten the victory over the AC unless they had been on the earth.

5. Because the book was addressed to the church to start with.

6. 33

7. 12

8. That the Gentiles should be fellow citizens or be together with the saved Jews in one body thus making peace.

9-10. Simon Peter and James

11. All 12 of them.

12-13. The 12 tribes of Israel, which were saved, were sealed in their foreheads and the Great Multitude (which were saved) were arrayed in white robes.

14. servants

15. Because the saved Jews had already been persecuted and killed in the church age as Jesus had said in John 16:33 they would have tribulation in the world and they had it.

16. 144,000

17. 12

18. 12

19. Jesus has made peace with the Jews and the Gentiles by making of two one new man and by putting both in the same body of Christ.

20. Only 144,000 entering into the city of New Jerusalem would truly be too restrictive.

Bonus Answer:

21. When you read portions of Isaiah 49 and 54, you will notice that Israel (or God's people) is growing exponentially as being MULTIPLIED (not as being subtracted, divided, or ADDED.)

On June 1, 2012 when Dr. James Dobson was still a part of Focus on the Family, he made this statement about being happy in marriage:

> "The best way to have love for a lifetime is at your wedding to have your eyes WIDE OPEN, and afterwards to have your eyes only HALF OPEN."

That might work well for marriage, but when it comes to the important doctrines of the Word of God such as prophecy, we not only need BOTH eyes wide open (as at the beginning of our marriage), but we need to make sure our EARS and HEARTS are wide open as well. That's why the Lord says seven times in Revelation 2 and 3, "He that hath an ear, let him hear what the Spirit saith unto the churches."

Chapter Five:
THE END—
WHEN IS IT?

WHICH CALENDAR NOW? ENDTIME TIME LINE

The Mayan calendar has taken center stage in the arena of secular attention. It left those looking at world events thinking the world would end December 21st, 2012, but it is now after that and guess what? The world is still here. The Mayan calendar is completed and what comes next? Which calendar will take center stage now? How about God's calendar? Does He have one? Yes, absolutely He does. The only thing left to do is to look at God's calendar and see what He has planned for this world. That might be easier said than done, because the majority of Christendom has been lulled into complacency with a few strands of end time dogma. Those who question the status quo rarely get to the forefront of serious consideration. The present "run of the mill" prophetic conundrum leaves too many questions unanswered. Who has the courage to break the deafening silence of the unaddressed mysteries? For the person who thinks he can correct the misinterpretations of other experts surely has a firing squad waiting to shoot him through with a million holes. It's quite a gamble, but it's worth the risk. So the rest of this chapter will unfold a view that, admittedly, is not widely held, but seriously Biblical. The reader will hopefully be left with the haunting question, "Could this be true?" Each will have to answer that for themselves, and only God knows if it will miraculously alter the landscape of accepted, Biblical interpretation. If the interpretations of the past have become stale and boring, get ready for a fresh, new, biblical look. The verses that are about to be explored will lead into a whole new arena of end time understanding.

The best place to start would be, like most end time Bible expositors, to start with the words of Jesus and not the words of Nostradamus, Edgar Cayce, Jeane Dixon, or the like. Such people, and them that are like them, are not prophets of God, and do not speak as instruments of God, contrary to what they might want the world to believe. They are the prophets of darkness. Their prophecies are only partially right. Hal Lindsey in his book THE LATE GREAT PLANET EARTH, starts his first chapter out the same way talking about these so called prophets, so it won't be necessary to go into great detail about them here. Time should be spent studying the words that are 100 percent always right, always come true exactly like they are written, and that means studying God's word. I must say from the middle to the end of this chapter it gets pretty deep. Take it slow. Study one section at a time, put the book down, rest your mind, and take the subject up again a little later. You'll find it more fun this way and your comprehension will increase. It's best to start in the New Testament by giving the entire 24th chapter of Matthew:

> Mat 24:1 "And Jesus went out, and departed from the temple: and his disciples came to him for to shew him the buildings of the temple."
>
> Mat 24:2 "And Jesus said unto them, See ye not all these things? verily I say unto you, There shall not be left here one stone upon another, that shall not be thrown down."
>
> Mat 24:3 "And as he sat upon the mount of Olives, the disciples came unto him privately, saying, Tell us, when shall these things be? and what shall be the sign of thy coming, and of **the end of the world?**"
>
> Mat 24:4 "And Jesus answered and said unto them, **Take heed that no man deceive you**."
>
> Mat 24:5 "For many shall come in my name, saying, I am Christ; and **shall deceive many**."
>
> Mat 24:6 "And ye shall hear of wars and rumors of wars: see that ye be not troubled: for all these things must come to pass, but **the end** is not yet."

Mat 24:7 "For nation shall rise against nation, and kingdom against kingdom: and there shall be famines, and pestilences, and earthquakes, in divers places."

Mat 24:8 "All these are the beginning of sorrows."

Mat 24:9 "Then shall they deliver you up to be afflicted, and shall kill you: and ye shall be hated of all nations for my name's sake."

Mat 24:10 "And then shall many be offended, and shall betray one another, and shall hate one another."

Mat 24:11 "And **many false prophets shall rise, and shall deceive many**."

Mat 24:12 "And because iniquity shall abound, the love of many shall wax cold,"

Mat 24:13 "But he that shall endure **unto the end**, the same shall be saved."

Mat 24:14 "And this gospel of the kingdom shall be preached in all the world for a witness unto all nations; and **then shall the end come**."

Mat 24:15 "When ye therefore shall **see the**

abomination of desolation, spoken of by Daniel the prophet, stand in the holy place, (whoso readeth, let him understand:)"

Mat 24:16 "Then let them which be in Judaea flee into the mountains:"

Mat 24:17 "Let him which is on the housetop not come down to take any thing out of his house:"

Mat 24:18 "Neither let him which is in the field return back to take his clothes."

Mat 24:19 "And woe unto them that are with child, and to them that give suck in those days!

Mat 24:20 "But pray ye that your flight be not in the winter, neither on the sabbath day:"

Mat 24:21 "For **then shall be great tribulation, such as was not since the beginning of the world to this time, no, nor ever shall be**."

Mat 24:22 "And except those days should be shortened, there should no flesh be saved: but for the elect's sake those days shall be shortened."

Mat 24:23 "Then if any man shall say unto you, Lo, here is Christ, or there; believe it not."

Mat 24:24 "For there shall arise false Christs, and false prophets, and shall shew great signs and wonders; insomuch that, **if it were possible, they shall deceive the very elect**."

Mat 24:25 "Behold, **I have told you before**."

Mat 24:26 "Wherefore if they shall say unto you, Behold, he is in the desert; go not forth: behold, he is in the secret chambers; believe it not."

Mat 24:27 "For as the lightning cometh out of the east, and shineth even unto the west; so shall also **the coming of the Son of man be**."

Mat 24:28 "For wheresoever the carcase is, there will the eagles be gathered together."

Mat 24:29 **"Immediately after the tribulation of those days** shall the **sun** be darkened, and the **moon** shall not give her light, and the **stars** shall fall from heaven, and the powers of the heavens shall be shaken:"

Mat 24:30 "And **then shall appear the sign of the Son of man in heaven:** and then shall all the tribes of the earth mourn, and they shall **see the Son of man coming** in the clouds of heaven with power and great glory."

Mat 24:31 "And he shall **send his angels with a great sound of a trumpet,** and they shall **gather together his elect** from the **four winds, from one end of heaven to the other.**"

Mat 24:32 "Now learn a **parable of the fig tree;** When his branch is yet tender, and putteth forth leaves, ye know that summer is nigh:"

Mat 24:33 "So likewise ye, **when ye shall see all these things, know that it is near, even at the doors.**"

Mat 24:34 "Verily 1 say unto you, **This generation shall not pass, till all these things be fulfilled.**"

Mat 24:35 "Heaven and earth shall pass away, but my words shall not pass away."

Mat 24:36 "But of that day and hour knoweth no man, no, not the angels of heaven, but my Father only."

Mat 24:37 "But as the days of Noe were, so shall also **the coming of the Son of man** be."

Mat 24:38 "For as in the days that were before the flood they were eating and drinking, marrying and giving in marriage, **until the day that Noe entered into the ark**,"

Mat 24:39 "And knew not until the flood came, and **took them all away;** so shall also **the coming of the Son of man be**."

Mat 24:40 "Then shall two be in the field; the one shall be taken, and the other left"

Mat 24:41 "Two women shall be grinding at the mill; the one shall be taken, and the other left."

Mat 24:42 "Watch therefore: for ye know not **what hour your Lord doth come**."

Mat 24:43 "But know this, that if the goodman of the house had known in what watch the thief would come, he would have watched, and would not have suffered his house to be broken up."

Mat 24:44 "Therefore be **ye also ready: for in such an hour as ye think not the Son of man cometh**."

Mat 24:45 "Who then is a faithful and wise servant, whom his lord hath made ruler over his household, to give them meat in due season?"

Mat 24:46 "Blessed is that servant, whom his lord **when he cometh** shall find so doing."

Mat 24:47 "Verily I say unto you, That he shall make him ruler over all his goods."

Mat 24:48 "But and if that evil servant shall say in his heart, My lord delayeth **his coming**;"

Mat 24:49 "And shall begin to smite his fellow servants, and to eat and drink with the drunken;"

Mat 24:50 "The lord of that servant **shall come** in a day when he looketh not for him, and in an hour that he is **not aware of**,"

Mat 24:51 "And shall **cut him asunder,** and

appoint him his portion with the hypocrites: there shall be weeping and gnashing of teeth."

Many different directions could be taken from this portion of scripture. Lots of prophecy teachers would like to start by saying that the next greatest event on God's calendar is the RAPTURE of the church, but this passage doesn't say that and neither does any other passage. A long discussion on the rapture, not happening until after the tribulation as it says in verses 29-31, might be in order, but that would be a LONG discussion, and so long that it would take a whole book (Revelation of the End, Volume II) to explain and prove it (yes, it can be proved). As stated elsewhere in this material, that book is almost completed and will be released at a future date. Many are interested in that, so a few thoughts on the subject will be included in this chapter (mostly at the end), but the book (Volume II) comes later.

A great discussion on how current events prove these are the last days might be interesting. The list could include earthquakes, famines, pestilences, wars, corruption in society, and the list goes on and on. Writers like Van Kampen, David Jeremiah, Hocking, Hutchings, Hagee, Salem Kirban, Van Impe, Larry Poland, Richard Perry and others have already discussed these kinds of events in great detail in their books, so I will not dwell on that.

This chapter will address the end time timeline that has not been discussed by many writers, especially, the time frames given in Daniel and Revelation. How many writers have explained the 2300 days of Daniel 8:13? How about the 1290 and 1335 days of Daniel 12? When the end comes these time frames will reveal that the door to this age is about to close and a new day will begin.

Know this for sure: this chapter does have to do with the END OF THE WORLD! As you can see, I highlighted those words in the passage above. Also, I want to repeat, the Lord warns us to be very careful not to be deceived. The Lord uses the word "DECEIVED" three times in this passage with several other hints about being caught off guard, in regards to His COMING and the END of the world. There are a lot of "experts" or church leaders who think they know what these words mean, and go around and teach thousands and thousands of people their understanding, and we believed them—thus one of the subtitles of this book, Betrayed by My Own Doctrine. How can I prove to you that I have the truth in regards to these future events and they don't? Let me say what John said:

> 1 Jn 4:6 "We are of God: he that knoweth God heareth us; he that is not of God heareth not us. Hereby know we the spirit of truth, and the spirit of error."

I cannot make anyone believe this exposition is the truth, but I can and will lay it out and confirm it with the verses themselves and leave the conclusion up to the reader. I want to encourage you to be in prayer as you read this material. Mark Twain said, "It is easier to fool people than it is to convince them they have been fooled." Many people are open to lies and closed to the truth, but I am believing that there will be some who read this that will close their minds to lies and open their eyes and hearts to the truth. The Word that I quote in this writing will interpret itself and witness to the fact that it is true. Notice how many verses I quote in every chapter. There are not many writers who quote the word more than I. I do that because the Word of God is more powerful than any word I could ever speak, and all quotes in this book are taken from the Authorized King James Version of the Bible.

My goal in writing this is five-fold:

1. It is to inform the believers in Christ that the end of the world is upon us.

2. We do not have to be surprised as it unfolds.

3. By knowing when the Abomination of Desolation (hereafter known as the A of D) sits or stands in the holy place, we will know when to get out of the big cities and out of Jerusalem itself.

4. To reassure the child of God that the pain of persecution and tribulation will only be for a defined period of time and then the Lord will come and rescue His people.

5. In this last point, "I am going to put my cards on the table," as R. C. Sproul puts it. I'll tell you, up front, of

my intentions and my hopes. I hope to change the minds of some of those who read this. Most have already made up their minds as to the timing of the rapture, when the A of D is set up, when the wrath of God will be poured out, etc. The timing of the rapture is the biggest of all the issues, because if the devil can mix us up on that, he will have defeated us in several areas. If all I do is create enough doubt to cause a person to take a second look at the issue, I will feel like I have accomplished my calling. More importantly, if I can, with my first book, prepare the reader for my second book, which will deal with the timing of the rapture in its entirety, then I will have even more fully completed my goal.

WHEN IS THE END?

In general terms, when is the end of the world? This chapter is written to help us determine how much time we have left. The most general indicators in scripture speak in the realm of thousands of years. How long has our world been here? Evolutionists say we have been here for millions of years mutating and changing into what and who we are today, but if we look at the Bible, we get a different picture. Through the Bible we understand man has been on this earth about 6000 years, and to us a thousand years seems pretty long, but to God a thousand years is like one day. Peter talks about that in II Peter 3:

2 Pe 3:8 "But, beloved, be not ignorant of this one thing, that one **day** is with the Lord as **a thousand years, and a thousand years as one day**."

That reminds me of a story of a man who was praying to the Lord. He said, "Lord how long is a thousand years to you?" The Lord said, "That's like a minute to me." The man goes, "How much is a million dollars to you?" The Lord responded, "a penny." The man continued, "Lord, would you give me a penny?" The Lord said, "Yeah, in a minute." Ha. It is true, though, that time is different to God than it is to us. You could say then, from God's standpoint, our world has been here for six days.

THE STUDY OF CALENDARS

The study of calendars is a big subject, so let me briefly say, everybody doesn't agree. In regards to the Jewish calendar, in the Magazine *Israel Today*, in the November 2014 issue, on page 17, David Lazarus in his article says, "The Jewish year 5775…began on September 25th, 2014…" According to that, our world at the beginning of 2019 is 221 years away from being 6000 years old. We Christians believe that the millennium will start at the end of 6000 years, because there were six days of creation and the Lord rested the seventh day. The millennium will be a thousand years of rest and peace and will begin after 6000 years of human history. So, are we 221 years away from the Lord coming and the beginning of the millennium? The Jewish people must have it right, right? Not necessarily. The Jews have their rabbis and scholars and the secular world has theirs.

Claus Tondering in Denmark monitors CALENDAR FAQ for Wikipedia. Under the heading of The Hebrew Calendar, there is a paragraph: How Does One Count Years, he says that creation took place in 3760 B.C. using the Gregorian calendar. (The world seems to have adopted the Gregorian calendar so everybody can be on the same page, except the Jewish people, as they have their own.) How did he come up with that date? It's a matter of subtracting 2019 from the Jewish year 5779 (at the time of this calculation). Simple, right? No, because there is more to consider.

On a broadcast on FM 106.7 on July 11th, 2019, at 9:30 p.m., I think it was, John MacArthur, in quoting an individual stated the creation took place at 4004 B.C. Many Christians have heard of Sir Robert Anderson and believe him, as I do, to be an authority on when Jesus entered into Jerusalem and when He started His ministry and died, etc. On page 224 of his book, THE COMING PRINCE, fifth edition, he says, "therefore the Creation will be B.C. 4141." If 2019 is added to his date of creation it comes out to 6,160. That puts us 160 years past the 6000 year mark, making us overdue for the millennium. So who is right? Maybe we will never know.

We do not have to know when the creation took place to know that we are close. All we have to know is when Jesus was born and died and that is easier to calculate than when the creation took place. If we know when He died and rose again we can know we are close to the end of this age because of the general indicators that are found in scripture.

THE THIRD DAY INDICATOR

There are four passages in the scripture—three in the Old Testament and one in the new—that give us a general indication when the resurrection will take place. They give us a birds eye view of what is ahead based on the symbolic use of the word "days". Let's start in Hosea 6 and see what it says:

> Hos 6:1 "Come, and let us return unto the LORD: for he hath torn, and he will heal us; he hath smitten, and he will bind us up."
>
> Hos 6:2 "After **two days will he revive us: in the third day he will raise us up,** and we shall live in his sight."
>
> Hos 6:3 "Then shall we know, if we follow on to know the LORD: his going forth is prepared as the morning; and **he shall come unto us** as the rain, as the latter and former rain unto the earth."

This is very much a prophetic passage. It is so beautiful as there is so much here. Here is my take on it: "He hath torn and smitten" refers to TWO things, or you could say it has a double application. Yes, the northern kingdom of Israel was to be shortly carried away into captivity by Assyria if they didn't repent, but secondly, this has to do with the smiting of the Jewish people during the two days or two thousand years after the rejection of their messiah. Also, there is a coming tribulation at the end of that two thousand years— specifically in our day— that will be a continuation of that punishing. It is known as "Jacob's trouble" in Jeremiah 30:7. In verse 3 above, it tells us who this passage is dealing with. It is the LORD...God...Father...the creator whose goings forth is as the morning, as the new rays of the sun—fresh and reviving. God will come to us like the rain. Not in America but in the nation of Israel the Lord sent the rain to soften the ground after the long summer to get it ready for plowing, planting, and preparation for seed germination. Then He would send the latter rain in the spring, right before the harvest to help the barley and wheat finish filling out to get it ready for the harvest. Basically, the rains came in two groupings, or you could say they came TWICE. God is coming to the earth twice! He came once already which could be called the former rain, to prepare the world to receive God's word.

There is more to this than what meets the eye. It's a play on words. Who was this one that came two thousand years ago? The passage says, "he shall come unto us..." It was the FATHER! He came in the form of a son and His name was Jesus to us Gentiles and as Yeshua Ha-Mashia to the Jews, but it was the same one. As 1 Timothy 3:16 says, "God manifest in the flesh" or you could say the FATHER was manifest in the flesh. When Moses asked God's name, He told him "I AM THAT I AM". In other words, I Am in existence now and a thousand years from now the one who is coming as a baby, THAT I AM also. In John 8:24 Jesus said, "...ye shall die in your sins: for if ye believe not that I am he, ye shall die in your sins." The word "he" is in italics which means it was inserted by the translators and accordingly, can be removed if it changes the meaning. When you remove it, Jesus is saying He is the "I AM" and unless you and I believe it, we will die in our sins! To make it even clearer, when you drop down to verse 27, it says, "They understood not that he spake to them of the Father." Wow! That is powerful. It's not over, though. This great Father God who came the first time, born as a babe, in the form of Jesus, will return as a conquering King Messiah as Jesus. That's the coming of the "rain" the second time, but Hosea, above, let's us in on a secret—it is really the Father ROBED IN FLESH!

Now let's concentrate, not on who the "He" is, but on the timing of His return. When will He return and what will He do? This passage tells us "in the THIRD DAY" He will raise us up. This is speaking of the resurrection from the dead which will happen at Jesus' second coming. (Erroneously, Pre-tribulationists call it the rapture, placing it before the Great tribulation.) The Lord often repeats Himself and when He does you know that He is trying to make a point. Similar type wording is given to us two more times in the Old Testament. Let's read them and make some more sense of this. Please look at Exodus 19:

> Exo 19:10 "And the LORD said unto Moses, Go unto the people, and sanctify them **to day and to morrow,** and let them wash their clothes,"

> Exo 19:11 "And be ready against **the third day:** for **the third day** the LORD **will come** down in the sight of all the people upon Mount Sinai."

Yes, I know that the Lord is talking to Moses about what the people were to do when they were standing at the foot of Mount Sinai, but the Lord has a strange way of giving prophetic words to future generations at the same time of giving words to the present generation. That is what He is doing here and it does apply. He is saying that you have TWO days to prepare before you meet your God and in the THIRD day you will see Him. As we have seen above in Hosea, that is exactly what the Lord is saying here. We have two days, 2 thousand years to get ready for the Lord to appear and in the beginning of the third day (third one thousand years) we must be ready to see our God coming back to the earth to meet His people and gather them together into one body.

Notice again, it's chapter 19 and the similarity of ideas:

> Lev 19:5 "And if ye offer a sacrifice of **peace offerings** unto the LORD, ye shall offer it at your own will."

Lev 19:6 "It shall be eaten **the same day** ye offer it, **and on the morrow:** and if ought remain until the **third day**, it shall be **burnt in the fire.**"

Lev 19:7 "And if it be eaten at all on **the third day**, it is abominable; it shall not be accepted."

Lev 19:8 "Therefore every one that eateth it shall bear his iniquity, because he hath profaned the hallowed thing of the LORD: and **that soul shall be cut off** from among his people."

Deciphering God's word can be a challenge at times, so let me help you. The passage has to do with peace offerings, but "lo and behold", prophecy is locked within the ceremony. The Lord is going to make peace with the earth. We will live our normal lives and eat regular food for TWO days. If any of the meat is left, it will be burnt at the end of the SECOND day or at the beginning of the THIRD day, but definitely it cannot be eaten on the THIRD day. The Lord is giving instructions for the Israelites in that present day, but at the same time He is speaking of a future time in our day. How does He do that? I do not know. All I know is that He DOES it. The truth is the Lord is giving us TWO days or TWO thousand years to lead normal lives and at the end of the TWO thousand years everything will be changed. There will be a sacrifice of fire on the earth that will cleanse it. This happens at the end of the tribulation and is called the WRATH OF GOD. The Lord will return to the earth and gather His people from the four corners of the earth, including the dead and the living. He will set up His kingdom. It will be the beginning of a new era of PEACE.

I am not alone in how I assess this verse. Ted D. Leavenworth III with goodnewspirit.com and goodnewsprophecy.org lists on his web site under THE THIRD DAY this last reference in Leviticus and the following reference entailing the same concept. This time it is in the New Testament and it is found in Luke 13 and it has to do with a message Jesus wants sent to Herod:

> Luk 13:32 "And he said unto them, Go ye, and tell that fox, Behold, I cast out devils, and I do cures **to day** and **to morrow,** and **the third day** I shall be perfected."

This verse is saying pretty much what Hosea 6 is saying. Again I am not the only one who sees this. Not only does Leavenworth see it, but Richard Perry agrees with us for in his book the LAST DAYS, short version page 21 he says, "Christ's prophecy seems to be saying that He will return from heaven after two days, and on the third day, He will achieve His goal." What is His goal or His perfecting? It is the day He perfects His people, or the day He harvests His people from the earth at His second coming, or you could say, the rapture. The late Chuck Smith, founder of the Calvary Chapel movement on his broadcast on KNKT in Albuquerque on April 3rd, 2015 also stated his belief in this concept. God has also revealed this concept to Marvin Byers in his book "The Final Victory: The Year 2000", published by Treasure House, 1994 on page 224 he talks about it.

WHEN DOES THE CLOCK START TICKING?

When does the clock start ticking? That's a good question and again, not everybody agrees. Let's see if we can figure it out. He said, "I do cures today..." Maybe the clock would start at the beginning of his ministry because that is when He started doing cures, which happened when? He was born between 6 and 4 B.C. because Herod the Great died in 4 B.C. Let's say He was born in 5 B.C. and started his ministry at about 30 years of age. That would put the date of Jesus' baptism or the beginning of His ministry at about 25 A.D., but there is a problem with these calculations. Luke tells us that the year Jesus was baptized was the 15th year of Tiberius Caesar:

> Luk 3: 1 "Now in the **fifteenth year of the reign of Tiberius Caesar,** Pontius Pilate being governor of Judaea, and Herod being tetrarch of Galilee, and his brother Philip tetrarch of Ituraea and of the region of Trachonitis, and Lysanias the tetrarch of Abilene,"

> Luk 3:21 "Now when all the people were baptized, it came to pass, that **Jesus also being baptized,** and praying, the heaven was opened,"

Luk 3:22 "And the Holy Ghost descended in a bodily shape like a dove upon him, and a voice came from heaven, which said, Thou art my beloved Son; in thee I am well pleased."

Luk 3:23 "And **Jesus himself began to be about thirty years of** age, being (as was supposed) the son of Joseph, which was the son of Heli,"

Sir Robert Anderson in his book THE COMING PRINCE on page 95 says, "Now the date of Tiberius Caesar's reign is known with absolute accuracy; and his fifteenth year, reckoned from his accession, began on the 19th August, A.D. 28." Remember, we figured his ministry started in A.D. 25, but if Anderson is right this would mean his ministry started in the year A.D. 28. On page 97 he continues, "And we are thus enabled to fix 32 A.D. as the year of the crucifixion." That would also mean that Jesus ministry was three and a half years long.

How can this be—where did we lose three years? The calendar has been tweaked down through the years. Sir Robert on page 128 in his footnotes says, "The Julian calendar, therefore, contains three leap years...", and in another place explains 1 B.C. to 1 A.D. is not two years but one year. At any rate the Lord's ministry began toward the end of 28 A.D. Generally speaking then, the two days or two thousand years would end about 2028, but if the clock starts ticking at the end of His life instead of the beginning of His ministry, then the end of this age would be around 2032 A.D., but personally, I prefer the previous date. This gives us a general idea of how much time we have before the end of this world. Keep in mind when the New Testament uses the words, "the end of the world", the Greek more perfectly is referring to the end of this age. (Remember, we are not just talking about the end of the Jewish age, but the end of the age of the world as we know it.) When the END comes, this world is not going to disintegrate and nothing be Left. No, a new age and a better world are coming. Now let's look at it from another angle.

HOW LONG IS A GENERATION?

In Matthew 24 the disciples asked Jesus the same question that is on our minds today:

> Mat 24:3 "And as he sat upon the mount of Olives, the disciples came unto him privately, saying, Tell us, when shall these things be? and what shall be the sign of thy coming, and of **the end of the world**?"

How did He respond? He commenced to give them a kaleidoscope of signs to look for and not until verse 32 does He give a time frame in which to specifically pinpoint these. They are all related to the budding of the "fig tree":

> Mat 24:32 "Now learn a parable of the **fig tree**; When

his branch is yet tender, and putteth forth leaves, ye know that summer is nigh:"

Mat 24:33 "SO likewise ye, **when ye shall see all these things, know that it is near, even at the doors.**"

Mat 24:34 "Verily I say unto you, **This generation shall not pass, till all these things be fulfilled.**"

I have pointed out in the chapter on the TWO WITNESSES that Israel is the true olive tree, but in this verse it is implied she is a fig tree. In the book WHY I STILL BELIEVE THESE ARE THE LAST DAYS, N. W. Hutchings, Mark Hitchcock, Robert Lindsted, Randall Price, Jimmy De Young, Kenneth Hill, Ray Yerbury, and I.D.E. Thomas on page 4 give us the title of chapter 1. "Israel—the Fig Tree God's Number One Sign of the Last Days". They go on to say: "If we were to list all the signs in the Bible identifiable with the 'last days,' or the 'latter years,' and the Second Coming of Jesus Christ, in order of importance we would have to put the return of a remnant of Israel and the re-founding of the nation as number one."

Jesus does not specifically mention that as one of the signs of the end, but it seems to be one of them. In this book these authors continue to point out that Israel faded away as a nation like the fig tree. Not only did the fig tree fade away, but most of the trees in Israel faded away with the fig tree. Today in Israel, not only is the fig tree budding and multiplying, but other trees are, as well. As the trees returned, so Israel returned as a nation. There are many prophecies that tell us that Israel will be regathered in the last days. First look at Ezekiel 20:

Eze 20:34 "And **I will bring you out from the people**, and will **gather you out of the countries** wherein ye are scattered, with a mighty hand, and with a stretched out arm, and with fury poured out"

Eze 20:41 "I will accept you with your sweet savour, **when I bring you out from the people**, and **gather you out of the countries** wherein ye have been scattered..."

What is the official date of the starting of the regathering of Israel? Hal Lindsey states in THE LATE GREAT PLANET EARTH page 43, "When the Jewish people, after nearly 2000 years of exile, under relentless persecution, became a nation again on 14 May 1948 the 'fig tree' put forth its first leaves", and we saw Isaiah 66:8 fulfilled, a nation was "born in a day". Jeremiah 24:1-7 ties it closer together because it says the remnant of Israel is like a good fig. Remember we saw above, Jesus specifically said the GENERATION that begins to see the first sign will not pass away until everything is fulfilled. Hal goes on to say, "A generation in the Bible is something like forty years." Hal was right in his first declaration, but his second declaration, which represents the sentiments of a lot of prophecy experts, give or take a few years, is not founded in scripture and should be dismissed. David Meade on page 21 of his book is undecided on how long a generation is whether it be 50, 75, 100, or 120 years long. He says that if it's a 100 years, it is based on when the Belfour Declaration was signed. Woodward states that Missler leans toward 38 years long, while others lean toward 40, but he might lean toward 70 years long for a generation. (Decoding Doomsday, 2010, Defender, pages 312-313). This is a very key concept. If we get confused on this it will totally throw us off from knowing how much time we have left. The enemy would like nothing more than to do that.

There are some prophecy scholars who say the end came during the generation that saw Jerusalem destroyed in 70 A.D., but her national destruction BEGAN at the same time which totally confirms her regathering did NOT happen then. We have to have her regathering before the end of the world, which confirms again that, the end Jesus was talking about, didn't happen in 70 A.D. This viewpoint is called preterism and we will look a little more into that in the section below labeled "The Abomination of Desolation", but knowing how long a generation is, gives us a clue on how much time we have left. It is a clue, because Jesus said, in so many words, the GENERATION that sees the regathering of Israel into a nation again, will not pass away until the end comes. (Jesus knew that the scriptures in Ezekiel would have to be fulfilled before the end.) We need not guess how long a generation is when the Bible plainly tells us. To get the key, one must go back to the book of beginnings or the book of Genesis. In chapter 15 He will tell us how long a generation is:

> Gen 15: 13 "And he said unto Abram, Know of a surety that thy seed shall be a stranger in a land that is not theirs, and shall serve them; and they shall afflict them **four hundred years;**"
>
> Gen 15:16 "But in **the fourth generation** they shall come hither again: for the iniquity of the Amorites is not yet full."

Write that down in your book of things not to forget. A generation in the Bible is 100 years. Jesus said, in so many words, the generation that begins to see the signs of the end time will not pass away until all be fulfilled. (Which generation was that? That is MY generation! I was born in 1951, three years after Israel had become a nation.) In plain language, that means the Lord will return before 2048! 2048 is 100 years after May 14, 1948.

Before we go any further I must stop here and make a point about the past to determine something about the future. Remember that the glory of God, or His characteristics, is revealed through Jesus as it tells us in II Corinthians 4:

> 2 Co 4:6 "For God, who commanded the light to shine out of darkness, hath shined in our hearts, to give the light of the **knowledge of the glory of God in the face of Jesus Christ.**"

There is a verse that tells us that Jesus does not change. It is found in Hebrews 13:

> Heb 13:8 "Jesus Christ **the same** yesterday, and today, and forever."

If Jesus does not change, then neither does God. Why do I say that? I say that because of the passage we just read in Genesis. God shows us a little about Himself here. He said that his (Abraham's) seed would remain in Egypt for four generations. Did He mean to the exact day? Did He mean to the exact year? Did He mean to the exact decade? No. What year was it when Israel came out of Egypt? Do you (the reader) remember? It is found in Exodus 12:

> Exo 12:40 "Now the sojourning of the children of Israel, who dwelt in Egypt, was **four hundred and thirty years.**"

> Exo 12:41 "And it came to pass at the end of the **four hundred and thirty years,** even **the selfsame day** it came to pass, that all the hosts of the LORD went out from the land of Egypt."

Here is the lesson we learn about God, since God does not change, but our perception of Him continues to change as we learn about Him. When He said to Abraham, "Your seed will be in Egypt for four hundred years..." (in so many words) He didn't mean exactly to the day, year, or decade. He meant approximately. In spite of the fact that Marvin Byers in his book, "The Final Victory: the Year 2000" (Published by Treasure House,, 1994) says that God is a perfect mathematician page 224, God does things rarely to the exact day. Now, in regards to the end of the world when God says He will return in the generation that sees Israel regathered to the land, He means APPROXIMATELY, just as He meant when He told Abraham that His seed would be in Egypt 400 years. Keep this in mind because it will come up again in regards to the Abomination of Desolation.

In our first section we saw that His coming would be after 2028 or 2032 depending on whether we take the beginning or the ending of Jesus' ministry. Believe it or not, this is consistent with that. 2028 is twenty years before 2048. This gives us a general idea how much time we have left—somewhere between 8 and 28 years. (This is based on the first publication of this book which is in 2020). The end of the world will not happen tomorrow, but it is getting close. 2020 plus 8 years puts it at 2028. Or if you add 28 years to that you get 2048. 8 to 28 years is not far off, but in some respects it gives us a bit of time. The scripture says it will happen BEFORE the generation is complete or before 2048. How much before, we do not know. There is a way to fine tune when the end will come, but even that is based on a floating date. It has to do with Daniel's prophecy, and the day the peace treaty is signed, and that will be talked about a bit later.

THE POSSIBLE EVENTS OF THE 70th WEEK

The best source for time events is the book of Daniel. This book really gives us our bearing when it comes to the end time format. Daniel chapter 9 gives us some valuable information:

> Dan 9:24 "**Seventy weeks** are determined upon thy people and upon thy holy city,": 1) "to finish the transgression," 2) "and to make an end of sins," 3) "and to make reconciliation for iniquity," 4) "and to bring in everlasting righteousness," 5) "and to seal up the vision and prophecy," (6) "and to anoint the most Holy." (Watch for those numbered points below.)

> Dan 9:25 "Know therefore and understand, that from the going forth of the commandment to restore and to build Jerusalem unto the Messiah the Prince shall be **seven weeks, and threescore and two weeks**: the street shall be built again, and the wall, even in troublous times."

> Dan 9:26 "And **after threescore and two**

weeks shall Messiah be cut off, but not for himself: and the people of the prince that shall come shall destroy the city and the sanctuary; and the end thereof shall be with a flood, and unto the end of the war desolations are determined."

Dan 9:27 "And **he shall confirm the covenant with many for one week**: and in the midst of the week he shall cause the sacrifice and the oblation to cease, and for the overspreading of abominations he shall make it desolate, even until the consummation, and that determined shall be poured upon the desolate."

Notice the first number in verse 24. Seventy is a BIG number, or you could say it is an important number in God's "economy". In this passage we see that 70 weeks is given to the nation of Israel. How long is a week? It is seven days, right? So that means we take 70 x 7 which makes 490 years, and this is the time frame given to the nation of Israel. This is based on every day equaling a year. During this period of time several things will happen: 1) **"to finish the transgression,"** could be thought of as putting the final touches on offending God. In other words the final great transgression will take place. This is a direct reference to the abomination of desolation (A of D). 2) **"make an end of sins"** is referring to a provision to take away sins, meaning the crucifixion. 3) **"make reconciliation for iniquity"** is referring to the sacrifice for sins that will be given, that is Jesus sacrificed for the world 4) "**...bring in everlasting righteousness**", is referring to the thousand year, or millennial reign of Christ at the end of the 70 weeks. A new era of righteousness will be ushered in at that time. After the thousand years it will not end but continue on forever. 5) "**...seal up the vision and prophecy**", is referring to the major events of prophecy for the end of the age being wrapped up or fulfilled. 6) "**...to anoint the most holy...**" By the time the 70 weeks are over, Jesus the Messiah will be crowned King of the world and universe. This will happen shortly after His second coming.

Daniel tells us in verses 25 and 26 that there is a time frame of 69 weeks or 483 years (69 x 7) in which a commandment to rebuild Jerusalem will go forth. At the end of that time frame, which works out to 173,880 days, the Messiah will be cut off and die. We go back to Sir Robert Anderson's book, on page 46 of the preface, he tells us that commandment went forth on March 14th, 445 B.C. The 69 weeks ended the day Jesus rode into the city of Jerusalem as recorded in Luke 19:28-40, and "ended upon that Sunday in the week of the crucifixion..." Folks, the 69 weeks have been fulfilled! What does that mean? That means according to verse 27, there is one remaining period of seven years that seems to be separated by 2000 years from the previous 69 weeks. This seven year time frame has not started nor ended. When will it start, and what will happen during that seven years? The rest of this chapter will deal with those questions. This is where it really gets interesting. The main thing to keep in mind is that this age cannot end until that seven year time span is completed. We need to be looking for that seven year time span to begin, but as stated earlier, it is a floating date. When it starts it will give us an "exact" time of the end. The rest of this chapter will deal exclusively with that seven years.

Many prophecy teachers have talked about the common time frames of 3-1/2 years or the 1260 days mentioned in Revelation and Daniel. How many teachers have discussed the 1290 and 1335 days of Daniel 12:11 and 12. Also, a few have tried to explain the 2300 days of Daniel 8:14, but not very many. But what about the starting and the stopping of the sacrifice? Many have discussed the A of D and when it happens, but few have tied it in with the rest of these dates. This is what we are going to do with the rest of this chapter. I try to deal with things very few have dealt with. This is going to get complicated, but I am going to go slow and methodical and try to organize it in such a way that it will be easy to understand.

It might help to make a list of the major events that will take place during this seven year period. A list of 33 chronological events follows based on what can be gleaned from studying and memorizing the prophetic text. I am not claiming to be a prophet so the order is not fool-proof, but can only be verified by the verses that will be given in the rest of this chapter. The list is as follows:

1. There will be a peace treaty signed between Israel, the Palestinians, and the Arabs. Provisions in the treaty will allow the temple to be rebuilt and animal sacrifices to be offered. Israel may have to give up half the city of Jerusalem for the treaty to be in effect.

2. The temple will be rebuilt.

3. The world will be brought under a one world government, with Sharia law.

4. Jerusalem will be declared the capitol of the world, the international city of peace, the eventual headquarters of the Antichrist (hereafter known as AC), the one world ruler.

5. A world trade center will be rebuilt in Jerusalem, and world trade will boom.

6. Excitement will mount over new found economic growth and prosperity due to the whole world uniting under a one world government.

7. Everyone will be asked to receive a chip, which will contain the mark of the beast, in their right hand or in their forehead.

8. True Christians will reject this chip and number, but pressure will increase to accept it.

9. Sacrifices will again be started in the temple.

10. Disunity erupts when half the world, possibly Russia and China, pull away and begin to act independently.

11. The one-world government—United Nations—will try to stop the uprising and world war III will erupt, during which, two billion will die.

12. An outcry over the sacrifices will be heard around the world from animal rights advocates.

13. The one world government will stop the animal sacrifices.

14. The Jews will realize they have been betrayed.

15. The Antichrist, with Persian descent (Daniel 11:2), will arise, to take the helm of the one-world government.

16. The AC will try to ease the turmoil the Jewish people are feeling.

17. Now Christians will be forced to take the chip which will contain the mark of the beast.

18. Persecution and execution of the Christians, Jews, and independent thinkers will ensue.

19. It is possible that at this time a great Christian revival will take place among the the Jewish people. If not at this time then for sure at the very end.

20. Great miracles will be performed by God's people who are the two witnesses.

21. All the nations of the world will gather at Megiddo to fight the final battle, the Battle of Armageddon to destroy Israel.

22. Israel threatens the unity by taking steps to restart the sacrifices.

23. To insure the sacrifices are not restarted, the A of D is set up on the altar/in the holy place.

24. Jewish and Gentile Christians will flee Jerusalem and the major cities of the world.

25. Within 12 hours or less, the 10 member Arab coalition agrees to nuke the major cities of the world including New York City and Jerusalem. Massive amounts of radiation are released into the atmosphere.

26. Destroying Jerusalem and killing the Jewish and Gentile Christians will anger God. The vials of God's wrath will be poured out.

27. The sun turns to darkness and the moon to blood.

28. The ANGER OF GOD in the form of a global catastrophe or heavenly disturbance such as Nibiru causes a pole shift and a global earthquake. As a result, the radiation is sucked off the earth, and the Lord saves mankind from total annihilation.

29. The Lord appears in the sky. The last enemy, Death, is destroyed. The dead in Christ arise and then the living saved are transformed and rise to meet them in the sky. They descend to the earth.

30. As the Lord descends, His feet touch down on Mt Olivet and the mountain splits—half to the north and half to the south as the earthquake, mentioned earlier, rocks the region.

31. The AC is killed and thrown into the lake of fire.

32. The Jewish nation recognizes Jesus as their Messiah. They ask Him how He got the nail prints in His hands. He tells them in the house of His friends. The surviving Jews, the remnant, as a nation, accepts Jesus as Lord. They ask if there is any way He could forgive them, and, of course, He does. They take His name in water baptism, and a cloud burst of His Spirit falls on them and tongues of fire sit on every one of them as at the beginning. They unanimously begin speaking, praying, and singing in other tongues as the Spirit gives them the utterance.

33. The thousand-year reign begins with the Marriage Supper of the Lamb.

Notice several of these events are in a different order than what has been commonly taught. Some of the events are certain, others are not. The order given is a conjecture based upon the few events that are set in concrete. Let's now go over some of those events starting with the first one, the seven-year peace treaty.

A SEVEN YEAR PEACE TREATY WILL BE SIGNED

Turmoil in the Middle East has been with us for decades. Will there ever be peace and if so how long will it last? As I have stated, Daniel has established the fact that there is going to be an agreement or a covenant of peace signed and he tells us how long it will last. It is found in Daniel 9 verse 27, but to understand it properly, ponder the three preceding verses:

> Dan 9:24 "Seventy weeks are determined upon thy people and upon thy holy city, to finish the transgression, and to make an end of sins, and to make reconciliation for iniquity, and to bring in everlasting righteousness, and to seal up the vision and prophecy, and to anoint the most Holy."
>
> Dan 9:25 "Know therefore and understand, that from

the going forth of the commandment to restore and to build Jerusalem unto the Messiah the Prince shall be **seven weeks,** and **threescore and two weeks:** the street shall be built again, and the wall, even in troublous times."

Dan 9:26 "And after threescore and two weeks shall Messiah be cut off, but not for himself: and the people of the prince that shall come shall destroy the city and the sanctuary; and the end thereof shall be with a flood, and unto the end of the war desolations are determined."

Dan 9:27 "And he shall **confirm** the **covenant** with many **for one week**: and in the midst of the week he shall cause the sacrifice and the oblation to cease, and for the overspreading of abominations he shall make it desolate, even until the consummation, and that determined shall be poured upon the desolate."

This is the only passage in the entire Bible that lets us know that there is going to be seven more years for the nation of Israel and for the rest of the world. It is referred to in verse 27 as "the covenant...for one week". It has been said many times, Israel is the time clock for the world, and it is true. Whatever happens to Israel affects the rest of us. The 7 weeks and the 62 weeks added together gives us 69 weeks.

The scripture is quite clear that those 69 weeks have already been fulfilled. Notice how verse 27 speaks of the last one week as a separate unit. It appears that in between the 69th and the 70th week there is an expanse of time lasting about 2000 years. We are at the end of that period of time right now. We are waiting for the 70th week to start. It has not started yet, but when it does we will know that we are at the very door of the end of this age.

How will we know when it starts? It is implied. (Many things in scripture are implied, but at the same time, very for sure.) It says the one who confirms the agreement will "cause the sacrifice and the oblation to cease". It appears that the one who initiates the agreement will be the same one who has allowed for the rebuilding of the temple, the re-instituting of the sacrifices, and even the ceasing of the sacrifices. (Now listen very carefully. Many prophecy teachers forget to clarify this one point. The AC only reigns for 42 months. If you will go to the fourth line of both graphs in the back of this chapter you will be able to understand and follow this explanation better. If 42 months is subtracted from the end of the seven year peace agreement, something becomes very clear. The list of events taking place in the first half of the week, including the signing of the peace treaty and the ceasing of the sacrifice is done BEFORE the AC is crowned world ruler!!!

The AC will somehow be involved with these events, but he doesn't perform them as the world Ruler. This is very significant and needs to be restated so it can be absorbed.

The AC signs the peace treaty or has it signed before he becomes the world ruler. The AC seems to be helping the Jews rebuild their temple, but he only does it to win the confidence of the Jewish nation. He only APPEARS to be their friend, but he is not. It also appears that this same one who has made it possible for all this to happen will also be the one who will cause these sacrifices to cease! These things will happen after the seven year peace treaty is signed, and since the Jews haven't been given the right to rebuild their temple yet, we know the treaty has NOT begun yet. Some have said that the agreement could have already been signed. No way. Believe me, when the Jews are given the right to rebuild their temple, it will reverberate around the world, and that will be the sign that the last seven years has begun!

In the section below, Jesus will confirm the fact that the A of D will occur, and in so doing He will, at the same time, be confirming the coming seven year peace treaty. In confirming the peace treaty, He will also be confirming the fact that the temple will be rebuilt, the sacrifices started, and then stopped. All of these events are markers, signs and indicators. Daniel is the one who has told us about the seven year peace treaty. He is also the one the Lord uses to give us the timing of when all these things happen. The main indicator preceding the wrath of God is the A of D and that has to do with the AC, but before we get to that, let's discuss how long the AC will reign, which is given to us in no uncertain terms.

42 MONTHS, 1260 DAYS, A TIME and TIMES and THE DIVIDING OF TIME, and THREE DAYS and a HALF

This time frame will also be discussed in the third book in the chapter entitled The Great Persecution and the Great Tribulation. It is evident from the section heading that this time frame is given to us in scripture in four different terminologies. The first one is found in Revelation 13:

> Rev 13:5 "And there was given unto him a mouth speaking great things and blasphemies; and power was given unto him to continue **forty and two months**."

The AC will reign for forty two months. He will be proclaimed as the Ruler or "King" of the World. Again, the AC will be discussed in greater detail in the third book under the chapter title, "Who is the Antichrist and from Where does He Come?". It appears that the Two Prophets, the Two Witnesses, or the people of God prophecy and witness to the inhabitants of the world the same period of time that the AC reigns. That period of time is given to us in "days" and is found in Revelation 11 and 12

> Rev 11:3 "And I will give power unto my two witnesses, and they shall prophesy **a thousand two hundred and threescore days, clothed in sackcloth**."

I have already discussed the TWO WITNESSES in a whole chapter of their own. Forty two Jewish months with 30 days apiece is 1260 days. As stated in that chapter, the people of God will testify to the world in miraculous ways during that period of time. The church, the bride of Christ, made up of Jews and Gentiles, and called the "woman" will be protected (and yet some will die) during the reign of the AC. (Many claim the woman in Revelation 12 to be only the Jewish nation. Others say, "no", it is just the Gentile bride. That is covered in greater detail in the chapter entitled WHO ARE THE 144 THOUSAND?) We know many will be beheaded and killed, but it sounds like some will be protected. It is a mystery how that will be played out. Since the reign of the AC is 1260 days, then that is the period of time the people of God are protected. That description, given to us in "days" is continued to be described in Revelation 12:

> Rev 12:6 "And the woman fled into the wilderness, where she hath a place prepared of God, that they should feed her there **a thousand two hundred and threescore days**."

In this very chapter, six verses later, the Lord changes the wording yet further:

> Rev 12:14 "And to the woman were given two wings of a great eagle, that she might fly into the wilderness, into her place, where she is nourished for **a time,**

and times, and half a time, from the face of the serpent,"

The book of Revelation is not the only book that tells us how long the AC reigns. Daniel, also, gives us the length of time which is also the amount of time he persecutes the saints of the Most High God. It is given to us as time, times, and the dividing of time. In scripture, time is one year, times is two years, and the dividing of time is half a year, making it three and a half years. It is found in Daniel 7:

> Dan 7:25 "And he shall speak great words against the most High, and shall wear out the saints of the most High, and think to change times and laws: and they shall be given into his hand until **a time and times and the dividing of time.**"

This wording changes only slightly when it is repeated in Daniel 12. (In regards to the A of D we will see the wording change for that event four times.) Please, look at chapter 12:

> Dan 12:7 "And I heard the man clothed in linen, which was upon the waters of the river, when he held up his right hand and his left hand unto heaven, and sware by him that liveth for ever that it shall be for **a time, times, and an half**; and when he shall have accomplished to scatter the power of the holy people, all these things shall be finished."

Notice two things: 1) The wording in Daniel 12 is very similar to the wording in Revelation 12. 2) The scripture confirms over and over again that the reign of the AC is 1260 days and the time the church is persecuted is the same. Watch this in Revelation 11. The wording will change again and it will change so much most prophecy teachers do not even catch it. It is not the fact that the phrase changes so much that many miss it, it is the fact that most believe that the Two Witnesses are TWO LITERAL PEOPLE and they believe the rapture of the church has ALREADY HAPPENED, so they dismiss the whole passage as a different event. This is a very real example how one's view of the rapture, if it is incorrect, can skew one's ability to put the pieces of the prophecy puzzle together. Look at verses 8, 9 and 11:

> Rev 11:8 "And their dead bodies shall lie in the street of the great city, which spiritually is called Sodom and Egypt, where also our Lord was crucified."

> Rev 11:9 "And they of the people and kindreds and tongues and nations shall see their dead bodies **three days and an half**, and shall not suffer their dead bodies to be put in graves."

> Rev 11:11 "And after **three days and an half** the Spirit of life from God entered into them, and they stood upon their feet; and great fear fell upon them which saw them."

Do you think the Lord is talking about three and a half literal days? No!!! Remember, you must be careful. The Lord switches the wording back and forth with no warning at all, and it will lead you into confusion or leave you in the dust unless you keep up with Him. That is why it seems like everybody thinks these TWO witnesses are literally two INDIVIDUALS when they are the two main parts of the body of Christ. He is referring to the CHURCH as I demonstrate for over 30 pages in my previous chapter on the TWO WITNESSES. The Lord is NOT saying these two people literally lay in the streets of Jerusalem for three and a half days, all though that could happen. He is only repeating what He said in verse three above, that their ministry will last for three and a half years and they will be persecuted the whole length of their ministry. Many will die and lay in the streets of the cities all around the world, but at the same time there will be some that will be protected.

Let me review this one more time, because all these verses come together here. Daniel 7:25 and 12:7 above tell us that, yes, the people of God, the saints are persecuted for three and a half years. Revelation 12:6 and 14 tell us, yes, some saints will be protected to a degree during this three and a half years. In other words, all the people of God will not be annihilated. A remnant will be miraculously preserved. After this three and a half years of persecution, the Lord will return and catch His people up into the air and they will be transformed in front of the eyes of their "enemies" (people remaining on the earth). Again, the three and a half days are three and a half years. Each day represents a year, and the verses dovetail together to give us the whole picture.

(Excuse me for digressing, but there are prophecy teachers like General James Green, and others who say the Lord is not going to catch us up into the air at His coming. They acknowledge the verse in I Thessalonians 4:17 says that, but since it is only one passage and it is not verified by another passage it can't be true. There is a verse in Matthew 18:16, which deals with the uncooperative Brethren that says, "…in the mouth of two or three witnesses let every word be established", and in this case, since there is not another verse that says it, it can't be true. Well, for those folks, here is your SECOND witness! The Lord uses Revelation 11:8-12 in a parabolic form and says that these two witnesses which represent the church will be told to "come up hither" and they ascend up to heaven in a cloud! This is talking about the second coming of Christ and our gathering together unto Him, the rapture. This is the second verse and therefore it is true, we will be caught up into the air.)

Getting back on track—once more it is confirmed that the AC reigns for three and a half years, or 1260 days. Write it down on your list of things never to forget; it is not 1261 nor 1259 days; it is 1260 days.

Here the Lord says what He means, and means what He says. This is NOT a general categorization. The Lord says it too many times, for it not to be exact. It will be 1260 days! At the end of the reign of the AC the AC will be destroyed by the return of Jesus. We will discuss that in greater detail below. It also appears that Jerusalem will be destroyed near the end of his reign, which is at the end of this 1260 days. Again in the third book I have a whole chapter on WHO IS MYSTERY BABYLON THE GREAT? In that chapter it is revealed that Jerusalem is Mystery Babylon the Great and it will be destroyed. I deal somewhat with Jerusalem being destroyed in the section below, in an encapsulated form, but along with that I will throw in some more insights on the subject. Before getting to that let me give more details on the 1260 days.

THE GREAT PERSECUTION, THE GREAT TRIBULATION, AND THE WRATH OF GOD

We have just said that the AC will reign for 1260 days. During this time he is going to persecute and kill, by means of beheading, thousands and thousands of Christians. The fake ones will cave in to the demands of this evil one, take his mark, and worship him and his image. The knowledgeable ones will run for their lives and hide. It appears that many will die for the Lord, but some will be spared. This will be the worst persecution of all times. We must console and encourage ourselves that it is only for three and a half years and then the Lord will come and rescue us.

It appears at the end of this 1260 days that the Lord will pour out his wrath upon the earth, for all the evil the AC has done and for all the lives he has destroyed. The Lord's wrath is incorporated in the Great Tribulation that will come upon the earth. The word tribulation has the idea of a time of trouble. We are not talking about just any time of trouble. We are talking about a time of trouble like no other time of trouble. This time of trouble starts out with a time of persecution like no other and extends to the wrath of God, like no other that has ever been poured out upon the face of the earth. There will, very likely, be geological changes and heavenly disturbances that will cause a pole shift and earthquakes that will disfigure the whole earth. These geological changes are the seven vials recorded in Revelation 16 and my last chapter will describe it better. It is difficult to place the exact timing of the Battle of Armageddon in the midst of all this disruption, but we know it will be somewhere near the end of the 1260 days. As mentioned before, the AC will be destroyed at the end of this time period, but before he is destroyed he will accomplish one of his most detestable acts, the A of D.

THE ABOMINATION OF DESOLATION

Daniel makes reference to the A of D FOUR times and uses different words and expressions each time. Jesus also verifies the A of D and is recorded in three of the four gospels. The character of the AC is most notably demonstrated in the destruction of Jerusalem and in desecrating the sacredness of the temple by means of the A of D. In the third book of this series, as mentioned earlier, a whole chapter on the AC, describes him in detail, so obviously, it will not be repeated here, except how he relates to the A of D. The timing of the end of the world is based on him coming to this world and setting up the A of D, or having it set up. It is difficult to segregate all the verses on the A of D in one section without doing a lot of repetition because the A of D plays center stage in the following three sections:

1. **The 2300 Days.**
2. **5 More Proofs the Abomination of Desolation is at the End of the Week** and
3. **So, What is the Abomination of Desolation?**

In this section only general information and one of the Daniel's passages will be given about the A of D. To get started it would be important to first examine the gospel accounts where the A of D is mentioned and see what can be learned from them, starting with Matthew 24:

> Mat 24:14 "And this gospel of the kingdom shall be preached in all the world for a witness unto all nations; and then shall **the end come**."

> Mat 24:15 "When ye therefore shall see **the abomination of desolation**, spoken of by Daniel the prophet, **stand in the holy place**, (whoso readeth, let him understand:)"

Mat 24:16 "Then let **them which be in Judaea flee into the mountains**:"

Mat 24:17 "Let him which is on the housetop not come down to take any thing out of his house:"

Mat 24:18 "Neither let him which is in the field return back to take his clothes."

Mat 24:19 "And woe unto them that are with child, and to them that give suck in those days!"

Mat 24:20 "But pray ye that your flight be not in the winter, neither on the sabbath day:"

Mat 24:21 "For **then shall be great tribulation**, such as was not since the beginning of the world to this time, no, nor ever shall be."

Mat 24:22 "And except those days should be shortened, there should no flesh be saved: but for the elect's sake those days shall be shortened."

As in the days of David, the time of judgment was shortened. So it will be at the end of time. What else can be learned from this passage? The subject matter is the END OF THE WORLD. General James Green with Aggressive Christianity Missions Training Corps along with other moderate preterists such as Hank Hanegraff, and R. C. Sproul say that this is referring to the sacking of Jerusalem in 70 A.D. To them it's all been fulfilled. See the cartoon below:

THE FALLACY OF PRETERISM

According to Prophecy Ministries, with Donald Perkins, "Preterism is a system for the interpretation of the book of Revelation. Its strange name comes from a Latin word meaning past tense. The word is appropriate because this view holds that either all or most of the book of Revelation was fulfilled in the First Century!"

(A personal comment: Some of this information was taken from *According to Prophecy Ministries* which talks about what preterists believe. I contacted Dr. R. C. Sproul and asked him if, indeed, he was a moderate preterist. He admitted that he was and at the same time he recommended his book, THE LAST DAYS ACCORDING TO JESUS, published by Baker Books, 1998. I found, acquired, and read the book. It was very informative and admittedly, it thoroughly explained the difference between a moderate and radical preterist. On page 68 he says, "Moderate preterism, though it sees the coming of Christ predicted in the Olivet Discourse as having been already fulfilled, still believes in a future consummation of Christ and his kingdom, based on other New Testament texts... Radical preterism, on the other hand, sees virtually the entire New Testament eschatology as having been realized already." After reading the book, it could be said there is merit in Sproul's position, but it's not convincing. Admittedly, there is a lot of things in history that appears, on the surface, to fulfill different prophetic passages, but some passages can have double and triple fulfillment. Many prophecy experts admit this is true. In other words, just because Jesus words were fulfilled once, doesn't mean they can't be fulfilled again, thus preterism isn't the final chapter. Take Jerusalem for example. Just because she was destroyed in Titus day, doesn't mean she can't be destroyed again in our day and she will be.)

Romans 11:25 talks about blindness happening to Israel. UPHOLDING OUR FUTURE HOPE, AN APOSTOLIC RESPONSE TO PRETERISM, compiled by G. Jorge Medina from eight writers, and published by Word Aflame Press in 2005, on page 131, says (full) "preterists, think that verse 25 teaches that God is through with Israel and that the promises to Israel in the Old Testament are being fulfilled in the church and that there will be no future kingdom on this earth in which Jesus Christ rules over Israel and the world." This is what you call Replacement Theology, and we reject this teaching.

To illustrate the moderate preterist view point, Hank Hanegraaff in his book, THE BIBLE ANSWER BOOK FOR STUDENTS, Thomas Nelson, 2007, page 264 gives a short answer to the question that comes out of Matthew 24:34 which is as follows:

> Mat 24:34 "Verily I say unto you, This generation shall not pass, till all these things be fulfilled."

The question is, "Which Generation Is 'This Generation'?" Hanegraaff, I would say, is a world renown figure, but especially in this country. I am not wanting to go too deep into preterism, but his answer to this question has circulated far and wide and needs to be addressed to some degree, because it represents what many preterists hold and believe, but it is NOT true. He says: "Which generation did Jesus have in mind? First, when Jesus says "**this** generation", **this** means **this**. **This** doesn't mean **that**. The phrase 'this generation' appears multiple times in the Gospels and **always** refers to Jesus' contemporaries. Allow me to say something obvious here: Jesus wasn't grammatically challenged. If He'd wanted to draw the attention of His disciples to a generation nineteen hundred years in the future, He wouldn't have confused them with the adjective **this**."

First, let me say, Hanegraaff is no dummy by any stretch of the imagination and I respect him highly. I am not going to dwell on the fact that the Greek word for "this" can also be translated "that", but taken in context, when Jesus said, "this generation shall not pass away, till all these things be fulfilled," He was speaking of the generation that SEES these things come to pass. Yes, it was 1900 years from then. Okay, maybe every other time He uses "this generation" He is referring to His contemporary generation, but this is different. He is giving signs of things far in the future. How do we know that? All we have to do is take the passage for face value. I agree Jesus was NOT grammatically challenged, but let me also say the obvious. Lots of things in prophecy cannot be taken logically. Some can and some can't. They have to be taken the way the Lord wants them taken, so how do you know? The context and other verses on the subject is what reveals the deciding factor. The disciples were asking about when the temple would be destroyed, the sign of His coming, and of the END OF THE WORLD. Many dismiss this and say they were asking about the end of the Jewish age. My comment: RIDICULOUS! Jesus answered the question and gave MANY signs in regards to the END OF THE WORLD, not the end of the Jewish age—"nation rising against nation, kingdom against kingdom, ...famines, and pestilences, and earthquakes, in DIVERS places," not just in Israel, "hated of ALL nations" not just in Israel, "for my name's sake...for then shall be great tribulation, such as was not since the beginning of the world to this time, no, nor ever shall be." Did all of this happen in the 40 years after Jesus' crucifixion? Not hardly. Was Jerusalem destroyed much like it was in Nebuchadnezzar's day? Yes, but not like it will be destroyed in the future with a nuclear bomb. I think my point is clear that "this" generation is the generation that sees all these things fulfilled. That has to be what Jesus meant or it doesn't make sense. (I expound on this in other sections of this chapter.) The point is, this has to do with the END OF THE WORLD and that just happens to be taking place in OUR day and that is over 1900 years later!

After giving Matthew 24:14-22, above, at the bottom of the section "The Abomination of Desolation", I asked, "What else can be learned from this passage?" and the first point was given, but there is more. 2) The Lord seems to use the A of D as a timing indicator that we are to watch for. 3) The A of D will be erected in the holy place, and possibly placed on the arc of the covenant, itself. Again, the temple will have to be rebuilt for this to happen. 4) The people living in Judea need to flee into the mountains. Why? There is going to be destruction. That is why the AC, as a man, is called the "the son of perdition". Perdition means "entire loss; ruin; especially utter loss of the soul, or of final happiness in a future state; damnation" (Webster's New Collegiate Dictionary, 1956 page 624).

When the AC takes control of the world there will be no hope for it, because the word "abomination" means, very detestable and abhorrent, but the word "desolation" means it is going to bring desolation with it, that is, destruction to the world and to Jerusalem. We are getting to the "nitty gritty" here. Very few, talk about this. This is why Jesus is instructing people to "high tail" it out of the city. Jesus is speaking like every second counts. Get to a place of safety. Fleeing to the mountains will be the only safe place. See how He talks about it. The people of God will not have much time. How long will it take to get to the mountains? It will take some time to get there, so leave immediately. Have your survival pack with you at all times. Grab it and run. Don't go out of your way to get any provision. You can't take anything out of your house? If you're in the field, you can't return home to get your clothes? What kind of examples are these? He is serious! You know some people. Some of us are like Boy Scouts, want to be ready for anything—you know, like spending half a day, just packing the car. Jesus is saying, "DO NOT DO THAT!" One would be wasting valuable time. If the survival pack isn't close at hand, just get out, NOW! That is what He is saying.

The father or mother should have already instructed every member of the family what to do. Again, there will not be much time to get to the mountains. In other words, get out of Jerusalem. The idea here, is whatever the people of Judea are doing, is what the rest of Christendom should be doing. (The people of Israel and Jerusalem because of the recent bombings, are trained to respond to emergencies within seconds, but what about the people of God scattered throughout the rest of the cities of the world? We need to learn to follow their example.) The people of God need to get to a place of protection just like those in Judea are going to do. It will be very, very bad. (Be looking for the third book which has a chapter in it called, The Great Persecution and The Great Tribulation. It will explain this in greater detail.)

5) This is the fifth point. There is going to be a time of trouble such as never was. All of this will happen when the A of D is erected in the holy place. It is very important to understand when this is going to happen, because as can be seen, this is the MAIN indicator the Lord uses to set the alarm off and to get the people of God into gear. Most prophecy teachers say this event will happen in the middle of the seven year agreement. Not so. It will be at the end of the seven year period, but proof for this will come below. We have been reviewing Jesus words about the A of D. Does Mark substantiate what Matthew says? Yes. Look at his account:

> Mar 13:13 "And ye shall be hated of all men for my name's sake: but he that shall endure unto the end, the same shall be saved."

Mar 13:14 "But when ye shall see **the abomination of desolation**, spoken of by Daniel the prophet, **standing** where it ought not, (let him that readeth understand,) then let them that be in Judaea flee to the mountains:"

Mar 13:15 "And let him that is on the housetop not go down into the house, neither enter therein, to take any thing out of his house:"

Mar 13:16 "And let him that is in the field not turn back again for to take up his garment"

Mar 13:17 "But woe to them that are with child, and to them that give suck in those days!"

Mar 13:18 "And pray ye that your flight be not in the winter."

Mar 13:19 "For in those days **shall be affliction, such as was not from the beginning of the creation which God created unto this time, neither shall be**."

Mar 13:20 "And except that the Lord had shortened those days, no flesh should be saved: but for the elect's sake, whom he bath chosen, he hath shortened the days."

Mark is repeating Matthew almost verbatim. Again, those that say this happened, already, in 70 A.D. have missed it because Jerusalem was destroyed much like she was in 587 B.C. by Nebuchadnezzar. The Lord foretold affliction such as "WAS NOT" from the beginning of creation. As in Matthew 24:21, Mark 13:19 says there will be "affliction" (Matthew uses the word tribulation) "such as was not..." Notice carefully, it doesn't say against Jerusalem. It just says, "affliction such as was not from the beginning of the creation..." and continues on, "And except the Lord had shortened those days, no flesh should be saved:..." It doesn't say no flesh should be saved in Jerusalem, but "no flesh..." period, should be saved. The destruction of Jerusalem in 70 A. D. doesn't cut it. The Lord is talking about something gargantuan here. It's bigger than the Middle East. This is global. This that is to come has NEVER happened before and will never happen again. Not only does Jerusalem get destroyed the third time (God works often in threes), but, again, it appears like the whole world is turned upside down at this time. (Verse 13 says, "he that shall endure unto the end, the same shall be saved." The end didn't happen in the 40 years after He gave this answer, and as I said earlier, neither did all those world events, which I deal with in greater detail in my final chapter.) We looked at Matthew's and Mark's account, but Luke's account has the wording quite different:

Luk 21:20 "And when ye shall **see Jerusalem compassed with armies**, then know that **the desolation** thereof is **nigh**."

Luk 21:21 "Then let them which are in Judaea flee to the mountains; and let them which are in the midst of it depart out; and let not them that are in the countries enter thereinto."

Luk 21:22 "For these be **the days of vengeance**, that all things which are written may be fulfilled."

Luk 21:23 "But woe unto them that are with child, and to them that give suck, in those days! for there shall be great distress in the land, and wrath upon this people."

Luk 21:24 "And they shall fall by the edge of the sword, and shall be led away captive into all nations: and **Jerusalem shall be trodden down of the Gentiles, until the times of the Gentiles be fulfilled**."

This is the passage that preterists use to say that all three passages were already fulfilled in 70 A.D., because it sounds exactly like what happened back in the days when Jerusalem was destroyed the second time. At the same time it is pretty obvious that the Israelites weren't lead into captivity into ALL nations in 70 A.D. It took hundreds of years for that to happen. Keep in mind each author uses different phrases to describe the same event. Here are all three accounts together:

1. **Luk** 21:22 "...the **days of vengeance**, that all things which are written may be fulfilled."

2. **Mat** 24:21 "For then shall be **great tribulation**, such as was not since the beginning of the world to this time, no, nor ever shall be." Mat 24:22 "And except those days should be shortened, there should **no flesh** be saved: but for the elect's sake those days shall be shortened."

3. **Mar** 13:19 "for in those days shall be **affliction**, such as was not from the beginning of the creation which God created unto this time, neither shall be."
Mar 13:20 "And except that the Lord had shortened those days, **no flesh** should be saved: but for the elect's sake, whom he hath chosen, he hath shortened the days."

Luke doesn't describe the days "of vengeance", "great tribulation", or "affliction" like Matthew and Mark does as:

"such as was not from the beginning of the creation which God created unto this time, neither shall be." Luke, in verse 22 throws in a phrase that the other two leave out: "...that all things **which are written** may be fulfilled." Luke must be referring to Daniel's description of those days in Daniel 12:1, because that is where it was written and it is as follows: "...and **there shall be a time of trouble, such as never was since there was a nation even to that same time**:..." That is why Luke doesn't repeat Daniel's exact words, he just refers to them by saying, "For these be the days of vengeance, that all things **which are written**" (in the book of Daniel) "may be fulfilled."

Yes, admittedly, the first half of Luke 21:24 seems to be saying exactly what happened at the destruction of Jerusalem in 70 A. D.: "And they shall fall by the edge of the sword..." That is what happened in 70 A.D. The Jews were massacred at the fall of Jerusalem, but that wasn't the end of the story. Besides being carried away captive into different parts of the world, the rest of the verse says, "Jerusalem shall be trodden down of the Gentiles, until the times of the Gentiles be fulfilled." The "times of the Gentiles" is referring to the ages of time in which the Gentiles rule the world. That didn't stop at 70 A.D.! Not only do the Gentiles still rule this world, but Jerusalem was still to be trodden down by the Gentiles even until 1967 (and believe it or not it will happen again). Therefore 70 A.D. wasn't the total fulfillment of what Jesus was saying in Luke 21! This is also in agreement with Matthew's and Mark's accounts. They are saying the same thing. The days of tribulation and affliction like has NEVER been, is yet to be fulfilled. Jerusalem was destroyed in 70 A.D. much like it was in 587 B.C., but the next time it happens will bring a time of trouble like no other time in history. All three passages will be fulfilled, to the letter, in the future.

Notice, also, Luke does not use the term A of D. He says when you see "Jerusalem compassed with armies," then get to the mountains. People in the countryside (he uses the word, "countries" in verse 21) should not enter into the city, but they should also head to the mountains. He is basically saying that at the same time the A of D is standing in the Holy place his armies will be surrounding the city. Remember, in 70 A. D. Titus's armies surrounded the city and for no apparent reason the armies pulled away from the city for a short period of time and that is when the Christians were able to escape. It happened in 70 A.D. just as Jesus had said and because of this preterists say, "See, this is the fulfillment, and there will be no other fulfillment." As I said earlier, and let me repeat, many prophecy teachers admit to the fact that some prophetic texts have double and triple fulfillment. In other words, history repeats itself, and since it does, one prophetic statement can be true two and three times in the saga of human history. (This was dealt with in great detail in the chapter on HOW IMPORTANT IS PROPHECY?) Yes, it did happen in 70 A.D., but everything was NOT fulfilled as it will be in the future. Armies again, in similar fashion, will be gathered around Jerusalem. The people who fear God and believe the prophets need to get out of "Dodge" as it were. None the less, Luke's account is plain. When the A of D is set up, the destruction of Jerusalem is very near. If the saints of God do not get out at that time, they will not get out at all! More about Jerusalem being destroyed in the section, JERUSALEM DESTROYED.

It bears repeating that Luke's passage uses the phrase, "the times of the Gentiles", and as stated earlier, this phrase is referring to an era of time in which the Lord allows the Gentiles to control the world. There is coming a time when the world will be controlled by the people of God. This will happen during the thousand year millennial reign of Christ. During that time the Gentiles will not be in control any longer. As you can see, the "times of the Gentiles" is the period of time that the world is in right now, but it is fast coming to an end. Jerusalem will constantly have armies in and out of the city until the END comes, and so far, the end has not come, but it is coming and it is coming fast!

Remember, we are in the section on the A of D. The three gospel accounts have been given. When talking about the A of D it is tempting like others, to throw in II Thessalonians 2:34, but that account doesn't mention the A of D directly, so it will be left out here and mentioned below. The next verse that should be considered is found in Daniel 11. It will reveal some interesting things:

> Dan 11:30 "For the ships of Chittim shall come against **him**: therefore **he** shall be grieved, and return, and have indignation against the holy covenant: so shall

he do; **he** shall even return, and have intelligence with them that forsake the holy covenant."

Dan 11:31 "And arms shall stand on **his** part, and **they** shall pollute the sanctuary of strength, and shall take away the daily sacrifice, and **they** shall **place the abomination that maketh desolate**."

Verse 30 talks about everything that the AC is going to do—he this and he that—and then it switches in verse 31 from "he" to "they", and then it says "they" are going to do THREE things:

1. They shall pollute the sanctuary
2. They shall take away the daily sacrifice.
3. They shall place the abomination that maketh desolate.

Why does the scripture switch like this? Remember, that the AC doesn't take his official position as the head of the world until later, but he still can use his influence, though not the head, to have it done. For now just keep in mind this passage is saying that "they place" the abomination that makes desolate. It will be discussed in greater detail in the third section below.

There are three more passages in Daniel that mention the A of D, that could be given here but to save a lot of repetition they will be given in the following two sections with revealing headings all their own.

The third section will cap it off. It will become evident that this event is the king pin in revealing how much time remains.

THE 2300 DAYS

The A of D is also mentioned in Daniel 8. This will be the second of Daniels four references to this subject. This is where it really starts to get interesting, because Daniel throws in specific timing factors. What if we could know the exact day that the A of D was set up? Would that be cool? Has anybody ever figured that out for you? Oh, yes, many have stated it would be set up in the middle of the week but has anyone ever given the exact day?!? Probably not, because the verses that give the exact day do not indicate that it takes place in the middle of the week, so they leave those verses out. Daniel does that in his account. He gives the exact day. Let's take a look:

> Dan 8:9 "And out of one of them came forth a **little horn**, which waxed exceeding great, toward the south, and toward the east, and toward the pleasant land."

> Dan 8:10 "And it waxed great, even to the host of heaven; and it cast down some of the host and of the stars to the ground, and stamped upon them."

Dan 8:11 "Yea, he magnified himself even to the prince of the host, and **by him the daily sacrifice was taken away, and the place of his sanctuary was cast down.**"

Dan 8:12 "And **an host** was given him against **the daily sacrifice by reason of transgression**, and it cast down the truth to the ground; and it practised, and prospered."

Dan 8:13 "Then I heard one saint speaking, and another saint said unto that certain saint which spake, **How long** shall be the vision **concerning the daily sacrifice**, and the **transgression of desolation**, to give both the sanctuary and the host to be trodden under foot?"

Dan 8:14 "And he said unto me, **Unto two thousand and three hundred days; then shall the sanctuary be cleansed.**"

Dan 8:15 "And it came to pass, when I, even I Daniel, had seen the vision, and sought for the meaning, then, behold, there stood before me as the appearance of a man."

Dan 8:16 "And I heard a man's voice between the banks of Ulai, which called, and said, Gabriel, make this man to understand the vision."

Dan 8:17 "So he came near where I stood: and when he came, I was afraid, and fell upon my face: but he said unto me, **Understand, O son of man: for at the time of the end shall be the vision.**"

Let's summarize this passage with six points:

1. It brings, especially, Luke's account along with Matthew's and Mark's together. An HOST was given him. In other words, the AC comes with his armies. They will be in and around the city of Jerusalem. (They will ensure his right to stand and sit in the holy place to desecrate it before it's destruction at the end.) Remember this is done BEFORE the AC takes the throne as the world ruler, and how he can do that without being the world ruler is somewhat of a mystery.

2. The little horn or the Antichrist will cause the sacrifice to cease. In other words verse 11 mentions the SANCTUARY. This refers to the temple and implies that it must be in existence. The rebuilding of it will have already been done. Others, including General James Green, disagree. They say it would take too long to rebuild, so it must be talking about something else,

but we have more modern building methods today than they had back then. Some have said that the temple is already built in pieces like a prefabrication building and could be assembled in a very short period of time. At any rate, the temple will be rebuilt and they will be given permission to start sacrificing again, and then the permission will be withdrawn and they will stop the Jewish nation from sacrificing. This man will also cast down the sanctuary or the temple and this will, most likely, be done when the whole city is cast down.

3. In verse 13 Daniel asks, "how long shall be the vision concerning the daily sacrifice, and the transgression of desolation…?" What is he asking? Watch the wording here. He is asking how much time is there between two major events. "Concerning the daily sacrifice" is really the starting of the sacrifice because you can't have anything concerning something unless that something is in existence, so "concerning the daily sacrifice" in reality is THE STARTING OF THE SACRIFICE! Okay. If that is the first event, what is the second event? The second event is called the "transgression of desolation". Transgression means sin, so it is the sin that brings desolation or the sin that destroys. Any sin that brings destruction with it is a sin that stinks to high heaven and, therefore, could be called an abomination. That is why this is just another phrase for the abomination of desolation (A of D). To summarize then, he is asking how much time is there between the

starting of the sacrifice and the A of D. The answer is given and it is 2300 days. The meaning of that will be given in a moment.

4. After 2300 days the sanctuary will be cleansed. Cleansed? Yes, it will be cleansed alright, by fire! It will be totally destroyed and burned up. That will be quite a cleansing. That is covered more fully below in the section on the Destruction of Jerusalem.

5. Remember, these events will all take place AT THE TIME OF THE END which is also discussed, more fully, below.

6. The most important factor in this passage is the 2300 days and it's time to center in on this. There are times when each day of God's calendar represents a year and at other times when each day is a literal day. If confusion happens here, it will mess up the whole time table. The Lord does not author confusion, but allows confusion in prophecy because He is hiding His calendar between the lines of the verses. If it is not time to let His secret out, He withholds human understanding. He allows confusion in many other subjects of the Bible as well. It is like He wants His people to seek after His truth in total hunger and sincerity, and if we don't, we will never see it. Prophecy teachers and researchers have tried to figure this 2300 days out for years and to no avail, as with the case of the Seventh Day Adventists.

The Seventh Day Adventists are one of the few that have made a concerted effort to explain this period of time. Hey, at least they're making an effort. They were founded May 21, 1863, according to Wikipedia. They were a branch off the Millerites. William Miller, born in 1782, found himself part of a movement of growing concern about the return of Jesus Christ. He was a Baptist farmer who delved into the prophetic scriptures for 15 years. Those who believed and followed his interpretation of the end days and other revelations were called Millerites. This comes from the churches Prophecy Seminar brochure entitled "What Happened on Earth in 1844" copyright 1989, exhibit 1, from Daniel's lesson 29. It appears that Miller's findings on the 2300 days became a foundational teaching in the Adventist Church. In their book, SEVENTH-DAY ADVENTISTS BELIEVE…, 1988, page 323 they show a graph of the 2300 day time line. They believe each of the 2300 days stands for a year. It began in "'the going forth of the command to restore and build Jerusalem' (Dan. 9:25), which took place in 457 B.C., the seventh year of Artaxerxes…", and it extends to the year 1844, when Jesus was supposed to have returned. Since Jesus did not return in that year they switch it from the day of His return to the day He started His cleansing of the sanctuary (church).

Jacques B. Doukhan appears to write for the Adventist movement and in his book, SECRETS OF DANIEL, published in 2000, page 189, he agrees that, "Historically, not a lot happened" in the year 1844, but points out that other movements were looking for their "messiahs" in the same year of 1843 to 1844. The Jews were looking for their messiah as well as the Muslims, and the Baha'i Muslims theirs. The Marxist movements at the same time "had begun to blossom". He seems to state this to give credence to the significance of this year, as though this was the year all have been waiting for, but as he states, it really didn't happen. Jesus did not return.

It is clear. The Adventists have missed it, and if the Adventists have missed it, what is the true meaning of the 2300 days in Daniel 8? If 2300 days is not representative of 2300 years, then what is it representative of? How about taking it exactly for what it says? That's a novel idea. It has been stated in regards to the principles of interpretation, "If the context of the text makes sense, seek no other sense." What if the 2300 days that the Lord gave Daniel in this verse literally means 2300 days? It would put a whole new spin on this verse, and just might reveal the exact day that the A of D takes place. How does that passage go?

> Dan 8:13 "Then I heard one saint speaking, and another saint said unto that certain saint which spake, **How long** shall be the vision **concerning the daily sacrifice**, and the **transgression of desolation**, to give both the sanctuary and the host to be trodden under foot?"
>
> Dan 8:14 "And he said unto me, **Unto two thousand and three hundred days; then**

shall the sanctuary be cleansed."

This verse is giving the length of time from the starting of the sacrifice until the A of D is set up. That period of time is 2300 days. That means from the day the sacrifice starts there will be six years, four months and twenty days until the A of D is set up and the altar and temple are desecrated! Wow!

If this explanation is true, then there are OTHER deductions that can be made from this. What else does this mean? If the 2300 days is subtracted from the seven year peace treaty, it reveals that seven months and ten days, or 220 days, after the seven year peace treaty is signed the temple will be rebuilt and the sacrifices will start. Wow, talk about being specific! This is the first proof, then that puts the A of D, as point 5 above states, at the end of the tribulation. (But this is not what has been taught.)

FIVE MORE PROOFS THE ABOMINATION OF DESOLATION IS AT THE END OF THE WEEK

The experts have been saying that the A of D will take place in the MIDDLE of the seven year peace treaty. According to the above interpretation, the A of D will not happen until the END of the peace treaty and this passage will be brought up and expounded on in the third point, but Who is right? Why do the majority of prophecy teachers teach this? The answer is, they get it from the Bible, but most incorrect doctrine comes from the Bible, but from misinterpreting it (thus the second subtitle of my book: Correcting the

Misinterpretations of Endtime Prophecy). In this case, the major tenets of it come from the last verse of Daniel 9. This will be the third of Daniel's four references to this subject. Look at it closely because it is not saying what they claim it says:

> Dan 9:27 "And he shall confirm the covenant with many for one week: and **in the midst of the week** he shall cause **the sacrifice and the oblation to cease**, and **for the overspreading of abomination**, he shall make it desolate, even until the consummation, and that determined shall be poured upon the desolate."

This verse contains two important phrases:

1. "...the sacrifice and the oblation to cease..." This, of course. is referring to the stopping of the sacrifice.

2. "...and for the overspreading of abomination..." The scripture keeps changing the wording to throw the unsuspecting off the trail. The arc of the covenant is going to be "overspread", or something will be placed on top of the arc, and possibly even upon the top of the temple itself. This, of course, will be done or authorized by the AC himself, even before he takes the official title of world ruler.

These are two different events used in the same verse that makes it difficult to decipher, and by this means the Lord can keep the meaning locked up until the very last days. These are the last days and God has opened this truth for His MYSTERIES to be revealed. The word "AND" is used here and because of that they say it all happens at the same time. Not only that, but if the A of D desecrates the temple, it "seems reasonable" to assume that that event would stop the sacrifices. Because of these two reasons most prophecy teachers have stated that these two events happen at the same time, but THEY DON'T!! Wait one minute. Can that be proven? Yes. "Fasten your seat belt" and keep in mind a preliminary principle found in II Peter 3:

> II Pe 3:16 "As also in all his epistles, speaking in them of these things; in which **are some things hard to be understood**, which they that are **unlearned and unstable wrest**, as they do also the other scriptures, unto their own destruction."

Yes, some things are hard to be understood, but that doesn't mean they can't be understood. It is just more difficult, but it can be done with prayer, fasting, hunger, sincerity, persistence, and even with memorizing, quoting and meditating in scripture. The Lord doesn't want His people to be reckless, but to take each step carefully. In the previous section the premise is given which could be called the first proof. FIVE proofs follow that will verify that these two things do not happen at the same time and thus substantiate the verses and the interpretation of the verses of the previous section:

1) For the first proof keep in Mind that Matthew 24:9-15 tells us Daniel 9:27 happens at the END! That is substantiated by looking at the last phrase, "even until the consummation, and that determined shall be poured upon the desolate." What does, "until the consummation" mean? This phrase is found in The Interlinear Bible, second edition 1986 by Jay P. Green, Sr., page 691. "even until the end. And that which was decreed shall pour out on the desolator." It is cumbersome, but at the same time it is clear. It is saying the A of D will be until THE END, or AT the end. What else happens at the end? Something has been decreed to fall upon the "desolate", or the desolator or the AC. What is that? Destruction. When will the AC be destroyed? He will be destroyed AT THE END, and more details about that are below. In other words the AC will reign as World Ruler for 42 months and only 42 months. That is set in stone. Nothing can stop that, so it is evident that he will be destroyed at the coming of the Lord, or at the End. Everybody knows that. So, by looking closely at the verse, it is giving the timing of TWO separate things: 1) the ceasing of the sacrifice will happen somewhere in the middle of the week, and 2) the A of D and the death of the AC will happen at the end. To say it another way, the word "AND" does not mean that the last event will happen at the same time as the first event. The timing of the second event, the setting up of the A of D, will happen, AS IT SAYS, at the consummation which means the END and that is exactly when the Desolator or AC will be

destroyed. To summarize then, the first proof of this section is Daniel 9:27 itself, which is a witness that the A of D will be at the end.

Some will say, "No, no, the A of D will happen in the middle of the 7 year agreement and it will desecrate the holy place for the rest of the three and a half years." Yes, it could be taken that way. The only way to know for sure which is the right way to take it and to verify our first proof, is to bring in another passage—another witness. Is there ANY other passage that deals with the timing of A of D? Yes there is, but before getting to that, remember, readers, how God speaks.

2) The second proof is understanding the word "and", and how God has spoken in the past. To illustrate, two examples follow in two other places in the Old Testament: one in Daniel and the second is a well-known one in Isaiah. Take a look at Daniel 12:2 first:

> Dan 12:2 "And many of them that sleep in the dust of the earth shall awake, some to everlasting life, AND some to shame and everlasting contempt."

The Lord states in this one verse that there will be two resurrections and joins them together with an "and", and just because they are joined with an "and" doesn't mean they happen at the same time. It is evident that the first resurrection happens a thousand years before the second, as per the rest of scripture on the two resurrections (John 5:28-

29; 11:24; Rev. 20; etc. Note: I have a chapter on this in my next book and when you read it you will find there are two and ONLY two general resurrections—not three or more as some prophecy experts contend. One reason they say this is to create a resurrection for the saints who died in the tribulation period because supposedly the rapture already happened three and a half years previously. I'm sorry, but that is making up scripture to fit their own interpretation!) This is what is happening with Daniel 9:27. Just because the two events are joined with an "and" doesn't mean they happen at the same time.

Many Bible expositors have used Isaiah 61 to show how God hides 2000 years in a small phrase in the middle of a verse. Jesus goes to a synagogue on the Sabbath, reads a passage and explains it. The verse that He read was in Isaiah, but see how He reads it in Luke 4 and explains it:

> Isa 61:1 "The Spirit of the Lord GOD is upon me; because the LORD hath anointed me to preach good tidings unto the meek; he hath sent me to bind up the brokenhearted, to proclaim liberty to the captives, and the opening of the prison to them that are bound;"
>
> Isa 61:2 "To proclaim the acceptable year of the LORD, and **the day of vengeance of our God**; to comfort all that mourn;"

"The day of vengeance of our God" is sandwiched in with all the things that will distinguish the ministry of Jesus while He is alive on the earth, but this day of vengeance is 2000 years after Jesus lived on the earth. Jesus reads this prophecy in Luke 4 as follows:

> Luk 4:17 "And there was delivered unto him the book of the prophet Esaias. And when he had opened the book, he found the place where it was written."

> Luk 4:18 "The Spirit of the Lord is upon me, because he hath anointed me to preach the gospel to the poor; he hath sent me to heal the brokenhearted, to preach deliverance to the captives, and recovering of sight to the blind, to set at liberty them that are bruised,"

> Luk 4:19 "To preach the acceptable year of the Lord."

> Luk 4:20 "And he closed the book, and he gave it again to the minister, and sat down. And the eyes of all them that were in the synagogue were fastened on him."

> Luk 4:21 "And he began to say unto them, This day is this scripture fulfilled in your ears."

Focus on verse 19 of Luke's account. Where does he stop reading? It's not at the end of the sentence. He stops reading right after the COMMA in Isaiah 61:2. Luke 4:19 has a period there, but Isaiah 61:2 has a comma. Why? It is because, as said earlier, He didn't keep reading because the next phrase is, "**the day of vengeance of our God**", and He knew that He would fulfill that 2000 years later, but in Isaiah it is sandwiched in the middle of the description of Jesus' ministry. This is what is going on here in Daniel 9:27—only it is not 2000 years—it is only three and a half years. There is approximately three and a half years between the ceasing of the sacrifice and the setting up of the A of D. This controversial principle is centered around the word "and", but first manifests itself in the previous chapter in 8:11. Here again this verse will imply that the two events happen at the same time, but two passages or not, they still must harmonize with the rest of scripture. With that in mind, let us look at Daniel 8:

Dan 8:11 "Yea, he magnified himself even to the prince of the host, and by him the daily sacrifice was taken away, **and** the place of his sanctuary was cast down."

This scripture says the AC will remove the sacrifice or will take it away AND he will cast down the sanctuary. The casting down of the sanctuary is tantamount to setting up the A of D. And yes, he will do both (ceasing the sacrifice and casting down the sanctuary), but NOT at the SAME time! It **appears** that it will be at the same time because these two events are mentioned in the same verse, in the same sentence, and connected with an "and", as Daniel 9:27 has it. It bears repeating again, Daniel 8:11 is saying almost exactly what Daniel 9:27 is saying, but they both still must harmonize with Daniel 8:13 and the rest of scripture! The Lord clarifies what He is saying two verses later and uh la la, He puts a whole new spin on it, only this time He nails it down and there is no way to mistake what He is saying because he uses something that can be calculated—2300 days. Before going to verse 13, realize this is proof number 3:

3) This passage was quoted above, but with different points emphasized and for quick reference it is repeated here:

> Dan 8:13 "Then I heard one saint speaking, and another saint said unto that certain saint which spake, **How long** shall be the vision **concerning the daily sacrifice**, and the **transgression of desolation**, to give both the sanctuary and the host to be trodden under foot?"
>
> Dan 8:14 "And he said unto me, **Unto two thousand and three hundred days; then shall the sanctuary be cleansed.**"

What was discovered about this verse previously? Two things were determined: 1) "Concerning the daily sacrifice" is the same thing as the **starting of the sacrifice** because one can't have anything concerning something unless that something is in existence. 2) The scripture is saying that there would be 2300 days BETWEEN the starting of the sacrifice and the A of D. Realize the first event of reference, unlike 9:27 and 8:11, is not the STOPPING of the sacrifice as in those verses, it is the STARTING of the sacrifice! That is why many teachers leave this passage out because it is somewhat confusing, but it need not be confusing, and it must be included because this is the verse that clarifies everything. There is a time line at the back of this chapter and from that it is easy to see in graph number two, on the seventh line, there are 1010 days in between the starting of the sacrifice and the stopping of the sacrifice. That forces the A of D by necessity, to be at the end of the week, not the MIDDLE! In other words it is impossible to fit 2300 days in a space that comprises only 1010 days. Again, the A of D will be, as it has to be, **at the end** of the seven year time span. In summary, this 3rd proof centers in on the days in between the starting and the stopping of the sacrifice and that demonstrates the A of D must be at the end of the week! This completes three proofs. A skeptic might say, "I am not convinced. Give me one more proof." ...Okay.

4) The fourth proof is that Jesus Himself specifically implies this is true. Look at Mark 13:

> Mar 13:14 "But when ye shall **see the abomination of desolation**, spoken of by Daniel the prophet, **standing where it ought not**, (let him that readeth understand,) then let them **that be in Judaea flee to the mountains**:"

Mar 13:15 "And let him that is on the housetop **not go down into the house, neither enter therein, to take any thing out of his house**:"

Mar 13:16 "**And let him that is in the field not turn back again for to take up his garment**."

Mar 13:17 "But woe to them that are with child, and to them that give suck in those days!"

Mar 13:18 "And pray ye that your flight be not in the winter."

Mar 13:19 "**For in those days shall be affliction, such as was not from the beginning of the creation which God created unto this time, neither shall be**."

Mar 13:20 "And except that the Lord had shortened those days, no flesh should be saved: but for the elect's sake, whom he bath chosen, he hath shortened the days."

The companion passage is given in Matthew 24:15-22 and says the same thing. What is He saying? He says when you see the A of D stand in the Holy Place, then leave and don't take anything with you— Nada, in Spanish—nothing. Why? He says it for two reasons. 1) you will not have much time to get out before the destruction of Jerusalem by means of a nuclear bomb and before the wrath of the Lamb begins. 2) It is implied that His people will not have to stay up in the mountains very long—for sure not three and a half years— or He would have told them to take provisions for a long stay. (Some will say, "Oh, God will take care of us like He did for Elijah, or the 5,000, or the 7,000 when He fed the multitudes in the wilderness." Yes, He could do that, but if that was the case He also could have just told us to take some provisions. Besides that, feeding one man for one meal by means of a raven from heaven is one thing and feeding thousands and possibly even millions for three and a half years is another story!) No. It will not be that long. The END is right around the corner. A NEW day will arrive SHORTLY. If the A of D was in the middle of the seven years, His people would have to stay up in the mountains with no provisions for the remaining three and a half years. That doesn't sound reasonable.

Somebody will say, "But Revelation 12 talks about the woman fleeing into the wilderness and being nourished there for 1260 days. Why so?" Look at the verses. They are as follows:

> Rev 12:6 "And the woman fled into the wilderness, where she hath a place prepared of God, that they should feed her there a thousand two hundred and threescore days."

> Rev 12:14 "And to the woman were given two wings of a great eagle, that she might fly into the wilderness, into her place, where she is nourished for a time, and times, and half a time, from the face of the serpent."

It could be summed up this way: whenever one finds truth there will always be verses that seem to contradict the main body of truth. This is the way it is with the truth of water baptism, salvation, the oneness of God, and the A of D. It can be explained this way: there is a difference between running from the AC, which is what Revelation 12:6 and 14 is dealing with and running from the time of trouble that Daniel 12:1 says is coming. The passages in Matthew 24:15-22, Mark 13:14-20, and Luke 21:20-23 are not talking about fleeing from the AC. They are talking about fleeing from a punishment coming upon the face of the whole earth. It could be called the WRATH OF GOD. Jesus calls it TRIBULATION. That tribulation will take place from one day to one, two, three or four weeks, but not longer than 45 days. It will not take very long.

(Many admit the child of God has to go through a time of persecution and they call it the tribulation, but they deny that the child of God will go through the wrath of God. This book and this chapter is not for the sole purpose of convincing the student of prophecy, either way. It is inevitable that subjects, like this will come up and these point one way or the other. Please, do not reject this chapter or book based upon preconceived and unverified eschatological studies. The pre and mid-tribulation rapture views have hindered the ability to unlock a lot of mysteries found in the book of Revelation, which could also be said of the post-trib, pre-wrath view point, as well. It is hard, but so important, for the prophecy student to keep an open mind and heart while perusing over this material. The subject is so large it is impossible to give convincing proof on all controversial subject matter in one book. Please, at least, consider this information. Proof for the Lord returning one time at the end of the world will come later. Also, a larger explanation of the difference between the Great Persecution and the Great Tribulation will come in the next book, the Lord willing. Now, back to the subject at hand.)

There is more than one way to understand Revelation 12. It could be taken "spiritually", literally, or both ways simultaneously. It could be talking about a spiritual or figurative place of safety—a place in God— where nothing that the child of God is going through in the flesh will cause them to lose faith in the Lord. In a literal or physical sense, the Lord could allow His people to find a place of protection from the desperate hand of persecution that comes from the AC to kill every Christian that can be found. The late Chuck Youngbrandt, although I don't agree with everything he says, but I do agree with this when he says there will be places of refuge set up in different parts of the United States. God will lead His chosen ones to those locations. Again, there is place for both of these ideas in the Word of God, but please don't think that one passage disannuls the other. Whether or not there is agreement on this point or not, the safest thing for the child of God to do is get in a safe place away from the cities for a short period of time before the nuclear bombs hit Jerusalem and multiple big cities around the world. Not only for that reason, but the child of God will want to get in a safe place before the cataclysmic heavenly disturbances and possible pole shift happens. Jesus is, in so many words, saying that this will not take very much time. This is called the wrath of the Lamb and it could be over within one day to four weeks, but definitely not longer than 45 days. Therefore, it bears repeating: the A of D will take place at the END of the seven year peace treaty. As I said, this is implied in both Mark's and Matthew's accounts. Still one might say, "I see what you mean, but do you have any other proof? Yes!

5) The fifth proof is the most clear and powerful verse and has been saved for the last proof. This is also Daniel's fourth and last reference to the A of D. Please, go back to Daniel 12 where, again, the Lord gets very specific:

Dan 12:8 "And I heard, but I understood not: then said I, O my Lord, **what shall be the end of these things?**"

Dan 12:9 "And he said, Go thy way, Daniel: for the words are closed up and sealed **till the time of the end.**"

Dan 12:10 "Many shall be purified, and made white, and tried; but the wicked shall do wickedly: and none of the wicked shall understand; but **the wise shall understand.**"

Dan 12:11 "And from the time that **the daily sacrifice shall be taken away**, and **the abomination that maketh desolate set up, there shall be a thousand two hundred and ninety days.**"

As can be seen from these verses, there is no question that this has to do with the time of the END. The Lord specifically says that from the time that the sacrifice is TAKEN AWAY until the A of D is set up, there is going to be 1290 days!!! Basically, in this section then, the Lord has given the timing from both events: 1) One timing scenario is taken from the STARTING OF THE SACRIFICE and 2) the other timing scenario is taken from the CEASING OF THE SACRIFICE, and they both culminate close to the end of the peace treaty! There is no question that the sacrifice cannot be taken away until the sacrifice has been restarted and there is no way to restart the sacrifices until the temple has been rebuilt, and there is no way the temple can be rebuilt until the seven year agreement is signed into being. All prophecy experts, at least, agree that the word of God is clear that the sacrifice is halted somewhere in the middle of the seven-year peace treaty. Therefore God Himself through the angel to Daniel gives the EXACT amount of days BEFORE the A of D is set up. That amount is 1290 days. Guess what? That puts the A of D at very close to the end of the seven year agreement. By turning to the second graph at the end of this chapter on page 433 on the sixth line down, it can be seen how this fits in with the other events taking place at this time. In review then, the Lord has told us the A of D will be set up 2300 days from the starting of the sacrifice and 1290 days from the ceasing of the sacrifice. This is a difference of 1010 days and that represents how long the sacrifices will continue. According to our calendar that will be two years, nine months and twenty days. Again, the A of D at the end, instead of the middle, is not what has been taught by the majority of the prophecy "experts", and that is too bad, because A LOT of people have been misled and misinformed. It is believed that this is not done intentionally. These teachers are sincere, but sincerity alone doesn't make one right.

The "cat has been let out of the bag", and the truth is now revealed. It is so important that the child of God be not deceived, and deception doesn't have to happen and shouldn't because it can affect one's salvation. There is enough scriptural proof here that should be able to convince any serious student of prophecy that the A of D is not set up at the time the sacrifice ceases, but occurs close to the end and the second coming of Christ. The A of D is a very key event and by knowing when that happens it will help determine when other events happen also. More about that below. At any rate, any interpretation as to the timing of the A of D that doesn't, at the same time, incorporate the 2300 days and the 1290 days should not be taken seriously.

Interpreting the Bible and prophecy in particular has its challenges. There are nooks and crannies in the road that can lead to misunderstanding. This can be illustrated by some rough terrain on Highway 41 from Moriarty to Santa Fe, New Mexico. Please, look at the following picture and tell me what you see:

Do you see a small mountain? Sure looks like it, huh? Now look at the next picture, and what do you see?

You now see that you were looking at two small mountains separated by about a quarter mile, but from the first picture it looks like one mountain. When I first saw this scene, I approached it from the view of the first picture and I truly thought it was one mountain, but it's two. (Keep in mind one more thing: the second mountain from this view appears to be the same height as the first one, when in actuality it is about twice as tall. That is verified by the first picture which was taken from a greater distance away.)

Now for the lesson: the first picture can be related to the two verses in Daniel that seem to imply that the A of D will be set up in the middle of the week at the ceasing of the sacrifice (Daniel 9:27 and 11:30). Some will say, "...in the mouth of two or three witnesses let every word be established." We have two verses, so therefore it must be true. Right? Wrong! One must get ALL the verses or passages on one subject before any conclusion can be made (like Daniel 8:13-14, and

12:11) If there is another passage on the subject and you don't understand it because it doesn't agree with how you took the first two passages, don't make any hard and fast conclusions about your first two passages. This is true in regards to any subject in the Bible especially prophecy. Keep in mind, if you mess up, and you are a pastor or teacher, etc., you not only mess yourself up, you mess up everybody else who hears you. That's tough to hear, but true.

SO, WHAT IS THE ABOMINATION OF DESOLATION?

Passage after passage has been given in regards to the A of D and the scripture never says what it is. It does seem mysterious, and if so, it is because the scripture keeps changing how it describes it. Isn't it interesting that the book of Revelation is totally quiet about the A of D, or you could say it doesn't even use the term. There are only six references to it in the rest of scripture—three in Daniel and three in the New Testament. It would have been nice if there were more verses to describe it, but the meaning of it will have to be deduced from these six. The main phrases from these references are as follows:

1. "...they shall **place** the abomination that maketh desolate" Daniel 11:31

2. "...the abomination that maketh desolate **set up**..." Daniel 12:11

3. "...and for **the overspreading** of abominations..." Daniel 9:27

4. "...see the abomination of desolation, spoken of by Daniel the prophet, **stand in** the holy place...," Matthew 24:15

5. "...see the abomination of desolation, spoken of by Daniel the prophet, **standing** where it ought not..." Mark 13:14

6. "...so that **he as God sitteth** in the temple of God, shewing himself that he is God." II Thessalonians 2:4

This last reference, II Thessalonians 2, says the AC sits "in the temple of God, showing himself that he is God." Because of this one passage many, including myself, have assumed that this verse interpreted the previous five references. Writing this chapter and getting all these verses together has enlightened my eyes and it is hoped that it will enlighten the eyes of the reader as well, but that is yet to be seen. The huge point is this: the II Thessalonians passage doesn't actually say, when the son of perdition sits in the temple showing himself to be God, that this is the A of D. It is important not to make assumptions. That is how students of prophecy and researchers get in trouble. The first five references use the following phrases: "Place, set up, overspreading, stand in, standing" and can all be true at the same time, whereas a man sitting (instead of standing) appears to be talking about something other than the A of D. Remember this also—just because it says "stand" or "standing" doesn't mean it is a person standing. It could be and probably is an object of some kind standing where it shouldn't. The II Thessalonians description of the AC sitting in the temple of God could transpire at the same time that the object of desecration (if so be that it is an object) was placed on the arc of the covenant, the brazen altar, and/or on top of the temple itself. There are good reasons to believe that it is an object, because of two main reasons: 1) Every single reference to the A of D could be true if it was an object. 2) What has happened in the past could be an indicator of what is to happen in the future. In the past, it was an object, and as said before, history repeats itself. It is revealing then, to look at history, to see that there have been **eleven** hypotheses of what the A of D could have been, that might be repeated in our day.

Those who record the past sometimes do not agree, but it is still revealing. The A of D is a good example of this. Although this event is yet future there was a time in the past when it seemed to have taken place. Also, keep in mind, it wasn't a person standing or sitting in the holy place. It was a THING in the holy place. It took place in the year 165 B.C. The pagan Syrian King Antiochus IV (Epiphanes) wanted to Hellenize, or make more Greek in nature, the eastern elements of his kingdom, including the Jewish nation, to strengthen it against Rome. To do this he felt he had to weaken the Jewish concept of there being only one God. Global Book Publishing in their book, written in 2008, Ancient Civilizations, the Middle East, on page 274, says that he "**sponsored** the construction of a PAGAN ALTAR in the Temple which was referred to as the Abomination of Desolation by the Jews." As a side point, this thought needs to be included: he didn't personally put it there. He "sponsored" the construction of the pagan altar. In other words, he did it by proxy. This might, very well, be how it happens in our day, but understand that a pagan altar is an object and it is the **first** possibility and expanded on below.

Isn't the AC going to stand and/or sit in the holy place? Yes, he is, but he or they are going to place something on the altar as well, so it could be the altar itself or something placed on the altar. The Zondervan Pictorial Encyclopedia of the Bible, volume Four M-P, page 5 also has its own account of greater detail of what happened on that December 16th day of 167 B.C. which was Chislev 25. Antiochus IV made the temple at Jerusalem a place to worship the Olympian Zeus, by "offering swine's flesh upon the altar Zeus which was erected on the altar of burnt offering... These were to be offered on the twenty-fifth day of each month after that, since that date celebrated the birthday of Antiochus Epiphanes; hence the sacrifices were offered to him." Yes, and while on the subject, is the AC going to require the people of the earth to worship him? Absolutely. As can be seen, Antiochus Epiphanes required people to worship him and so will the AC, and by doing so will illustrate that history, indeed, does repeat itself. Thus, it could be said the A of D could be a sacrifice, as a pig, or something else on the altar. (Some denounce the idea of a pig being used as a sacrifice because a true Muslim, if he were the AC would never even touch such an unclean thing himself, but then again, what if he has it done?)

In talking about the A of D, Wikipedia says the rabbis as a whole feel "the expression refers to the desecration of the Second Temple (Herod's Temple) by the erection of a ZEUS STATUE in its sacred precincts by Antiochus IV Epiphanes." Wikipedia continues: "Some scholars, including Hermann Detering...see it as another... attempt to install the STATUE OF JUPITER CAPITOLINUS on the site of the ruined Jewish Temple in Jerusalem leading to the Bar Kokhba rebellion of 132-135 AD." Still others see the A of D being fulfilled by two more different things: "the worship of the Roman Standards on the Temple Mount under Titus in 70 AD and/or the building of the Dome of the Rock by the Umayyad Caliph Abd al-Malik ibn Marwan in 691 AD" on the holy mount. Some come up with another option and say it was the changing of the Sabbath from Saturday to Sunday. What some are saying by these last two views is that the A of D has already happened and the prophecy that Jesus gave has already been fulfilled and there is no need to continue anticipating it in the future. This is a result of the preterist view point. (This has given us a total of **five** options so far, but more about the first two.)

Unger in his dictionary, 16th printing in 1970 page 10 says "the reference is to the act of Antiochus Epiphanes...who in

June, 168 B.C. (instead of 165 or December 167) desecrated the temple at Jerusalem. He built an altar to JUPITER OLYMPIUS on the altar of burnt offering...and offered swine's flesh." As can be seen historians do not agree on what happened in the days of Antiochus Epiphanes, and in fact, neither do the prophetic theologians agree on how they interpret it. Whether it was 165, 167 or 168 BC doesn't matter that much. Zeus or Jupiter are irrelevant also, because it was the same god. Zeus is the god of the sky and the god of thunder. He was the king of gods to the Greeks, but the Romans worshiped him as Jupiter. A bigger question is, was swine's blood offered on the altar or wasn't it? Some accounts include it, while others leave it out, but whatever happened back there could happen again. It is interesting that it is never referred to in Daniel or the gospels as any PERSON sitting or standing in the holy place. Wikipedia says, "In both biblical and rabbinical Hebrew, the word "abomination" is a familiar term for an idol..." Unger again on page 10 says that this term "is interpreted by premillennialists as the idolatrous IMAGE to be set up by the final Antichrist...in the restored temple at Jerusalem..." If Unger or the premillennialists are right and the A of D is not a person sitting on the arc of the covenant, or standing in the holy place, and it is not a swine being offered on the altar (even if it happened, and it probably did), but it is an image being set up in the holy place, then what image would it be? Is this the image Revelation 13:14 and 15 talks about?

David C. Pack who heads up the Restored Church of God, in his writings and videos, indicates that this image, which is to be labeled the A of D, is directly related to the Catholic church. He indicates that the image of Jupiter has been altered. His head has been removed and the head of St. Peter has been put on it and that this will be the idolatrous image placed on the alter or in the temple. It is interesting and he uses a lot of history to verify his view, and it could be possible. This is the **sixth** option.

There are **five more** possibilities. The first two are similar and will be discussed more in detail in the next book under the chapter title, "Who is the Antichrist and from Where Does He Come?" If the AC is a Muslim, whether he is Obama or not as some suggest, what is the symbol of the Islamic religion? It could be two different things. The most popular symbol of Islam is the half moon and star. Many of the Islamic countries fly flags with these symbols on them. Where have these symbols come from? About.com under the heading, "Islam, the Crescent Moon", says: "The city of Byzantium (later known as Constantinople and Istanbul) adopted the crescent moon as its symbol. According to some reports, they chose it in honor of the goddess Diana. Others indicate that it dates back to a battle in which the Romans defeated the Goths on the first day of a lunar month. In any event, the crescent moon was featured on the city's flag even before the birth of Christ." When the Turks conquered Constantinople they adopted their flag, and it spread from there. Many Islamists have accepted it as their symbol, while others have rejected it.

The magazine, *Israel Today*, in the December 2014 Issue on page 27 says, "A huge crescent-shaped monument, larger than a football field, dedicated to Sin, has been uncovered in Israel close to the shores of the Sea of Galilee. The massive 150-meter long tribute to the Mesopotamian **moon god** is over 5,000 years old, according to Israeli archaeologist Ido Wachtel who made the discovery." Could this be where the symbol of the Islamic religion came from?

Walid Shoebat discusses this symbol quite extensively in his book, *God's War on Terror*, 2010, Top Executive Media, on pages 384 and 387. He says the symbol goes back to Judges 8:21 where the symbol around the camel's neck was in the shape of the moon. This is explained in the center column reference in some King James versions of the Bible as when Gideon conquered the kings of Midian. Walid continues to explain the name of Lucifer in Isaiah 14:12 has a link to an Arabian word for "Son of the Morning" to include the **crescent moon**. The implication he gives is that the crescent moon and star is a symbol of Satan and has been used for a very long time. (My thought is, is Satan trying to take the place of Jesus as being the morning star as He is referred to in Revelation 2:28 and 22:16. This grows bigger when considering Barack Obama's logo. Some have interpreted it as the sun arising from the west—the U.S. is the greatest power of the west. The Muslims have stated that the Mahdi will come when the sun rises from the west and remember the sun is a star!) Will this crescent moon and star be placed over the temple and/or upon the altar? It could be.

Secondly, another Islamic symbol is much like a hollow circle. It is seen on top of the Dome of the Rock. Some symbols have a solid circle in the middle with a ring around it. What would this symbol indicate? It could be indicative of a solar eclipse. What is a solar eclipse? The moon passes between the sun and the earth. This could have special meaning. If it is true, the Islamists who support this image might be saying the moon will blot out the sun. Could they be saying that the moon represents the Muslim religion and the sun represents Christianity, and that the Islamic religion will surpass Christianity in America and the world? There might be something to this.

Whenever the Muslims conquer a country, they take churches and make them into mosques, as they did the Greek Orthodox church, Hagia Sophia, in Istanbul in 1453, before it was made into a museum in 1935. There is another Hagia Sophia in Iznik (Nicaea) Turkey. It also was made into a mosque, but for the last 90 years has been operated as a museum, until November 6th, 2012 when it was turned back into a mosque. (Note: that was the day Obama was put in the White House for a second term. Was this done on that day by accident? Maybe not.) Turning churches into mosques happens a lot. A recent article in the Tulsa Beacon, November 23, 2012 by Randy Bright, states, "In England, over a thousand churches have already been converted to mosques…" What happens when churches are turned into mosques? Minarets are raised and the half moon and star or some other symbol appears somewhere on the building, letting the public know of the change.

In reality, Christianity has taken pagan symbols and "sanctified" them for its own use. In the dome of Hagia Sophia is a painting of the virgin Mary and the Christ child. To the pagans it is the goddess Isis and her child Horus. The circle behind their head is showing they are saints, but to the pagans, the circle is in honor to the sun god. Could the A of D be a symbol of Islam: a half moon and star, or a full moon, passed off to the pagans as a symbol of the sun god and to the Christians as the Son of God? Could one of these symbols be placed over the newly, rebuilt, Jewish Temple or even placed on the altar of burnt offering or the arc of the covenant? (Armageddon News agrees with this concept as they show this on their YouTube video.) In other words, after the Jews have been granted the privilege to rebuild their temple, and they do, could it be possible at some future date that it will be confiscated and turned into a mosque?!!? The AC will perpetrate himself to be on the side of the Jewish nation, but after this is done, it will be a sign of betrayal to the Jews and will show his true colors. This will be the "last straw" and will decimate the seven year covenant that was drawn up between the Jews, Arabs, and Palestinians. The use of the crescent and eclipsing moon represents options **seven and eight**.

There is a **ninth** option to what the A of D could be. If you recall in Revelation 13 it talks about a second beast rising and causing the world to worship the first beast, the AC. This second beast is considered to be the False Prophet, and he makes an IMAGE of the AC and causes the earth to worship it. The exact wording is as follows:

Rev 13:11 "And I beheld **another beast** coming up out of the earth; and he had two horns like a lamb, and he spake as a dragon."

Rev 13:12 "And he exerciseth all the power of the first beast before him, and causeth the earth and them which dwell therein to **worship the first beast**, whose deadly wound was healed.

Rev 13:14 "And deceiveth them that dwell on the earth by the means of those miracles which he had power to do in the sight of the beast; saying to them that dwell on the earth, that they should make an **image to the beast**, which had the wound by a sword, and did live."

Rev 13:15 And he had power to give life unto the **image** of the beast, that the **image** of the beast should both speak, and cause that as many as would not worship the **image** of the beast should be killed."

This image which could speak and cause that as many as would not worship it, should be killed, might be the image that is placed on the altar of burnt offering, or the arc of the covenant and be the image of a man. This image might be set up after the AC enters the holy place, stands, and sits on the arc of the covenant. Could it be that all of this is the A of

D? If this is true, it would desecrate their holy place, brake the seven year covenant, and be the sign of the destruction of Jerusalem and of the end.

Going along with that thought, think about the technology of Hollywood. Many have visited Disney Land. I remember as a child seeing an image of Abraham Lincoln sitting and standing and giving a speech. It looked just like him. I saw that in the 1960's. If they had that technology back then, what could they do today? ...a lot more! I have already talked about how Hollywood uses fictional movies to tell the country what is coming in the future. They have already shown human androids on the screen. Will the AC be a human android or a transhuman? Tom Horn and Chris Putnam suggest the AC will be half human and alien, or half human and demon in their book EXO VATICANA, published in 2013 by Defender. In fact on page 529 he quotes a Father Ludovicus Maria Sinistrari de Ameno and concludes "...how the coming of Antichrist represented the biological hybridization of demons with humans." He continues, "Thus, as Jesus Christ was the 'seed of the woman,' the 'Man of Sin' will be the 'seed of the serpent,'" the devil. The AC could also be a cyborg, part human and part machine, uniting humans with artificial intelligence (AI).

Maybe the AC will act something like what happened in the movie "Equilibrium" where the "Father" was in charge of all operations of the new government, but was never seen, because he was afraid of being assassinated. It comes out later in the movie that in fact he had died and no one even knew it, because his representative did all the negotiations. Could this be something like what the AC will do in the future—show himself as an android, or half alien, or half demon or through some image, and be only seen by a few people and operate in the shadows?

As you can see, there are many ways the AC could bring about the A of D. Is it just 1) an erected altar, 2) a pig slain on the altar, 3) the Roman standards, 4)a Sunday Sabbath, 5) the dome of the rock, 6) the image of Zeus with the head of Peter, 7) the half moon and star, 8) the full moon, 9) the image of a man as an android, 10) a half human half alien, or 11) a demon possessed transhuman sitting on the arc of the covenant. It is the last huge sign that the Lord has given to let us know that the end of the world, as we know it, is only hours away. As children of God we need to be very alert as to how this prophecy could be fulfilled, and be ready for anything. Hopefully, this section will suffice to alert you to some of those possibilities to what actually, could happen.

JERUSALEM DESTROYED

Daniel DOES tell us that Jerusalem will be destroyed. Let's give these two verses together:

> Dan 9:26 "And after threescore and two weeks shall Messiah be cut off, but not for himself: and **the**

people of the prince that shall come **shall destroy the city and the sanctuary** and **the end thereof shall be with a flood**, and unto the end of the war **desolations are determined**.

Dan 9:27 "And **he shall confirm the covenant with many for one week**: and in the midst of the week he shall cause the sacrifice and the oblation to cease, and for the overspreading of abominations **he shall make it desolate**, even until the consummation, and **that determined** shall be **poured upon the desolate**."

In book three I have a chapter on WHO IS MYSTERY BABYLON THE GREAT? In that chapter there are 33 proofs that Jerusalem is Mystery Babylon the Great. Everything cannot be put in one book, but if it is true that Jerusalem is Mystery Babylon the Great, which it is, then Revelation 18 will be fulfilled in her destruction. She shall receive double wrath, be burned, and come to nothing in an hour. A nuclear holocaust is one of the few ways this could happen. If the word of God says it, it is set in stone—Jerusalem will be destroyed in one hour: Verse 26 states that quite clearly: "…the people of the prince… shall destroy the city and the sanctuary, and until the end of the war desolations are determined."

Most prophecy experts believe and teach that when Jerusalem was destroyed in 70 A.D. it was the fulfillment of this scripture. Jerusalem, they say, will not be destroyed again, but if you look carefully you will see the scripture was only half fulfilled. Jerusalem will be destroyed again even though few admit it. This sounds vaguely familiar. Remember nothing is new. Back in Jeremiah's day the same thing was happening. Jeremiah told of the coming doom as in chapters 9 and 19:

> Jer 9:11 "And **I will make Jerusalem heaps**, and a den of dragons; and I will make the cities of Judah **desolate, without an inhabitant**."

> Jer 19:8 "And **I will make this city desolate**, and an hissing; every one that passeth thereby shall be astonished and hiss because of all the plagues thereof."

There were men, a lot of men, so called prophets who disagreed with Jeremiah. Jeremiah denounces these false prophets throughout his writings and especially in chapter 23. See what they said:

> Jer 23:17 "They say still unto them that despise me, The LORD hath said, **Ye shall have peace**; and they say unto every one that walketh after the imagination of his own heart, **No evil shall come upon you**."

Hananiah in chapter 28 was among those who said similar things. It actually sounds like preachers today, "We will all be raptured out of here before the tribulation. Jerusalem will not be destroyed again. She was already destroyed in 70 A. D. It's not going to happen again." But Jeremiah spoke against them over and over again. In so many words he said they were betraying their own people:

Jer 12:10 "**Many pastors have destroyed my vineyard**, they have trodden my portion under foot..."

Jer 23:1 "Woe be unto **the pastors that destroy and scatter the sheep of my pasture!** saith the LORD."

This is happening today, the church, by its leadership, is hurting their own people by not telling them the truth about future events. The Lord wants to help His people by letting them know what is going to be in the future so they can be prepared. They aren't preparing; they're getting ready to go up in a great fanfare, in a pre-tribulation rapture. They don't realize the church is going to have to suffer first, and the more we make preparation, the easier it will be on us, but who is preparing for the coming destruction? The Mormons? Yes, but what about fundamental Bible believing children of God? Why shouldn't they be forewarned and be prepared as well? They should be and that is why this book and the ones to come are so important! Jeremiah called them false prophets and denounced them over and over again, but the people wanted to believe them:

> Jer 5:31 "The prophets prophesy falsely, and the priests bear rule by their means; and my people love to have it so: and what will ye do in the end thereof?"
>
> Jer 29:9 "For they prophesy falsely unto you in my name: I have not sent them, saith the LORD."

Please, believe me. Jerusalem will be destroyed again. If you will look at verses 26 and 27 closely you will see that it says, "The people of the prince that shall come shall destroy the city... And he shall confirm the covenant with many for one week..." The prince who confirms the covenant for one week is the same prince whose people destroy the city. Let me repeat this more simply. The prince who makes the peace treaty is the one who destroys the city. Therefore if the peace treaty has not been signed, then neither has the city yet been destroyed by him. If Titus, supposedly is that prince where is the seven year peace treaty that was signed by him back in 70 A.D.. There was no peace treaty because Titus wasn't that prince and the third destruction of Jerusalem is yet to happen!

There is another reason we can know that it will happen again because there are other details in the verse, as stated above, that were never fulfilled in Titus's day. For one, it says, "...the end thereof," speaking of the destruction of the city, "will be with a flood." Was there a flood in Titus's day? No. In the end day battle over this city, there is going to be a flood. Is this flood spoken of in other places? Yes, but it is hidden in the wording and sometimes implied. Look at Revelation 14:

> Rev 14:20 "And the winepress was trodden **without the city**, and **blood** came out of the winepress, even **unto the horse bridles**, by the space of a thousand and six hundred furlongs."

This verse doesn't specifically mention a flood, but what does it mean? From the very first time I read this passage it befuddled me, and for years afterward. Even after reading account after account on the book of Revelation, writers would mention verse 20, but would not offer an explanation. Is so many people going to be killed that the blood will be four or five feet deep? I knew that was impossible. I knew it could not happen, at least, not without some help. While memorizing, quoting, and meditating on these verses over and over again, the answer came. Although this passage doesn't say there is going to be a flood, it is implied as I said. Daniel does mention it. A flood could erupt by a dam breaking, but that is not too likely. It is more likely derived from a sudden cloud burst when a storm breaks forth. This could be the same storm that soon releases hail stones of 100 pounds in weight. This could be the same storm that erupts right before the pole shift. The dead bodies will be laying everywhere in the valley of Jehoshaphat. When the water gushes into the valley, it will wash across the dead bodies lying in the field. Because of so many bodies and so much water washing across them, it will turn the water red. Remember the side of Jesus was pierced while on the cross and out came WATER AND BLOOD, so this water will be mixed with men's blood, will look like blood, and will reach to the bridles of the horses, which would make it about four or five feet deep. This never happened in Titus's day, but it is going to happen in the day of the third destruction of Jerusalem.

Is there any other place in the Bible that hints to this kind of a storm? Yes. Isaiah verifies this great abundance of water. Look at chapter 30:

> Isa 30:25 "And there shall be upon every high mountain, and upon every high hill, **rivers and streams of waters** in the day of the great slaughter, when the towers fall."

> Isa 30:28 "And his breath, as **an overflowing stream, shall reach to the midst of the neck**, to sift the nations with the sieve of vanity: and there shall be a bridle in the jaws of the people, causing them to err."

Notice in verse 25 that the "rivers and streams of waters" will be "upon every high mountain, and upon every high hill…" It happens in the "day of the great slaughter, when the towers fall." This is talking about the Battle of

Armageddon, the day of tribulation, and the wrath of God. It is at the time of the pole shift when the tall buildings or "towers" are knocked over. How will there be so much water on top of the mountains and hills? I only know of one way—a cloud burst from the sky. This is the flood that Daniel and Revelation are referring to. In verse 28 there is a metaphor about the Lord's breath being as "an overflowing stream". Again, this is a play on words to refer to the flood just mentioned in verse 25, but this time it says it reaches "to the midst of the neck…" That is about the same height as a horse's bridle as it is mentioned in Revelation 14, implying that it must be the same flood mentioned there. Look at how Zephaniah describes that day:

> Zep 1:15 "That day is a day of wrath, a day of trouble and distress, a day of wasteness and desolation, a day of darkness and gloominess, **a day of clouds and thick darkness**,"

Several places in Revelation refer to this storm. One such place is found in chapter 16:

> Rev 16:18 "And there were voices, and **thunders**, and **lightnings**; and there was a great earthquake, such as was not since men were upon the earth, so mighty an earthquake, and so great."

Every storm, especially bad ones, come with thick, dark clouds, thunder, and lightnings and these verses are there for a reason. There's going to be a storm. It's going to rain and it's going to be bad, and the Lord is telling us in advance so we can expect it and be ready. As stated earlier, this flood **did not** happen at the time of the first two destructions of Jerusalem, so we know there is coming a future destruction of the city that will have an accompanying flood.

ANOTHER MISUNDERSTOOD PROOF. There is another powerful proof that Titus' destruction of Jerusalem was not the final fulfillment of this prophecy. It would be good if we revisited the very words of Jesus' prophecy. Those words are found in Matthew, Mark, and Luke. Let us start with Matthew's words first:

> Mat 24:1 "And Jesus went out, and departed from **the temple**: and his disciples came to him for to shew him **the buildings of the temple**."

> Mat 24:2 "And Jesus said unto them, See ye not all **these things**? verily I say unto you, There shall not be **left here** one stone upon another, that shall not be thrown down."

Why do I bring this subject up? Many prophecy experts, including the preterists, declare that Jesus said the temple would be destroyed and not one stone would be left upon another, and many believe that was fulfilled when Titus destroyed Jerusalem in 70 A.D. Ray C. Stedman gives a

TYPICAL account of this in What's This World Coming To?...Discovery Publications of Palo Alto, California, 94306, 1970:

> "There were great quantities of gold and silver there which had been placed in the temple for safekeeping. This melted and ran down between the rocks and into the cracks of the stones. When the soldiers captured the temple area, in their greed to obtain this gold and silver they took long bars and pried apart the massive stones. Thus, quite literally, not one stone was left standing upon another. The temple itself was totally destroyed, though the wall supporting the area upon which the temple was built was left partially intact and a portion of it remains to this day, called the western wall."

I have a problem with this account. He doesn't quote his sources. Secondly, if the soldiers had taken control of the temple and went in and first searched out all its treasures before burning it, they would have found the gold and silver, and would have just carried it out. Thirdly, if they had have burned the temple first and melted the gold, it would have been in one or more choice locations and not in the walls, but in the floor and foundation stones which were massive and no pry bar would have been able to budge them. Fourthly, he conveniently says this fulfilled the prophecy of not one stone being left on another, but then admits part of the building remains to this day. You can go to templemount.org/destruct2.html, and see the article on the Destruction of the Second Temple, under the heading, Visible Remains of the Temple, in his day, "Eusebius, bishop of Caesarea (A.D. 260-340) testified that he could still see the remains of the sanctuary." You can Google the "wailing wall construction" and click on the "Western Wall Jerusalem". On that web site it says, "The western wall is the surviving part of the second Temple, which was destroyed by Romans in 70 CE." A site called "wiseGEEK" came up and it declared in regards to the wailing wall, "…it also is a source of much dispute regarding it's true history…Jews and many people consider the wall to have been a part of a Jewish temple, also called the second temple." Listen, if Jesus was talking about just the temple when He said one stone would not be left on another, sorry to bust your bubble, but it was not fulfilled in the days of Titus! It is yet to be fulfilled!

To continue this same train of thought, there is a bigger question that needs answering. Was Jesus talking about the temple or the temple AND the buildings surrounding the temple? Just by looking at this verse alone, if we look at it carefully, we get a different view. Jesus walks OUT of the temple and his disciples start talking to him about "the building**S** of the temple". Notice it doesn't say the building (singular) of the temple. Then He says in my words, "Don't look on these things." He doesn't say, "Don't look at this thing (the temple)". Then He says there will not be left "HERE" one stone upon another. Okay, was He talking about the temple, AND the buildings surrounding it or was He talking about the very CITY in which they were standing? Does Mark verify the, "more than the temple concept"? Yes, and even reinforces it! Let's look at his rendition of this prophecy:

> Mar 13:1 "And **as he went out of the temple**, one of his disciples saith unto him, Master, see what manner of stones and what **buildings** are **here!**"
>
> Mar 13:2 "And Jesus answering said unto him, Seest thou these **great buildings**? there shall not be left one stone upon another, that shall not be thrown down."

Remember this is before He goes to the mount of Olives and this is not part of the Olivet discourse. He walks out of the temple and one of His disciples says, look at how magnificent **these buildings** are. The subject is more than the temple. It included the magnificent buildings that were around the temple. We know Jesus understands his statement because He repeats, "Seest thou these **great buildings?** There shall not be left one stone upon another, that shall not be thrown down." Both accounts agree that it is more than the temple that He is talking about. I think we could all agree that all the buildings surrounding the temple were not taken apart stone by stone, so therefore the prophecy Jesus gave was not totally fulfilled in the days of Titus.

We now come to the main point. Jesus was really talking about the WHOLE CITY of Jerusalem. Luke's account is very insightful. In fact Luke's account seems to take place apart from the temple mount! Let's look at it in Luke 19:

> Luk 19:41 "And when he was come near, he beheld **the city**, and wept over it,"
>
> Luk 19:42 "Saying, If thou hadst known, even thou, at least in this thy day, the things which belong unto thy peace! but now they are hid from thine eyes."
>
> Luk 19:43 "For the days shall come upon thee, that thine enemies shall cast a trench about thee, and compass thee round, and keep thee in on every side,"
>
> Luk 19:44 "And shall **lay thee even with the ground**, and thy children within thee; and they shall **not leave in thee one stone upon another**; because thou knewest not the time of thy visitation."

Luke's account is plain—He wasn't just talking about the temple, because He wasn't standing in front of it. He was talking about the CITY. This prophecy is given to us as Jesus is possibly on a donkey and is approaching the city of Jerusalem. One account (Search for Truth #2 Home Bible Study by Jerry Twentier and Marcella Willhoite, 1985, page 135) says it like this: "Two distinct sights of Jerusalem are viewed on the route Jesus took. After the first glimpse, the city is temporarily hidden by the rough terrain. Then suddenly; the whole city bursts into view. At this turn of the road, Jesus paused momentarily to behold its splendor. The festivity quietened as He loudly wept." That's when He "beheld the CITY (my caps) and wept over IT (my caps), saying…thine enemies shall…lay thee even with the ground, and …shall not leave in thee one stone upon another…" It is quite clear that the subject is the "city" and not the temple. All three passages tell us it is more than just the temple, and the third passage crimps the nail on the other side of the board, He was talking about the very city of Jerusalem itself! It will be laid even with the ground, not just the temple, or the immediate buildings around the temple. The stones of the wailing wall are screaming to us that there is more to this prophecy than what "meets the eye". God has not left us without a witness that this prophecy will come to pass EXACTLY as Jesus foretold. It is yet to happen. Jerusalem will be totally decimated!

Yes, the Holy Word is plain as day, the Lord is saying Jerusalem will be leveled, but am I the only voice out there saying that. No, there are other voices like Michael Drosnin for instance, who wrote three books on the Bible code, which many feel are "way out there", but it is interesting. In his first book, page 130, he states, "Jerusalem, the most fought-over city in history…is clearly encoded in the Bible as the target of the predicted nuclear attack. Only one world capital is encoded anywhere in the Bible with either 'atomic holocaust' or 'world War'—Jerusalem'." He continues on page 197 "Both Daniel and Isaiah 29 make it clear that the ultimate danger is in a time yet to come, that the destruction of Jerusalem is not only in the past, but also in the future." In his second book the Bible Code II page 226 he says, "'Atomic attack' was encoded with 'missile'. The two most likely immediate targets appeared to be 'New York' and 'Jerusalem.'" On page 235 he continues: "I fear that one morning we will wake up to the news that a whole city has been destroyed—not two big buildings, but an entire city—that New York, or Tel Aviv, or Jerusalem just does not exist anymore."

There are other voices. In the last 10 years or so a multitude of films have come out depicting the end of the world. There is an apocalyptic craze right now. In many of these films they depict Jerusalem being nuked. It is like there are many voices saying the same thing. Even though it is "Hollywood", these are voices speaking to warn us of the end and reminding us of the truth that, truly, Jerusalem will be destroyed.

There is another way we can know that Jerusalem, being destroyed in 70 A.D., was not a complete fulfillment of Jesus' or Daniel's prophecy. I mentioned this above, but let me repeat it in more detail here. In Daniel 8:25, talking about the AC, "he...by peace shall destroy many..." In Daniel 11:21 it says,

"he shall come in peaceably...", and again in verse 24, it says, "He shall enter peaceably even upon the fattest places of the province..." Titus didn't, by peace, do anything, and as mentioned above he certainly didn't sign a peace treaty for seven years. He and his army took the city by force. In the future, the AC will enter the city under the guise of peace. The last seven years of the world as we know it, will be a PEACE treaty, but the city will be betrayed without warning except for the sign of the A of D. And remember, Dan 9:26 says, "...the people of the prince...shall destroy the city and the sanctuary...". This confirms once more that the prophecy is yet future.

Also, as I said before, Jerusalem will probably not be alone. Dumitru Duduman, a man greatly used of God in Romania, prophetically pronounced that the major cities of America will burn. There was also a TV series that ran in 2006 – 2008 called Jericho. At the time of this writing it could still be found on Netflix. The executive producer was Jon Turteltaub and the creators were Steven Chbosky, Josh Shaer, and Johnathan E. Steinberg. By the end of the first season it garnered 9.8 million viewers. It gives a possible end of the United States as we know it scenario. The nation is suffering a takeover. It is split in two. The drama began when 13 or more cities were nuked. Is Hollywood warning us what might happen. Is there anything in scripture that hints to this? Yes, but in the following reference it is not just the major cities of America, but the "cities of the NATIONS". Let's look at it:

> Rev 16:19 "And the great city was divided into three parts, and **the cities of the nations fell**: and

great Babylon came in remembrance before God, to give unto her the cup of the wine of the fierceness of his wrath."

This could happen at the exact same time that Jerusalem is destroyed. Dumitru calls America Babylon. Could it be when Jerusalem the Babylon is destroyed so will America the Babylon be destroyed? Yes, it could be. Strategic nuclear devices could be placed in the cities that they want to take out as it showed in the movie, Jericho. This is one way this prophecy could be fulfilled, but the cities of the nations could fall more than one way. They could, also, fall because of the pole shift that is coming. 400 mile an hour winds or greater would be the worst hurricane in history sweeping across the whole world destroying every high structure in every city in existence. (More about this in the next chapter.) At any rate, it is very likely that Jerusalem will not be alone, but alone or not, Jerusalem will be nuked. Look at what God says to Ariel or Jerusalem in Isaiah 29:

> Isa 29:4 "And thou shalt be brought down, and shalt speak **out of the ground**, and thy speech shall be low **out of the dust**, and thy voice shall be, as of one that hath a familiar spirit, **out of the ground**, and thy speech shall whisper **out of the dust**."

> Isa 29:5 "Moreover **the multitude of thy strangers** shall be **like small dust**, and the

> multitude of the **terrible ones** shall be **as chaff** that passeth away: yea, it shall be **at an instant suddenly**."

Notice how it says out of the ground and out of the dust twice. The Lord doesn't waist words. Jesus was referring to this very passage when He, in Matthew 24:2, said, "There shall not be left here one stone upon another, that shall not be thrown down", In Luke 19:44 He said, "lay thee even with the ground". Jesus was just repeating Isaiah to us. Basically, He is saying that JERUSALEM will just be dust, before it is all over. The "STRANGERS" and "TERRIBLE ONES" will have the same judgment. That's why I say other cities in the U.S. and around the world will be taken out at the same time. It will be "at an instant suddenly"—sounds like a nuclear holocaust. This same idea is repeated in the next chapter, also.

> Isa 30:13 "Therefore this iniquity shall be to you as a breach ready **to fall**, swelling out in a **high wall**, whose **breaking** cometh suddenly **at an instant**."

> Isa 30:14 "And he shall **break it** as the breaking of the potters' vessel that is **broken in pieces: he shall not spare**: so that there shall **not be found** in the bursting of it **a sherd** to take fire from the hearth, or to take water withal out of the pit."

Jerusalem will be broken like "a high wall" that, through freezing and thawing the bricks and mortar start to bulge outward. Then one day without warning, a section of the wall brakes out and falls to the ground, suddenly bringing destruction with it. Isaiah is making a play on words and at the same time referring to a type of destruction that came from a wall in the past. Remember when David had Joab put Uriah the Hittite on the front lines in the battle against the royal city of Rabbah of the children of Ammon? Joab lost some men in the siege, besides Uriah, and he sent a messenger to King David. He was anticipating David's wrath and the scripture records the thought pattern of Joab. It is recorded in II Samuel 12 and it goes like this:

> 2 Sa 11:20 "And if so be that the king's wrath arise, and he say unto thee, Wherefore approached ye so nigh unto the city when ye did fight? knew ye not that they would **shoot from the wall**?"

> 2 Sa 11:21 "Who smote Abimelech the son of Jerubbesheth? **did not a woman cast a piece of a millstone upon him from the wall, that he died in Thebez**? why went ye **nigh the wall**? then say thou.. Thy servant Uriah the Hittite is dead also."

> 2 Sa 11:22 "So the messenger went, and came and showed David all that Joab had sent him for."

2 Sa 11:23 "And the messenger said unto David, Surely the men prevailed against us, and came out unto us into the field, and we were upon them even unto the entering of the gate."

2 Sa 11:24 "And the shooters **shot from off the wall** upon thy servants; and some of the king's servants be dead, and thy servant Uriah the Hittite is dead also."

The scripture verifies that death can come from a wall, or from something like a wall. Isaiah says it is a "HIGH wall". Could this be referring to something up in the air, like a plane or missile with a warhead on it, from an enemy. From that wall, plane, or missile something falls and breaks. A bomb "falls" and "breaks". The Lord will NOT SPARE in that day. If He is referring to a nuclear missile in this Isaiah 30 passage, then for sure, nothing would be spared. He says there will not even be a piece of pottery left. Sounds nuclear to me. Sorry, but Titus, didn't have one of them. This is yet future. The bigger question is WHEN will Jerusalem be destroyed? We have actually already discussed that when we discussed the 2300 days in Daniel 8, but I didn't emphasize it. It should be addressed directly, because it is a big deal. The point is, we know that it will happen at the end, and there is more than one passage that verifies that. Revelation 16 is one of those passages:

Rev 16:17 "And **the seventh angel poured out his vial** into the air; and there came a great voice out of the temple of heaven, from the throne, saying, It is done."

Rev 16:18 "And there were voices, and thunders, and lightnings; and there was a great earthquake, such as was not since men were upon the earth, so mighty an earthquake, and so great"

Rev 16:19 "And the **great city** was divided into three parts, and the **cities of the nations** fell: and **great Babylon came in remembrance before God, to give unto her the cup of the wine of the fierceness of his wrath**."

I have given proof that Jerusalem will be destroyed and if that is true, it is true because Jerusalem is Mystery Babylon the Great. Much more proof of that will be given in the third book as mentioned earlier—33 proofs! These verses tell us that destruction will be at or **after the pouring out of the 7th vial**, and the 7th vial is at the end of the seven year peace agreement. Jesus attests to this timing, as you may recall, in Matthew 24 when He discusses the A of D. We read this several times before in an effort to establish different points, but let's read it again with the idea of determining the timing of the destruction of Jerusalem:

> Mat 24:15 "When ye therefore shall see the abomination of desolation, spoken of by Daniel the prophet, stand in the holy place, (whoso readeth, let him understand:)"

The A of D will stand or be placed in the holy place. As I said earlier, the holy place is referring to the sanctuary in the temple where the arc of the covenant will be kept. The temple has to be there for the A of D to stand or be placed in it. Jerusalem **cannot** be destroyed before this time because if it was, the temple would also be destroyed, but as you can see in this verse, Jerusalem and the temple are still there. So, Matthew 24:15 and Revelation 16:17-19 are telling us that Jerusalem's destruction will be at the end. Daniel 8 couples with these two passages and continues to verify the same thing:

> Dan 8:9 "And out of one of them came forth **a little horn**, which waxed exceeding great, toward the south, and toward the east, and toward the pleasant land. "

> Dan 8: 10 "And it waxed great, even to the host of heaven; and it cast down some of the host and of the stars to the ground, and stamped upon them."

> Dan 8: 11 "Yea, he magnified himself even to the prince of the host, and **by him the daily sacrifice was taken away, and the place of his sanctuary was cast down**. "

> Dan 8: 12 "And an host was given him **against the daily sacrifice** by reason of transgression, and it cast down the truth to the ground; and it practised, and prospered."

This little horn, which we know to be the AC will cause the sacrifices to cease and will cause the sanctuary or the temple and even Jerusalem to be "cast down". The destruction of Jerusalem will follow the ceasing of the sacrifice three and a half years later. (We discussed that earlier). As we discovered above, when we continue reading into verse 13, the Lord tells us the very day the A of D is set up:

> Dan 8: 13 "Then I heard one saint speaking, and another saint said unto that certain saint which spake, How long shall be the vision concerning **the daily sacrifice**, and the **transgression of desolation**, to give both the sanctuary and the host to be trodden under foot?"

> Dan 8:14 "And he said unto me, Unto **two thousand and three hundred days**; then shall the sanctuary be cleansed."

There will be six years, four months and 20 days from the time the sacrifices start until the A of D. How long is it after the A of D is set up until the destruction of Jerusalem? That is a good question.

Jesus in Matthew 24 gives us the scenario, and I have already given these verses before but since we are trying to pinpoint when destruction comes to Jerusalem, it might be a good time to repeat those verses one more time:

Mat 24:15 "When ye therefore shall **see the abomination of desolation**, spoken of by Daniel the prophet, **stand in the holy place**, (whoso readeth, let him understand:)"

Mat 24:16 "Then **let them which be in Judaea flee into the mountains:**"

Mat 24:17 "**Let him which is on the housetop not come down to take any thing out of his house:**"

Mat 24:18 "**Neither let him which is in the field return back to take his clothes.**"

Mat 24:19 "And woe unto them that are with child, and to them that give suck in those days!"

Mat 24:20 "But pray ye that your flight be not in the winter, neither on the sabbath day:"

Mat 24:21 "For **then shall be great tribulation,**

such as was not since the beginning of the world to this time, no, nor ever shall be."

We have seen above in Revelation 16 that Jerusalem is destroyed after the 7th vial, which is at the end of the wrath of God. Jesus verifies this timing to His disciples, because He says as soon as you see the A of D stand in the holy place, then get out. He tells His people to flee to the mountains. There is NO safe place except in the mountains. He acts like you have no time to lose—not even a second. It is like He is saying, "Don't take anything out of your house if it is going to delay you—don't even worry about your clothes. Your life is more important than anything you may possess. You're going to lose it all anyway and you won't need it, because as soon as I get there, I will give you everything you need." I say that because we end Jesus' discourse right there, talking about the "great tribulation", and we race over to Daniel 12 where Daniel picks up the subject of this terrible "time of trouble" and finishes it's description and explains more of its timing:

> Dan 12:1 "And at that time shall Michael stand up, the great prince which standeth for the children of thy people: and there shall be **a time of trouble**, such as never was since there was a nation even to that same time: and **at that time thy people shall be delivered**, every one that shall be found written in the book."

Dan 12:2 "And many of them that **sleep in the dust of the earth shall awake, some to everlasting life**, and some to shame and everlasting contempt."

Dan 12:3 "And **they that be wise shall shine as the brightness of the firmament**; and they that turn many to righteousness **as the stars for ever and ever.**"

As you can see, Daniel gives more details of this same tribulation that Jesus mentions. It is a time of trouble that has NEVER been, but he says, "at THAT time thy people shall be delivered". This is the coming out of the graves. This is the changing of our bodies. This is the resurrection which I talk about more below, but somewhere in between the A of D standing in the holy place and the coming of the Lord, Jerusalem is destroyed. As Revelation 16 says, it is at the 7th vial. It appears that Jerusalem is destroyed at the end of the vials, but as Daniel 12 puts it, right before the worst and final part of it—the pole shift. From what it sounds like, it could be a matter of hours—8, 12, maybe as long as 24 hours, but probably not even that long—after the A of D is set up until Jerusalem goes up in smoke.

Is it possible to pinpoint the day of the destruction of Jerusalem? Who could know that for sure? According to Gary Hedrick with Messianic Perspectives, on his June 18th, 2012 broadcast, the first two destructions of the city happened in 586 B.C. and 70 A.D., BOTH on the 9th of Av. He also stated that not only for this reason has this day become a day of fasting and mourning for the nation of Israel, but also for the reason that on this day other terrible events happened. Wikipedia also speaking about it, has it under "Tisha B'Av" which is the same as "the Ninth of Av". In regards to our western calendar it falls in July or August. Five more events that happened on that day include: 1) The twelve spies returned from spying out Canaan and because ten of them gave an evil report they were turned back to the wilderness. 2) In 132 A.D. the Romans crushed Bar Kokhba's revolt and destroyed the city of Betar leaving 100,000 Jews dead. 3) A year later in 133 A.D. the Roman commander Turnus Rufus returned to plow up the sight of the Temple and surrounding area and sow it with salt. 4) In 1290 the Jews were expelled from England. 5) In 1492 on the 8th and 9th of Av all the Jews were expelled from Spain. Other calamities followed these. Could it be that the third destruction of Jerusalem might take place on this very day? Michael Drosnin agrees. He says in his first book on page 162, "And now the Bible code stated that on the "9th of Av" a third world War might start, with the third destruction of the Holy City, a nuclear attack on Jerusalem." It is possible. Whether it happens on the 9th of Av or not, we know Jerusalem will be destroyed right before the Lord comes, but so will the AC. Now, let's talk about that.

THE ANTICHRIST DESTROYED

At the end of the 1260 day reign of the AC, after he has tried to wipe out the Jews and the church, he will be destroyed by the return of the Messiah, Jesus. How do we know this? Of course, Daniel is the first one to reveal this. It starts in chapter 7 and continues into chapters 8, 11, and 12:

> Dan 7:25 "And he shall speak great words against the most High, and shall **wear out the saints** of the most High, and think to change times and laws: and they shall be given into his hand **until** a time and times and the dividing of time."

> Dan 7:26 "But the judgment shall sit, and they shall **take away his dominion**, to consume and to destroy it **unto the end**."

The AC makes war with the saints UNTIL the Lord returns. Again, it is at the Lord's return the AC's reign ends. If the saints are given into the hands of the AC UNTIL "a time, and times, and the dividing of time", or three and a half years, that is another way of saying that is when his reign ends, or it is at the END that his reign ends. Now, let's go to chapter 8:

> Dan 8:24 "And his power shall be mighty, but not by his own power: and he shall destroy wonderfully, and

shall prosper, and practise, and shall destroy **the mighty and the holy people.**"

Dan 8:25 "And through his policy also he shall cause craft to prosper in his hand; and he shall magnify himself in his heart, and by peace shall destroy many: he shall also stand up against the Prince of princes; but **he shall be broken without hand.**"

Yes, the AC will destroy the holy people, but he will be broken without hand—referring to the coming of the Lord. The Lord will personally destroy him.

Dan 11:35 "And **some of them of understanding** shall fall, to try them, and to purge, and to make them white, even to the time of **the end**: because it is yet for a time appointed."

Dan 11:45 "And he shall plant the tabernacles of his palace between the seas in the glorious holy mountain; yet **he shall come to his end, and none shall help him.**"

It is only for an APPOINTED TIME that the saints are destroyed and then the AC will also come to his end and none will help him. Now, we will go to chapter 12:

Dan 12:7 "And I heard the man clothed in linen, which was upon the waters of the river, when he held up his right hand and his left hand unto heaven, and sware by him that liveth for ever that it shall be for **a time, times, and an half**; and when he shall have accomplished **to scatter** the power of **the holy people**, all these things shall be finished."

Dan 12:10 "**Many** shall be **purified**, and **made white**, and **tried**; but the wicked shall do wickedly: and none of the wicked shall understand; but **the wise shall understand**."

Dan 12:12 "Blessed is **he that waiteth, and cometh to the thousand three hundred and five and thirty days.**"

Dan 12:13 "But go thou thy way **till the end be**: for thou shalt rest, and stand in thy lot **at the end of the days**."

Again and again Daniel repeats the words. It is at the end of this age, after the three and a half years that the Lord returns, stops the persecution, rescues His people from the world, and from the AC. Paul knows these words of Daniel very well and with the revelations given to him, gives us even greater clarity about the destruction of the AC in II Thessalonians 2:

> 2 Th 2:3 "Let no man deceive you by any means: for that day shall not come, except there come a falling away first, and that man of sin be revealed, the son of perdition;"

> 2 Th 2:4 "Who opposed' and exalteth himself above all that is called God, or that is worshipped; so that he as God sitteth in the temple of God, shewing himself that he is God."

> 2 Th 2:5 "Remember ye not, that, when I was yet with you, I told you these things?"

> 2 Th 2:6 "And now ye know what withholdeth that he might be revealed in his time."

> 2 Th 2:7 "For the mystery of iniquity doth already work: only he who now letteth will let, **until he be taken out of the way.**"

> 2 Th 2:8 "And then shall that Wicked be revealed, whom **the Lord shall consume with the spirit of his mouth, and shall destroy with the brightness of his coming:**"

> 2 Th 2:9 "Even him, whose coming is after the working of Satan with all power and signs and lying wonders,"

Actually this passage is very clear, especially if we set aside our preconceived notions about it. The AC will be taken out of the way. He will he destroyed or consumed. Of course, this will happen AFTER he has worked all of his deceptive practices to destroy the Jews and the people of God worldwide. This is another reason why there is not a pre-tribulation rapture. The AC wants to and will destroy BOTH the Jewish people AND the church. If the church was raptured BEFORE the AC came, it would wreck one of his main purposes in coming. Again, he wants to destroy BOTH the Jews and the Christians and then he, himself, will be destroyed by the Lord. Notice the passages in Daniel: He doesn't say, "the Jews" or "the Jewish people". He uses such phrases as: "the saints; the mighty and the holy people; some of them of understanding; many; and the wise". Daniel had a "revelation" that the people of God in the last days would be made up of Jew and Gentile, and his prophecy was for the people of God, worldwide. So, yes, the AC will try to destroy the saints and AFTER that he will be destroyed. The passage in Revelation 19 spells out his doom:

> Rev 19:20 "And **the beast was taken**, and with him the false prophet that wrought miracles before him, with which he deceived them that had received the mark of the beast. and them that worshipped his

image. **These both were cast alive into a lake of fire burning with brimstone."**

As I stated earlier, this happens when Jesus returns to the earth, and I will discuss that more after I discuss the last remaining time frame which has to do with more of the same, Jesus' return.

THE 1335 DAYS

This time frame is a direct reference to the very last event of our era, the return of the Lord, and it is found in Daniel 12, but let's give the previous verse to get the setting:

> Dan 12:11 "And from the time that the daily sacrifice shall be taken away, and the abomination that maketh desolate set up, there shall be a thousand two hundred and ninety days."

> Dan 12:12 "Blessed is he that waiteth, and cometh to **the thousand three hundred and five and thirty days.**"

Now, the Lord in verse 11 just got done saying that there is 1290 days from the time that the sacrifice is taken away until the A of D is set up, and then in verse 12, he pulls this 1335 days "out of the hat", sort to speak. What is He saying? If the 1290 day "event" starts at the ceasing of the sacrifice, then so does the 1335 day event. There is going to be a blessing for those people who are alive and can get to the 1335 day event. What is it? He does not tell us, does He? So, how do we know? We can surmise and take an educated guess. We are coming down to the end of time. There is not much of anything left that has not been fulfilled except one thing: that is the coming of the Lord. 1335 days after the ceasing of the sacrifice is when the Lord comes! When that happens do you think the people of God will be blessed? You better believe it. They will be blessed "right out of their socks" literally!

Somebody will say, "Wait a minute. No one knows the day or the hour of His coming." Yes, I know it says that in Mathew and Mark, but we can't get around the fact that He tells us in advance when He is going to come. There are some things in scripture that are hard to explain as 2 Peter 3:16 tells us. It appears contradictory. There are other things that seem contradictory in scripture as I have stated before and as I will mention again, such as:

1. Whatever you ask in my name that will I do and yet we ask sometimes and it doesn't happen. How come?

2. There is one Lord, one faith, one BAPTISM, and yet the wording of Matthew 28:19 doesn't match up with the wording of how the Apostles baptized in Acts 2, 8,10 and 19. Are there two or more water baptisms? No.

3. John 3:16 says whoever believes in Jesus will have everlasting life, and yet verse 5 says that unless you are

born of water and spirit, which is more than just "believing", you cannot enter the kingdom of God. So what is it?

4. Paul says we are not saved by works, and yet James says we are saved by works, so how can they both be true?

There are a "ton" more seeming contradictions, but there is an answer to every one of them and there is an answer to this one too. Until the seven year agreement is signed, and the sacrifice ceases, we do NOT know when that day is, so in that sense we do not know the day or the hour at this time. Yes, when the agreement is signed, we will know the day of His coming.

One man said, "If we knew the day of His coming, some would want to party right up to the day of His coming." I have four responses to that:

1. Even if a person knew what day the Lord was coming for His church, he still does not know the day that God is coming for him, personally. In the parable of the rich man, the Lord said to him in Luke 12:20, "Thou fool, this night thy soul shall be required of thee..." God could come individually for anyone of us at any time. It behooves us to be ready.

2. No one is going to heaven unless that person is saved and loves the Lord with all his or her heart and if he or

she loves the Lord, they are going to want to serve Him now, not just five seconds before the Lord comes. That reasoning doesn't make sense.

3. Remember this too; no man can come to Jesus unless He draws him. We do not choose when the Lord calls us. The Lord calls us and we answer His call. If we postpone our coming to Him, the Lord may not call us ever again and we will be lost forever.

4. Besides that, God said in Daniel 12:10, "none of the wicked shall understand; but the wise shall understand." If a person isn't serving the Lord, they won't even know how to put the verses together to find out when the Lord is coming back, no matter how many other verses they know.

Think about this. When Jesus said those words in Mat 24:36: "But of that day and hour knoweth no man, no, not the angels of heaven, but my Father only," Jesus was speaking to them in his humanity and not as the Father, which he was, also. After He rose from the dead, he said in Mathew 28:18 "...All power is given unto me in heaven and in earth." If He had all power, He also had all knowledge (Jn. 21:17), because knowledge IS power. Then He ascended up into heaven. Does He know NOW when He is coming back? Yes. Just because He didn't know at that moment in his flesh, doesn't mean He wouldn't eventually know. He does know now, and if so, then it can also be true of us. Just because we do not know now, doesn't mean we will not know at some future point! Consider also I Thessalonians 5:

> 1 Th 5:1 "But **of the times and the seasons**, brethren, ye have no need that I write unto you."

> 1 Th 5:2 "For **yourselves know perfectly** that the day of the Lord so cometh as a thief in the night."

> 1 Th 5:3 "For when they shall say, Peace and safety; then sudden destruction cometh upon them, as travail upon a woman with child; and they shall not escape."

> 1 Th 5:4 **"But ye, brethren, are not in darkness, that that day should overtake you as a thief.**"

The Lord is talking to us through Paul and telling us that we know the times and seasons and we will not be surprised as the wicked will be. (We will not be surprised because when the treaty is signed we will know the very day Jesus will return.) Watch this. Look at Acts 1:

> Act 1:7 "And he said unto them, **It is not for you to know the times or the seasons,** which the Father hath put in his own power." (I have already expounded on this in great detail in the first chapter, How Important is Prophecy.)

You see, one verse says you know the times and the seasons and the other verse says you don't. It applies the same with the day of His coming. One verse says you do not know the day and the other verse gives us the day of His coming. Remember also what Amos has told us:

> Amo 3:7 "Surely the **Lord GOD will do nothing, but he revealeth his secret unto his servants the prophets.**"

The Lord said He would reveal His secret to His servants the prophets...even the day of His coming? We don't actually know it yet, but we will know it when the peace treaty is signed. Why would the Lord let us know the day of His coming? He will do that because at that time, we will need to know. The people of God will be going through so much turmoil and death, knowing when He comes will give His people the strength to endure. Basically, then, He is saying, "Just hold on. It won't be long until I appear in glory to take you home to be with Me! Don't give up. It will be worth it all in a matter OF DAYS!" And of course that is, 1335 days from when the sacrifice ceases.

S. Douglas Woodward agrees with me wholeheartedly. He deals with this in his book, DECODING DOOMSDAY, 2010, Defender, on page 315, he says, "As to the admonition, 'no one will know the day nor the hour,' we have already suggested a number of reasons, biblically, that this warning was NOT (my caps) for believers who are 'children of the day' but for those who are 'children of the night' who will be caught unawares."

I cannot resist expounding on this passage in regards to the timing of the rapture. My pre-tribulation, mid-tribulation, and post-tribulation pre-wrath friends would say, "This is not the rapture. This is the second advent of Christ. The rapture took place 7 years, 3 and 1/2 years, one month, or 7 days before this." My response to this is, what did that verse say?

> Dan 12:12 "Blessed is **he that waiteth**, and cometh to the thousand three hundred and five and thirty days."

Who is "he that waiteth" and why would he be Blessed? If the rapture already occurred, there wouldn't be anybody left that was a child of God. They would all be gone and they would be in heaven. Could there be any greater blessing than being in the very presence of God? I don't think so. It doesn't make sense if the rapture already happened. It only makes sense if the rapture has NOT already happened and the people of God are still WAITING for His coming!

This next thought is in my next book, but let me give you a little taste of it. This is the thought: There is only one second coming of Christ and only one resurrection of the just—not two or three, just one. Notice the wording in scripture. It is always singular, not plural. A lot of emphasis is placed on the wording of Matthew 28:19, "be baptized in the NAME of the…" Name is singular. There is just one name of all three and that is the name Jesus. The fact that the word "coming" is singular is just as significant. So many people want to split the coming of the Lord into two parts or more and it's crazy. The Bible says what it means and means what it says. "Men of God" are betraying their own people by trying to make the scripture say, either what their prejudice is saying, or what their own man-made doctrine is saying, but they are hurting the very people of God. And that is why my own doctrine betrayed me, because of what I was taught. Folks, let me say it again, there is only one second coming of the Lord and one resurrection of the just and they are both found in Daniel 12: verse 12 and verse 2 respectively. But, you are blessed if you wait until 1335 days after the ceasing of the sacrifice, because that is when you are going to be raptured! More about His return next.

THE RETURN OF JESUS

One can hardly talk about the return of Jesus without talking about WHEN it happens. Everybody wants to know, is it before, in the middle, or at the end of the tribulation? The 1290 and 1335 day events along with other sections of this chapter verify that Jesus will return AFTER the AC is revealed, and the ceasing of the sacrifice has happened. In 2 Thessalonians 2:9, as we have seen, the Lord's coming is "AFTER the working of Satan with all power and signs and lying wonders". When Paul says the preceding words, he is referring to the 1260 day reign of the AC. When that reign of

1260 days is completed the AC will then be thrown into the lake of fire, along with the false prophet. We saw that when we read Revelation 19:20 earlier (at the end of the section entitled The Antichrist Destroyed). Jesus is coming at the end of the world to destroy the AC and to rapture His people.

Many who believe in a pre-trib rapture, call it the end, but it's not. Seven years BEFORE the end, is not the end. Let's look at it a little closer. The disciples in Matthew 24 asked Jesus how they would know when He was coming, and somehow they knew it would also be the end of the world. See how they ask the question in verse 3:

> Mat 24:3 "And as he sat upon the mount of Olives, the disciples came unto him privately, saying, Tell us, when shall these things be? and what shall be **the sign of thy coming, and of the end of the world**?"

From Jesus' response, we can tell they asked the right question the right way because He uses the word "END" three times in His answer to their question:

> Mat 24:6 "And **ye** shall hear of wars and rumours of wars: see that ye be not troubled: for all these things must come to pass, but **the end** is not yet."

He doesn't say, "the rapture is not yet". He says, "the END is not yet".

> Mat 24:13 "But he that shall endure unto **the end**, the same shall be saved."

> Mat 24:14 "And this gospel of the kingdom shall be preached in all the world for a witness unto all nations; and then shall **the end come**."

He doesn't say, "he that shall endure unto the rapture shall be saved." No, He says, "He that shall endure unto THE END, the same shall be saved." Then He describes His coming using several key words:

> Mat 24:29 "Immediately **after** the tribulation of those days shall the sun be darkened, and the moon shall not give her light, and the stars shall fall from heaven, and the powers of the heavens shall be shaken:"

> Mat 24:30 "And then shall **appear** the sign of **the Son of man** in heaven: and then shall all the tribes of the earth mourn, and they shall see **the Son of man coming** in the clouds of heaven with power and great glory."

> Mat 24:31 "And he shall send his angels with a great sound of a trumpet, and they shall **gather together his elect** from the four winds, from one end of heaven to the other."

We are talking about the return of Jesus to get His people. This is the first resurrection, or the rapture of the church. Friend, this happens AT the end NOT seven years BEFORE the end. He is coming AFTER the Great Tribulation, not before, as so many voices have heralded. As you can see verses 29-31 definitely tell us that Jesus comes AFTER the tribulation to gather His elect. At the same time, He comes to destroy the AC, making it clear that this is the end. I want to give THREE more points to strengthen the argument and challenge those who have believed the other way to closer examine the scripture. (I am compelled to say again, many more points could be given, but that's in the next book.)

1) We are discussing the last event, the rapture, but what about the last enemy? Does the last enemy have anything to do with the last event, the rapture? Yes, it does, but does the scripture identify the LAST enemy? Yes, it does, and it is in I Corinthians 15:

> 1 Co 15:26 "The **last enemy** that shall be destroyed is **death**."

The question is, then: "Is the AC an enemy?" Absolutely he is, so therefore he must be destroyed BEFORE the very last enemy, right? Right! So, when is the last enemy, DEATH, destroyed? Please look at verses 51-55:

> 1 Co 15:51 "Behold, I shew you a mystery; We shall not all sleep, but **we shall all be changed**,"

1 Co 15:52 "In a moment, in the twinkling of an eye, **at the last trump**: for the trumpet shall sound, and **the dead shall be raised** incorruptible, and we shall be changed.

1 Co 15:53 "For this corruptible must put on incorruption, and this mortal must put on immortality."

1 Co 15:54 "So **when** this **corruptible** shall have **put on incorruption**, and this **mortal** shall have **put on immortality, then shall be brought to pass** the saying that is written, **Death is swallowed up in victory.**"

1 Co 15:55 "O death, where is thy sting? O grave, where is thy victory?"

Is this clear? Let me summarize. We are talking about the ENDTIME time line. I am showing you that the Lord is going to return to this world at the end of time. He is going to appear in the clouds above the earth and raise the righteous DEAD first, and then pull the righteous LIVING off the earth to meet Him, and them, in the air. This is what we call the RESURRECTION, or if you like, the RAPTURE. The resurrection will only happen AFTER the Great Tribulation and the Great Persecution. It will only happen AFTER the AC is destroyed, because the AC is an enemy, but not the last enemy! According to this verse in I

Corinthians, death is the LAST enemy and will be defeated when the saints get their glorified bodies at the rapture, which is the FIRST resurrection!

The majority of prophecy teachers would say, "No, no, no, that is wrong. The Lord raptures His people, the dead and the living, at the beginning of the tribulation." They use a variety of verses to say this, but they are ALL just inferences, and if it were true it would violate I Corinthians 15:26, along with other verses, so it can't be true.

2) Let me boldly say, there is NOT ONE verse that plainly says the Lord is coming before the Great Tribulation. Not one! Just as an example, let me give two of the strongest popular verses that many use to say this as they are found in I and II Thessalonians, and they are both inferences. First, let's look at I Thessalonians 4:

> 1 Th 4:16 "For the Lord himself shall descend from heaven with a shout, with the voice of the archangel, and with the trump of God: and **the dead in Christ shall rise first:**"

> 1 Th 4:17 "Then **we which are alive and remain shall be caught up together with them in the clouds, to meet the Lord in the air: and so shall we ever be with the Lord.**"

They use this passage to say we go to heaven for seven years to celebrate the Marriage Supper of the Lamb and then we come back with the Lord to save Israel, after that. Let me ask you, does this verse say we go to heaven for seven years? NO!! It says we will ever be with the Lord. Where will the Lord be? He will be ON THE EARTH and we will be with Him. Let me illustrate. When loved ones, from out of town, call and tell you they are coming to visit, you are expecting their arrival. When they pull up in your drive way, what do you do? You go out to meet them. Then after hugs and kisses, where does everybody go? They don't go back to the city where the visitors came from. They go into YOUR house! When the Lord returns to receive His bride, He is on His way to the earth. We are expecting His arrival, because He has told us He is coming. When He appears in the sky, we rise to meet the Lord in the air and then where do we go? We don't go back to heaven. He is on His way to the earth to **set up His new kingdom**. We descend with the Lord to the earth. This verse is, plainly, NOT saying that we go back to heaven for seven or three and a half years. If it said that plainly here, or somewhere else, then it could mean that, but it doesn't say or mean that, and it's not stated anywhere else.

Now, let's go to a second "strong" passage in II Thessalonians 2 that many pre-tribers use. Some may think we're opening up a "can of worms", but let's open it up anyway:

> 2 Th 2:6 "And now ye know what **withholdeth** that he might be revealed in his time."

2 Th 2:7 "For the mystery of iniquity doth already work: only he who now **letteth will let**, until he be taken out of the way."

2 Th 2:8 "And **then** shall that Wicked be revealed, whom the Lord shall consume with the spirit of his mouth, and shall destroy with the brightness of his coming:"

R. C. Sproul on page 180 of his book, THE LAST DAYS ACCORDING TO JESUS, accurately details their beliefs (the majority of pre-tribers) in regards to this verse:

"...the rapture must occur before the Antichrist is unleashed. For the Antichrist to operate without restraint, the Holy Spirit must be first removed. For this to occur the Christian community must be physically removed from the earth, because as long as Christians are present in the world the Holy Spirit who indwells them is likewise present. Whoever the restrainer is, he must be taken out of the way before the lawless one can be revealed."

In other words, they say that the Holy Ghost is the restraining force in the earth. As long as the church is on the earth the Holy Ghost will not allow the AC to be revealed. After the church is raptured to heaven, then the AC will be revealed, but does this verse say that? The passage is quite vague, but doesn't say this at all. 80% of the King James Version (KJV) was taken from Tyndale's 1534 A.D. translation, but here is one place where "they" get totally away from it. Admittedly this is a difficult passage and the only way to get to the bottom of it is to go to the Interlinear Greek-English Lexicons. One by George Ricker Berry, Baker Book House Company, 1981 and another by Jay P. Green, Sr., Sovereign Grace Publishers, Second Edition 1986 both have it very similar. The major part of the misunderstanding can be boiled down to five words that are embolden in the verse above, but those five words are reduced to two Greek words in the Lexicon. "Withholdeth" and "letteth will let" both come from the same Greek word, #2722 "katecho" in the Strong's Concordance. In the Lexicon they use the word "restrains", but the Strong's doesn't even list that as one of the meanings! That word can also mean, "possess, retain, seize on, stay, or take", besides the word, "withhold". Keep that in mind as we center in on the next word, "then". That Greek word #5119 "tote" can also mean "at the time that" referring to the future OR the past as the previous verse or thought. (I am not a Hebrew and Greek expert, but I can read English out of the Lexicon. Here it does add credence to the point, but the context itself bears witness to the meaning as I also point out shortly. Greek as Hebrew doesn't seem to be written in complete sentences as in English, but is written in segments of thought patterns.) Now, let's put this together. I am going to quote the Lexicon and insert the meanings of the words we discussed:

II Thes. 2:6. "And now that which 'possesses, seizes

on, and takes' ye know, for to be revealed him in his own time."

II Thes. 2:7. "For the mystery already is working of lawlessness only there is he who 'possesses, seizes on, and takes' at present until out of the midst he be gone,

II Thes. 2:8. "And 'at the time that' will be revealed the lawless one, whom the Lord will consume with the breath of his mouth, and annul by the appearing of his coming;"

One might say that these verses are not very clear, and it's true, but for sure there is no inference to the Holy Ghost or Spirit of God being taken out of the world before the AC can be revealed. The eighth verse is actually restating what verses 6 and 7 are trying to say, and that is Satan through the AC will not stop seizing all power and authority on earth until he be removed or destroyed. That's it! For sure it is not saying the rapture has to happen before the AC can be revealed!

3) Next we expound more on the resurrection and ask again, how many resurrections are there, and as a result, how many groups labeled the "dead in Christ" are there, and the timing of these? There are two resurrections: ONE for the just and one for the unjust. Jesus tells us that in John 5:

Joh 5:28 "Marvel not at this: for the hour is coming, in which all that are in the graves shall hear his voice,"

Joh 5:29 "And shall come forth; they that have done good, unto **the resurrection of life**; and they that have done evil, unto **the resurrection of damnation**."

Now, let's jump ahead six more chapters and listen to Martha repeat back to Jesus, in John 11, from the evidence, what He taught her and we will see that from all indications, she had it right:

Joh 11:24 "Martha saith unto him, I know that he shall rise again in **the resurrection at the last day**."

Martha reminds us that the resurrection takes place at the last day. Do you know what that means? If that is when the resurrection takes place, then that is when the "dead in Christ" are raised, because they are a part of the resurrection. They are not raised up seven years or even three and a half years before the end. They are raised up **at the last day**. Compare that with those who have died in Revelation 14:

Rev 14:13 "And I heard a voice from heaven saying unto me, Write, Blessed are **the dead which die**

in the Lord from henceforth: Yea, saith the Spirit, that they may rest from their labours; and their works do follow them."

If these people have died "in the Lord", then they must be the "dead in Christ" because the Lord is Christ. Just as the AC in known by more than one name, so are the "dead in Christ". In other words, "the dead which die in the Lord", are the same as the "Dead in Christ" and they are continuing to die up and until the coming of the Lord. The point is, chapter 14 is past the middle of the book of Revelation and the wrath of God (mentioned in chapter 6) is being poured out and the "dead in Christ" have not been raptured? How could that be? How many "dead in Christ" are there? According to the multitude of prophecy teachers, the "dead in Christ" were taken at the beginning of the book of Revelation at 4:1, so who are these in chapter 14? The experts, erroneously, call these the "tribulation saints".

On September 25th, 2014 Janet Parshall was on the radio in Albuquerque on channel 730 AM at 4:00 p.m. She was interviewing Ron Rhodes who had just put out one of his latest books, THE EIGHT GREAT DEBATES OF BIBLE PROPHECY. I respect this man highly, as the author of over 60 books, and receiving three silver Medallions. Who could match that? Not many. Since they were discussing Bible prophecy what was I to do? I mean, it is a "call in program". Should I sit idly by and not call in? Come on; this is my forte! So I called in and believe it or not, she took my question. I must say that Ron was very respectful to those who didn't believe as he did, but he said that he was a pre-triber because it was a belief system that had more answers and less questions than the other two viewpoints, if you know what I mean. (By the way, that's why I am a post-triber.) Let me set the stage. Remember pre-tribulationist say the rapture happens by Revelation 4:1. The dead in Christ have already been raised, so I reminded him of the verse I just quoted above—Revelation 14:13. It's the middle of the book of Revelation and it says, "...blessed are they which die in the Lord from henceforth..." I asked, How could these be dying in the Lord or be the dead in Christ if the dead in Christ have already been raised?" Then I had to shut up (that was hard) and let him answer the question. Of course he said exactly what I said they say, in so many words—"these are tribulation saints." On a program like that you only get to ask one question and that's it. All these guys, including Noah Hutchings, say the same thing, but they "open a can of worms", by saying they are "tribulation saints".

It's easy to say the saints who die during the tribulation are tribulation saints, but when do these so called "tribulation saints" get raised up? It appears nobody has ever asked them this question. If you say they get raised up at what they call the "second advent", when Jesus returns to save the Jews, then you get two resurrections, and two groups, "dead in Christ". You can't have that and be consistent with scripture. Remember there is only one resurrection of the Just. Do they get raised up at the end of the thousand year reign? That wouldn't make sense, because they would have been persecuted and killed and refused to take the mark of the beast and wouldn't be raised up until AFTER the thousand year reign of Christ? No way. Maybe, they just missed it and they will never be raised up, but that doesn't make sense, either. The answer is, they will be raised up at the END when the Lord returns to set up His kingdom and thousand year reign, and that is when the rest of us meet the Lord in the air, as well.

The fact is, if there is only one resurrection of the just and it happens at the last day, and there is only one group labeled "dead in Christ", then there is no way that the rapture will take place before the tribulation. Let me repeat it again, at the resurrection, the living saints will meet the "dead in Christ" in the air, and this will happen when Jesus physically returns to this world AFTER the AC's reign of 1260 days. To seal this thought and crimp the nail on the other side, the Book of Revelation actually tells us when these so called tribulation saints get raptured. It is found in Revelation 20:

> Rev 20:4 "And I saw thrones, and they sat upon them, and judgment was given unto them: and I saw the SOULS of them that were **beheaded for the witness of Jesus**, and **for the word of God**, and which had **not worshipped the beast, neither his image, neither had received his mark upon their foreheads, or in their hands**; and they lived and **reigned with Christ a thousand years.**"

> Rev 20:5 "But the rest of the dead lived not again until the thousand years were finished. This is the **first resurrection**."

This is pretty plain. These souls that were beheaded, did not worship the beast (the AC), neither his image, and refused to take the mark of the beast. These are the tribulation saints and they will get their glorified bodies at the FIRST RESURRECTION, but that is when us living saints get ours also! Yes! It is all at the same time! There is only ONE resurrection of the JUST! In other words, there are NOT two comings, or two resurrections! Never is the return of Christ given in a plural sense. It is always "coming", not "coming**S**". Many defend their position by saying, "There is only one coming but it is in two phases." Sorry, that doesn't "fly". These people are trying to get around the clear cut voice of scripture. Any two phase coming of Christ separated by 7 years, three and a half years, or even one week is TWO comings! We are talking about the endtime time line. The coming of the Lord, the rapture of the church, which is the first resurrection, is the last event before the starting of the new era—the thousand year millennial reign of Christ.

THE CRUX OF THE MATTER

It appears the greatest timing factor in this whole time line is the A of D. That was the crux of the matter to Jesus. In Matthew, Mark and even in Luke, where it is inferred, Jesus gave a list of signs such as famines, earthquakes, persecutions, etc., and when He came to the sign of the end itself, He said in Mark 13:14:

> Mar 13:14 "...But **when ye shall see the abomination of desolation**...standing where it ought not,...flee to the mountains..."

As in a three ring circus, this was the BIG EVENT. If you get the timing wrong on this it throws everything out of whack. What do I mean by everything? Let me give you a list, and then I will go over each one in detail:

1. The timing of the Great Tribulation is skewed.

2. When to flee to the mountains is wrecked.

3. The AC acceptance with the Jews is ruined.

4. The peace treaty for 7 years is meaningless.

5. The timing of the vials or the wrath of God is messed up.

6. The 1290 days is senseless.

7. Forget trying to figure out the 2300 days.

1) THE TIMING OF THE GREAT TRIBULATION IS SKEWED.

I just quoted Mark 13:14 and five verses later Jesus says in Mark 13:19 "For in those days shall be affliction, such as was not from the beginning of the creation which God created unto this time, neither shall be." Jesus' words are verified by Matthew in 24:21 "For then shall be great tribulation, such as was not since the beginning of the world to this time, no, nor ever shall be." This is referring to a global chaos. This is not just an escalated time of persecution as some would say is typical of the tribulation. Again this is world chaos. Daniel 12:1 also verifies this: "And at that time shall Michael stand up, the great prince which standeth for the children of thy people: and there shall be a time of trouble, such as never was since there was a nation even to that same time: and at that time thy people shall be delivered, every one that shall be found written in the book." This, according to Jesus is to follow hard on the heels of the A of D, and will be right before the resurrection. If the A of D took place in the middle of the seven year peace treaty, then so would this great affliction, tribulation, and chaos. That, my friend, is NOT going to happen in the MIDDLE of the peace treaty. It is at the end. Let me be super clear here. If the A of D happened in the middle of the week, then the world disturbances would happen then, too, which from all indications happens at the END, and so the A of D must also be at the end.

2) WHEN TO FLEE TO THE MOUNTAINS IS WRECKED.

If we flee from the cities to the mountains BEFORE it is time, we're sunk. We'll be wondering around in the mountains waiting for something to happen that won't happen for another three and a half years—with no preparation? We would die up there and it wouldn't be the Lord's fault, it would be ours because we didn't read the word carefully enough. Remember, He said don't take anything with you—run for your life. It will happen quickly and once it starts, it won't take long to be completed. If you have eyes to read, let these words sink in!

3) THE AC ACCEPTANCE WITH THE JEWS IS RUINED.

The scripture says in Daniel 8:25 he "...BY PEACE shall destroy many..." Also, Daniel 11:21 says, "...he shall come in PEACEABLY, and obtain the kingdom by flatteries." Daniel 11:24 says, "He shall enter PEACEABLY even upon the fattest places of the province." As you can see by these verses, the AC will appear, at first, as a man of peace. The scriptures also tell us that he ONLY reigns for 42 months or three and a half years. This is where it gets ticklish because Daniel 9:27 says, "he shall confirm the covenant with many for one week: and in the midst of the week he shall cause the sacrifice and the oblation to cease..." Here's the dilemma: The AC doesn't take the world ruler position until half way into the seven year agreement in order for his reign to end at the end of the agreement. Many verses witness the fact that he starts his reign with peace, but other verses say he stops the sacrifice in the middle of the agreement. How can both passages be true? The only answer that I have been able to come up with is: He has the sacrifices stopped without him being tagged as the instigator of it, and then he is able to start his reign of 42 months as a man of peace, but this also means he wouldn't be setting up the A of D at that time. He would wait until he has the Jewish nation firmly in his grasp and do it at the end of his reign, not the beginning! The reverse would wreck his peace efforts. Also, keep in mind when the Lord says the AC stops the sacrifice in the middle of the week, He doesn't mean exactly. It is "close" to the middle of the week.

4) THE PEACE TREATY FOR 7 YEARS IS MEANINGLESS.

As mentioned in 3, the AC, either overtly or covertly, will establish a peace treaty for seven years. If he sets up the A of D in the middle of this peace treaty, it will destroy it immediately. It must not be done until the end of the treaty, or it's doomed to fail.

5) THE TIMING OF THE VIALS OR THE WRATH OF GOD IS MESSED UP.

You could say that the catastrophic events that will follow the A of D are, or are a part of, the wrath of God that is coming. The vials don't start until the very end and are completed at the same time as the 7th seal and 7th trumpet. If the A of D was in the middle of the week the vials would ultimately be started at the same time. This would mess up the, already established, order of the vials as found in Revelation.

6) THE 1290 DAYS IS SENSELESS.

The Lord tells Daniel in 12:11 that there are 1,290 days from the time the sacrifices ceases until the A of D. If the A of D is set up in the middle of the week, that would be at the very same time the World Ruler or AC begins his reign, and would by necessity be the first act of his reign. By looking at Time Line 2 below, the fourth line, you can see that would put 75 days between the ceasing of the sacrifice and the A of D. It doesn't work! The Lord said there would be 1,290 days—not 75 days—between those two events. If you keep the A of D there in the middle of the week and you place 1290 days in front of or before it, the ceasing of the sacrifice would take place 105 days before the 7 year peace treaty was even signed! That also would put it 280 days before the temple was built! That's ludicrous. Therefore the A of D can't be in the middle of the week.

7) FORGET TRYING TO FIGURE OUT THE 2300 DAYS.

In Daniel 8:13 and 14, there is supposed to be 2300 days between the starting of the sacrifices and the A of D. If the A of D is in the middle of the week, you lose the ability to generate 2300 days between these two events.

As you can see, knowing when the A of D transpires is knowing when everything happens. It is seen more clearly by looking at the events in one picture, as I show in the time line below:

THE TIME LINE

We have discussed several events having to do with the last seven years before the end of this age. I have listed each event with a code in front of it. Those codes will be used because of a restriction of space in the two time lines below. Those events include:

1. (PTB) Peace Treaty Begins. That will give the Jews the right to rebuild their temple. They will also have the right to start animal sacrifices.

2. (STS) Starting The Sacrifices.

3. (CTS) Ceasing The Sacrifices.

4. (WRB) World Ruler Begins. The reign of the AC starts and lasts for 1260 days.

5. (GPB) Great Persecution Begins. All are required to take the mark of the beast. The Two Witnesses, the people of God, manifest the power of God to the world.

6. (AOD) Abomination Of Desolation is set up in the Holy place.

7. (GTB) (WOG) Great Tribulation Begins, including the Wrath Of God. The Battle of Armageddon is fought, the major cities of the US (and possibly the world) are nuked along with Jerusalem, and there is a pole shift and/or a catastrophic global disaster, possibly caused by Nibiru, and/or a solar disruption.

8. (JR) Jesus Returns to destroy the AC and every enemy. The dead in Christ rise first, the living saints are raptured to meet them in the air, and descend to start a new era, the thousand year reign of Christ. The Jews, as a nation, accept Jesus as their Messiah.

The two time lines that follow will help you assimilate the flow of events as they happen. I have placed the event codes at the bottom of each graph, all on the same line, to help you see it in one glance. The first graph only gives the time frames that are spelled out in scripture, and because of that, you will notice there are quite a few gaps left in the graph. Then I give the second graph where I do the calculations to fill in the missing numbers. Remember all the time frames are based on a 360 day Jewish calendar year.

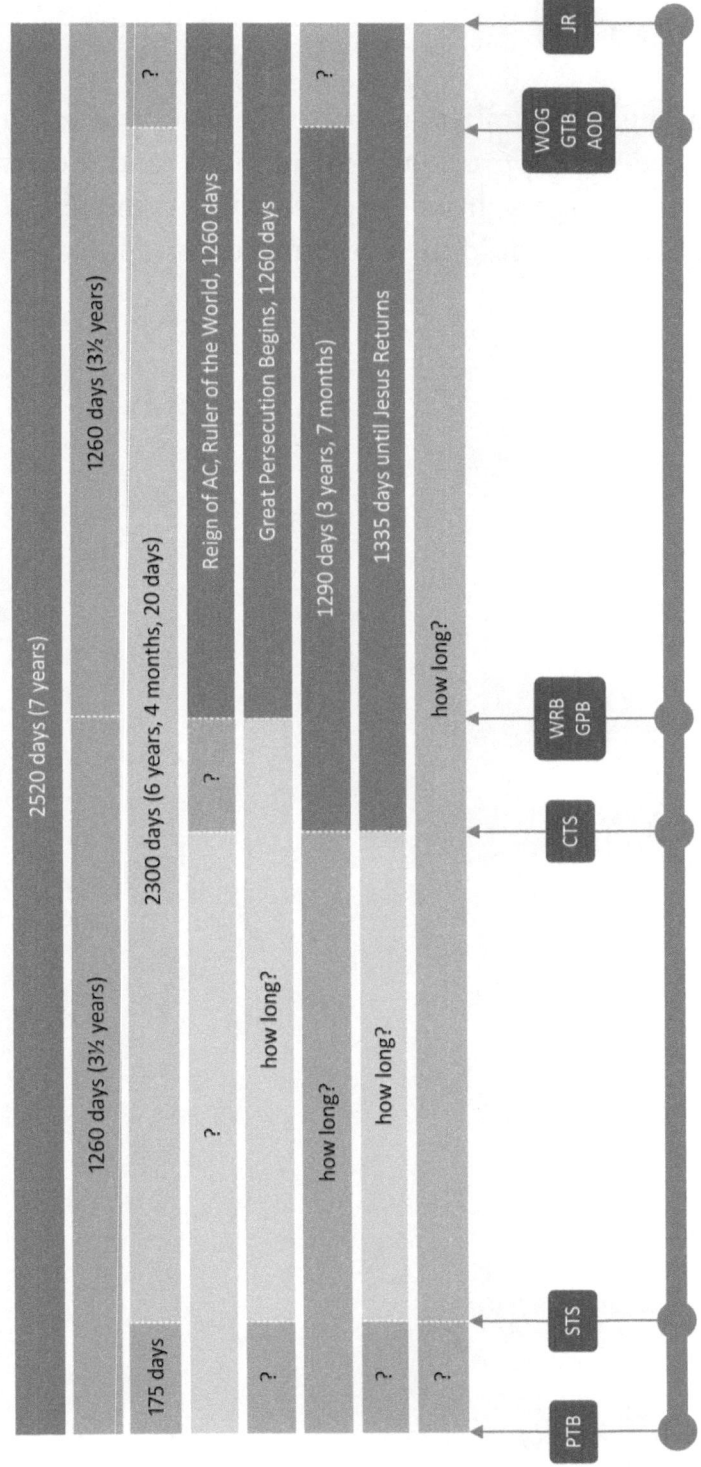

By taking the numbers given to us in scripture, we are able to make the appropriate calculations and determine the missing numbers. If we insert the new numbers, Time Line Number Two would then be complete and look like this:

TIMELINE TWO

2520 days (7 years)

1260 days (3½ years)

1260 days (3½ years)

2300 days (6 years, 4 months, 20 days)

45 days

Reign of AC, Ruler of the World, 1260 days

75 days

Great Persecution Begins, 1260 days

1290 days (3 years, 7 months)

45 days

1335 days (3 years, 8 months, 15 days) until Jesus Returns

2345 days (6 years, 6 months, 5 days)

175 days

1185 days (3 years, 105 days)

1085 days (3 years, 5 days)

5 m, 25 dys

1185 days (3 years, 105 days)

1010 days (2 years, 9 months, 20 days)

175 days

175 days

PTB • STS • CTS • WRB / GPB • WOG / GTB / AOD • JR

CONCLUSION

In this chapter we have determined that God has a calendar and according to Sir Robert Anderson we are 152 years overdue for the millennium to start. You could say we are living on borrowed time. According to the four passages in the scripture giving us the third day indicator Jesus could come anytime after 2028. We found out that a generation is a hundred years and if Israel became a nation in 1948, then Jesus must of necessity come back before 2048! Israel is our timing indicator overall and the seven year peace treaty that is coming will signal the final seven years. The saints will be persecuted for three and a half years while some are protected. We don't accept the 70 A.D. destruction of Jerusalem as the final one as the preterists do. 220 days after the peace treaty is signed the temple will be rebuilt and the sacrifices started. 2300 days later the A of D will be set up. We gave five proofs why the A of D would be at the end of the seven year peace agreement. I give the six references to the A of D and give eleven possible explanations what it could be. I give more proofs why Jerusalem's destruction in 70 A.D. wasn't the final one. After the AC reigns for 1260 days he will be destroyed, and 1335 days after the sacrifice ceases the Lord will return. If one gets the timing of the A of D wrong it throws 7 things into confusion. The time line maps out eight events. The peace treaty starts it all out. After the temple is rebuilt, 175 days later the sacrifices begin and 1010 days after that they are stopped. 75 days after the sacrifices cease or 1260 days into the peace treaty the AC is crowned world ruler. 1215 days from then the wrath of God and the Great Tribulation start. 45 days later the Lord returns to gather His people home and start the new age — the millennial reign of Christ. In other words, the graffs at the end of this chapter have answered the ultimate question, "The end, when is it?"

I have illustrated my best assimilation of all the time periods in Daniel and Revelation, showing what is on God's calendar. What will you do with this information? Are you ready for the end of the world and the return of Jesus to rescue His people? The best way to be prepared is two-fold: 1) be in the know when the end time events are going to happen by reading this book and studying the endtime time lines and 2) believe in the Lord with all your heart and be saved. In Acts chapter 2 Peter told the multitude on the day of Pentecost how to do just that:

> Act 2:38 "Then Peter said unto them, REPENT, and be BAPTIZED every one of you in the NAME of Jesus Christ for the REMISSION of sins, and ye shall RECEIVE THE GIFT of the HOLY GHOST."

"THE END, WHEN IS IT?"
STUDY QUESTIONS
(*Open Book Quiz*)

1. What is a thousand years to the Lord?

2. According to Sir Robert Anderson, what year did the creation take place?

3. According to the four passages that give us the "third day indicator" what happens on the third day?

4-5. There are two possibilities as to when the "clock" might start ticking in regards to the ministry of Jesus. What are they?

6. According to Genesis, how long is a generation?

7. According to Daniel 9:27, how long will the AC confirm the covenant?

8. What will be the sign that will reverberate around the world that will let us know that the last seven years has started?

9. Very likely in Revelation 11, what are the three days and a half a type of?

10. The wrath of God will be incorporated in what major event?

11. In a nut shell, what do preterists believe?

12. What is the timing factor that alarms all the people of God, Jews and Gentiles, worldwide to flee to the mountains or to a place of safety?

13. In Daniel 8 the angel tells us that there will be how many days between the starting of the sacrifice and the A of D?

14. Daniel 12 says there will be 1290 days between what event and the A of D?

15. Under the topic of the A of D there are 11 possibilities offered. Why?

16. In Luke 19 what was Jesus looking at when He said, "...thine enemies...shall lay thee even with the ground...and...shall not leave in thee one stone upon another..."?

17-18. How does II Thessalonians 2:8 say the AC will be consumed and destroyed?

19. In regards to the meaning of the 1335 days, what is the only event left that has not happened?

20. The AC is an enemy, but he is NOT the LAST enemy. What or who is the last enemy?

Bonus Questions:

21. How do we know that the "dead in Christ" have not been taken up to heaven in Revelation even as late as chapter 14?

22. How many events are tracked in the Endtime Time Line graph?

"THE END, WHEN IS IT?"
(Quiz Answers)

1. One day

2. 4141 B.C.

3. The day He will raise us up—the resurrection of the just.

4-5. Either, 28 A.D. when He started His ministry, or 32 A.D. when He ended His ministry.

6. 100 years

7. For one week

8. When the Jews are given the right to rebuild their third temple because of a peace treaty with the Palestinians.

9. Three and a half years

10. It will be incorporated in the Great Tribulation

11. They believe that all or most of the book of Revelation was fulfilled in the first century.

12. It is the A of D.

13. 2300 days

14. The ceasing or stopping of the sacrifice

15. So that we as the children of God will be very alert as to how this prophecy will be fulfilled.

16.   The city of Jerusalem

17-18. The AC will be consumed "with the spirit of His mouth", and shall be destroyed "with the brightness of His coming:"

19.   The coming of the Lord (or the rapture)

20.   Death

Bonus Answers:

21.   Because Revelation 14:13 says, "...blessed are the dead which die in the Lord from henceforth..." Those who have died in the Lord ARE the DEAD IN CHRIST.

22.   8

Chuck Swindol, May 3, 2011, on his radio program said, "A well-dressed stern-looking man was in the checkout stand at a grocery store and a woman putting her food up on the moving belt cast a glance backward and said, 'Excuse me, are you a minister?' No ma'am, I've just been sick the last three weeks.'" He was trying to illustrate the fact that ministers have a tendency to be among the saddest looking people on earth, but at the same time it illustrates how it is so easy to misunderstand things that we SEE. It's that way with prophecy, also. We must be careful not to project our bias into the scripture!

Chapter Six:
THE END—
HOW BAD WILL IT GET?

> Mat 24:3 "And as he sat upon the mount of Olives, the disciples came unto him privately, saying, Tell us, when shall these things be? and what shall be the sign of thy coming, and of **the end of the world**?"

This verse uses the phrase, "the end of the world". The end of the world is coming whether you believe it or not. Chuck Missler was teaching in his "Learn the Bible in 24 hours" and he said something significant (as he usually does, and not that I agree with everything) if the world had a beginning it also has an ending. (End of his thought). If you don't believe it is coming in your life time, think again. You will believe it when you find yourself in it! The previous chapter, The End, When Is It? provides a lot of rational for this and a lot of future events, but how bad will it get?

The end has been talked about from the beginning. When was it first talked about and who first mentioned it? Already in Genesis chapter 5 it tells us that Enoch was so close to God that He, God, translated him. The book of Jude in the New Testament expounds on the message Enoch brought to his generation. Where Jude got his information we will never know, but it is powerful:

> Jud 1:14 "And **Enoch also, the seventh from Adam**, prophesied of these, saying, **Behold, the Lord cometh with ten thousands of his saints**,"
>
> Jud 1:15 "**To execute judgment upon all**, and to convince all that are ungodly among them of all their ungodly deeds which they have ungodly committed, and of all their hard speeches which ungodly sinners have spoken against him."

It has been said as soon as a baby is born it begins to die. It is almost like that in regards to the creation of this world. This seventh person from Adam, Enoch, was born a prophet, and as notated, almost as long as there have been humans there have been prophets calling people back to the Lord. Although it is inferred here that it has to do with the end of the world, the meaning is still clear, and Jude inserts, He is not coming alone this time, as He did when He came the first time. This is His SECOND COMING. Someone will say, "Yeah, but He's coming with His saints. Isn't that the church?" (This will be dealt with in detail in the next book, but here are some teasers.) Matthew 13:41 lets us know they are angels. If you didn't know it, angels are called saints in Daniel 8:13 and Deuteronomy 33:2 and it is letting us know, to restate it, that He is coming with His angels (maybe you could call them extra-terrestrials) to judge this world.

Judgment usually follows God's established time frames (many call them dispensations). Remember God did judge the world in Noah's day, which we'll discuss shortly, but here He was talking about the end of the world that was to come. Many are interested in this subject and most of this book has dealt with the mysteries related to it, and the amount of time that is left before it happens. This chapter, though, will deal with the events that comprise what we call THE END, but we are not the only ones who are interested in the end of the world. The book of Mark tells us that it was Peter, James, John and Andrew who had approached Jesus and asked Him about this question. Matthew, Mark, and Luke all deal with the events that led up to the end and they all give us almost a full chapter on the subject. Daniel probably would take the prize for giving the most open discussion on it with the least amount of words in the whole Old Testament. In his 12th chapter alone, he uses the word "end" six times in 13 verses. There are a lot of movies, films and DVD's out there that picture for us what the End might look like, but there may not be as much written material, so a chapter detailing the scriptural basis what the end might look like is in order. In Daniel chapter 12, Daniel tells us:

> Dan 12:1 "And at that time shall Michael stand up, the great prince which standeth for the children of thy people: and **there shall be a time of trouble, such as never was since there was a**

nation even to that same time: and at that time thy people shall be delivered, every one that shall be found written in the book."

What does it mean, "a time of trouble, such as never was since there was a nation even to that same time"? This sounds BAD and it is bad, but Jesus mentions this time capsule in verses 21 and 22 of Matthew 24:

Mat 24:21 "For then shall **be great tribulation, such as was not since the beginning of the world to this time, no, nor ever shall be.**"

Mat 24:22 "And except those days should be shortened, there should no flesh be saved: but for the elect's sake those days shall be shortened."

Daniel calls it a time of trouble, but Jesus calls it great tribulation and because of Jesus' words this time period is called The Great Tribulation. Most of Christendom is saying the "church" will be up in heaven during this time. Sorry to be the bearer of bad news, but all the people of God—the living saints—are going to be here on the earth during this time, just like Noah was on the earth during the flood. God has called me to shake the pillars of Christendom and wake up the church. Most of the leaders of Christianity have maimed their own people by leading them astray on this matter, even if it's been done "innocently". They have led them to adopt a doctrine that will eventually betray them. It was done in Jesus day at the time of His first coming and it is being done now in regards to His second coming. (The next book will give more proof of that.) We are not alone in dealing with this situation. Jeremiah, as stated earlier, had to deal with this same issue.

> Jer 5:26 "For **among my people are found wicked men**: they lay wait, as **he that setteth snares; they set a trap, they catch men**."

> Jer 5:27 "As a cage is full of birds, so are their houses **full of deceit**: therefore they are become great, and waxen rich."

> Jer 5:28 "They are waxen fat, they shine: yea, they overpass the deeds of the wicked: they judge not the cause, the cause of the fatherless, yet they prosper; and the right of the needy do they not judge."

> Jer 5:29 "Shall **I not visit for these things? saith the LORD**: shall not my soul be avenged on such a nation as this?"

> Jer 5:30 "A wonderful and **horrible thing is committed** in the land;"

> Jer 5:31 "**The prophets prophesy falsely**, and

the priests bear rule by their means; and **my people love to have it so: and what will ye do in the end thereof**?"

As in that day so it is today that there are many that are misleading multitudes (some of them ignorantly) in regards to the end times and they are getting rich doing it. It says they set snares and catch men. They do it to catch men in deception, but we do it to catch men in the truth that they may escape the coming "night", thus the name of this ministry—E.S.C.A.P.E. Ministries. There is another verse that summarizes the mission of this ministry in Psalms 124:

Psa 124:7 "**Our soul is escaped as a bird out of the snare of the fowlers: the snare is broken, and we are escaped.**"

It is this ministries' mission to expose the lies of the enemy and set many free from deception. To put it succinctly, the enemy wants the church to be in darkness and confusion so that when the end comes they will not be aware of, or ready for it. Knowledge is power and just knowing the truth about the end times will help many out of the trap. Many are resting on their laurels, thinking they will miss the Great Tribulation and be in heaven during that time, but sadly they are wrong. The Lord has said a "horrible thing is committed…the prophets prophesy falsely…and my people love to have it so." Some want to believe this kind of lie because it's easier on the flesh. Thank God, there are some who want the truth no matter what it contains and hopefully this book will help many awake to that truth and be prepared.

IN NOAH'S DAY

The end is coming and it is coming fast and there is not much time left to prepare. Just looking at the past at times, can help prepare one for the future. One might ask, "How can that be?" It can be, as you might not know, because history repeats itself. The proof of that is found in Ecclesiastes 1:

> Ecc 1:9 "**The thing that hath been, it is that which shall be; and that which is done is that which shall be done: and there is no new thing under the sun.**"
>
> Ecc 1:10 "**Is there any thing whereof it may be said, See, this is new? it hath been already of old time**, which was before us."

There is coming a destruction to this earth, so it might pay us to take a glance back to see how it came about in Noah's day. Jesus mentioned Noah in Luke 17:1, in regards to the end days:

> Luk 17:26 "And as it was in the **days of Noe,** so

shall it be also in the days **of the Son of man.**"

Luk 17:27 "They did eat, they drank, they married wives, they were given in marriage, until the day that Noe entered into the ark, and **the flood came, and destroyed them all**".

What was it like in the days of Noah? Look at Genesis 6:

Gen 6:5 "And **GOD saw that the wickedness of man was great in the earth, and that every imagination of the thoughts of his heart was only evil continually.**"

Gen 6:6 "And **it repented the LORD that he had made man on the earth**, and it grieved him at his heart."

Gen 6:7 "And the LORD said, **I will destroy man** whom I have created from the face of the earth; both man, and beast, and the creeping thing, and the fowls of the air; for it repenteth me that I have made them."

Gen 6:8 "**But Noah found grace in the eyes of the LORD.**"

Man was wicked and the thoughts of his heart was evil continually and God was fed up with it all and decided to destroy every living creature. But Noah found grace in the eyes of the Lord. Will you and I find grace in the eyes of the Lord? The Lord showed Noah how to escape the coming flood. The Lord is merciful and always gives a way of escape up to a period of time and if people don't listen, then time runs out and it's too late and then there's no escaping His judgment.

> Gen 6:17 "And, behold, I, even **I, do bring a flood of waters upon the earth, to destroy all flesh**, wherein is the breath of life, from under heaven; and **every thing** that is in the **earth shall die.**"

God had Noah prepare for this coming event:

> Gen 6:14 "**Make thee an ark of gopher wood**; rooms shalt thou make in the ark, and shalt pitch it within and without with pitch."

> Gen 6:19 "And **of every living thing of all flesh, two of every sort shalt thou bring into the ark, to keep them alive with thee; they shall be male and female.**"

> Gen 6:21 "And **take thou unto thee of all food**

that is eaten, and thou shalt gather it to thee; and it shall be for food for thee, and for them."

FIRST, Noah prepared an ARK and then he (by God's help) brought two of every living creature into the ark and then he stocked it with food. So Noah prepared for the inevitable! Are you preparing for the end of the world?

The best way to prepare for the end is to get right with God first and foremost. Get saved so that if you die, at least, you will go to heaven and be with God and be protected forever. But then again, how do you get saved? Everybody has a different message, right? Peter had it right in Acts 2:

> Act 2:38 "Then Peter said unto them, **Repent, and be baptized every one of you in the name of Jesus Christ for the remission of sins, and ye shall receive the gift of the Holy Ghost.**"

While on the subject of salvation, notice that Noah is used as a visual lesson to teach important truths about it:

> 1 Pe 3:20 "Which sometime were disobedient, when once **the longsuffering of God waited in the days of Noah, while the ark was a preparing, wherein few, that is, eight souls were saved by water.**"

1 Pe 3:21 "The like figure whereunto even baptism doth also now save us (not the putting away of the filth of the flesh, but the answer of a good conscience toward God,) by the resurrection of Jesus Christ:"

Several things can be gleaned from this passage:

God was longsuffering in waiting for Noah to preach for a hundred years to get people in the ark. He started preaching when he was 500 years old and stopped when he was 600 years old. Jesus said in Matthew 24:34 that this generation would not pass away until all be fulfilled. When Israel became a nation in 1948 and all the Jews began returning to their homeland, all the prophecy experts came out of the woodwork and began declaring that this is the end times. Noah preached to his generation for a hundred years before the flood came. Maybe God will allow this generation to be preached to for close to a hundred years before the end comes! Interesting huh?

1. "Few souls were saved" could be taken two ways. There will be few people who will actually be saved by the atonement and true New Testament salvation. And there will be few humans spared death during the time of trouble that's coming. More will be said about that later.

2. "Eight souls were saved by water." Most say water baptism doesn't save you and they say this because it doesn't agree with their theology, so they trample the word of God to make it fit. No one is saved by water baptism by itself, but it is part of the born again process according to Jesus. John 3:5 says one has to be born of water and Spirit to enter heaven. Mark 16:16 says, "he that believeth AND IS baptized shall be saved…" Acts 22:16 "…be baptized and wash away thy sins calling on the name of the Lord…" If water baptism is the one way in which the blood is applied to take away our sins, no wonder it's part of the salvation process! (More on this vital subject in a future publication.)

3. "Not the putting away of the filth of the flesh, but the answer of a good conscience toward God by the resurrection of Jesus Christ:" All of this plays a part of salvation. It is a birth process as Jesus put it. Just repenting and stopping the acts of sin and having a clear conscience, doesn't save you by itself. And receiving the Holy Ghost typified by the resurrection of Jesus doesn't save one by itself either, but don't be mistaken, water baptism is a part of salvation! Peter had it right, it takes all three, death, burial, and resurrection to save us. I Corinthians 15:1-4 tells us this is the gospel. Jesus did all three and so must we in a spiritual sense!

SECONDLY, Noah brought his family and all other living creatures into the ark. When one gets saved, the natural thing to do is to share the knowledge of the truth with as many people who will listen. The Lord wants us to win the lost and show them why it's so important to be saved NOW.

> 2 Co 6:2 "(For he saith, I have heard thee in a time accepted, and in the day of salvation have I succored thee: behold, **now is the accepted time; behold, now is the day of salvation**.)"

Today is the day of salvation especially since we are so close to the end of the world. Find a church that teaches salvation correctly and get saved!

THIRDLY, Noah brought provisions and food into the ark. Some have said, "Oh, I will let God provide food for me like He did for Elijah in I Kings 17." Yes, the ravens brought him food and the widow woman's flour and oil was multiplied. That is true. But what about Joseph in the land of Egypt when he interpreted Pharaoh's dream in Genesis 41? There were no ravens or widow women there to help him out. Joseph interpreted Pharaoh's dream and God didn't tell Joseph to tell Pharaoh to store up food. God only gave Joseph the interpretation and left it up to him to make the proper deductions on what to do. Joseph made the right deductions WITHOUT God telling him to start storing up food. Will you prepare like Joseph and Noah? There are several other things worth noting here:

1. The beginning of the flood is talked about in Genesis **6**.

2. Noah was **600** years old when he entered the ark

3. The words "destroy" and "destroyed" are used **6** times in chapters **6** and 7 of Genesis.

4. The word "end" is used **6** times in Daniel 12.

Why is the number "6" repeated so many times? It is because man and beast were created on the 6th day and all of this has to do with man and beast being destroyed. Revelation 13:18 tells us this number is the number of man and beast, and this BOOK tells us about their destruction, but 2 Peter 2 deals with the angels that sinned and the END of the old world:

2 Pe 2:4 "For **if God spared not the angels that sinned**, but cast them down to hell, and delivered them into chains of darkness, to be reserved unto judgment;"

2 Pe 2:5 "**And spared not the old world**, but saved Noah the eighth person, a preacher of righteousness, **bringing in the flood upon the world of the ungodly**;"

If God judged the angels that sinned and spared not the old world by bringing a flood upon it to destroy them, guess what? He is not going to spare our world today. There is one tiny bright spot in all this. He has promised to not destroy the world with a flood again:

> Gen 9:11 "And I will establish my covenant with you; **neither shall all flesh be cut off any more by the waters of a flood; neither shall there any more be a flood to destroy the earth.**"

Let me clarify. This promise doesn't mean He won't destroy the earth again. It just means He won't do it by means of a flood. By the way the film "2012" depicted the destruction of the world by a worldwide flood. Sorry, Hollywood was wrong. The Lord will not destroy the earth with a flood again, He will do it by means of fire and could that be a global nuclear fire from world rulers? (See Psalms 110:5)

> 2 Pe 3:6 "Whereby the world that then was, being overflowed with water, perished:"

> 2 Pe 3:7 "But **the heavens and the earth, which are now,** by the same word are kept in store, **reserved unto fire against the day of judgment** and perdition of ungodly men."

2 Pe 3:9 "The Lord is not slack concerning his promise, as some men count slackness; but is longsuffering to us-ward, not willing that any should perish, but that all should come to repentance."

2 Pe 3:10 "But **the day of the Lord will come as a thief in the night; in the which the heavens shall pass away with a great noise, and the elements shall melt with fervent heat, the earth also and the works that are therein shall be burned up.**"

2 Pe 3:11 "**Seeing then that all these things shall be dissolved**, what manner of persons ought ye to be in all holy conversation and godliness,"

2 Pe 3:12 "Looking for and hasting unto **the coming of the day of God, wherein the heavens being on fire shall be dissolved, and the elements shall melt with fervent heat**?"

It appears that the references to a great noise, elements melting with fervent heat, and the heavens being on fire and being dissolved are all referring to a nuclear Holocaust and will hasten the END.

REVELATION 6 & THE 6TH SEAL

Revelation 6 reveals to us how the future will take place. It starts off talking about the six seals. The first four seals deal with the four horsemen of the Apocalypse which takes us through verse 8. Verse 9 starts describing the great persecution that is coming to all true believers. The sixth seal is opened in verse 12 and is as follows:

Rev 6:12 "And I beheld when he had opened the sixth seal, and, lo, **there was a great earthquake; and the sun became black as sackcloth of hair, and the moon became as blood**;"

Rev 6:13 "And **the stars of heaven fell unto the earth, even as a fig tree casteth her untimely figs, when she is shaken of a mighty wind**."

Rev 6:14 "And **the heaven departed as a scroll when it is rolled together; and every mountain and island were moved out of their places**."

Rev 6:15 "And the kings of the earth, and the great men, and the rich men, and the chief captains, and the mighty men, and every bondman, and every free man, hid themselves in the dens and in the rocks of the mountains;"

Rev 6:16 "And said to the mountains and rocks, Fall on us, and **hide us from the face of him that sitteth on the throne, and from the wrath of the Lamb:**"

Rev 6:17 "For **the great day of his wrath is come; and who shall be able to stand?**"

This passage lets us know that there will be extreme geological changes in the earth, including the worst earthquake of all times, and what many have called a pole shift where the earth rolls over and a new axis is formed. If this happens while one is looking at the stars at the axis, it will look like they are swirling in a circle. Mountains and islands will move out of their places. There is much information on the internet about scores of underground cities set up all across the United States for such a time as this. It sounds like many will be running for them, but will they really be able to hide from God as this passage says it is the wrath of God? I doubt it. Similar events are described in Revelation at the 6th trumpet in 9:14-21, the 7th trumpet in 11:15-19, and the 6th and 7th vials in 16:12-21. (For a cross reference on Rev. 6:14 see Isa. 34:4.) It appears that Isaiah 24 describes these events in more detail:

ISAIAH 24

> Isa 24:1 "Behold, the LORD **maketh the earth empty**, and **maketh it waste, and turneth it upside down**, and scattereth abroad the inhabitants thereof."

If the earth is turned upside down, wouldn't you call that a pole shift?

> Isa 24:3 "The **land shall be utterly emptied, and utterly spoiled**: for the LORD hath spoken this word."

> Isa 24:4 "The **earth mourneth and fadeth away, the world languisheth and fadeth away**, the haughty people of the earth do languish."

> Isa 24:5 "The earth also is defiled under the inhabitants thereof; because they have transgressed the laws, changed the ordinance, broken the everlasting covenant."

> Isa 24:6 "Therefore hath **the curse devoured the earth**, and they that dwell therein are desolate: therefore **the inhabitants of the earth are burned, and few men left**."

As you can see, this passage is very descriptive. Many things are going on here. The whole earth is cursed being emptied, spoiled, fading away, people are burned, and few are left. More will be said about how few is few. It's not a very nice picture, huh? It tells us that all joy and gladness are gone. It continues in verse 10:

> Isa 24:10 "The city of confusion is broken down: **every house is shut up, that no man may come in.**"

> Isa 24:11 "There is a crying for wine in the streets; **all joy is darkened, the mirth of the land is gone.**"

> Isa 24:12 "**In the city is left desolation**, and the gate is smitten with destruction."

It says, "In the city..." much like it is really talking about every city. The cities are desolate and every house is shut up. Nobody is out walking or traveling or having fun. There is no joy nor happiness. The cities are all destroyed. It is bad. Reader, are you ready for this? It's hard for us to picture this, but Hollywood with its end time scenarios has depicted how severe the END will be. They may have gone too far in some areas, but God might be using them to shake America and the world awake.

> Isa 24:17 "Fear, and the pit, and the snare, are upon thee, O **inhabitant of the earth**."

> Isa 24:18 "And it shall come to pass, that he who fleeth from the noise of the fear shall fall into the pit; and he that cometh up out of the midst of the pit shall be taken in the snare: for the windows from on high are open, and the **foundations of the earth do shake**."

Again, some say the destruction here is only in Israel or the Middle East. Hey, this is not just Jerusalem. In verses one through six the word "earth" is used six times and nine more times in the rest of the chapter. It is talking about the inhabitants of the earth—not just the Middle East. It is world-wide to the place where it feels like the foundations of the earth are shaking, but it continues:

> Isa 24:19 "The earth is utterly broken down, the earth is clean dissolved, **the earth is moved exceedingly**."

> Isa 24:20 " **The earth shall reel to and fro like a drunkard, and shall be removed like a cottage**; and the transgression thereof shall be heavy upon it; and it shall fall, and not rise again."

Again, it is describing the world wobbling as in a pole shift. At the same time another phenomena is happening. It is as follows:

> Isa 24:23 "Then **the moon shall be confounded, and the sun ashamed**, when the LORD of hosts shall reign in mount Zion, and in Jerusalem, and before his ancients gloriously."

This is exactly what Revelation 6:12 was describing:

> Rev 6:12 "And I beheld when he had opened the sixth seal, and, lo, **there was a great earthquake; and the sun became black as sackcloth of hair, and the moon became as blood**;"

As can be seen, this is the same event that is described in Isaiah 24. It is also described in Joel 2:

> Joe 2:30 "And **I will shew wonders in the heavens and in the earth**, blood, and fire, and pillars of smoke."

> Joe 2:31 "The **sun shall be turned into darkness, and the moon into blood, before the great and the terrible day of the LORD come.**"

God will show signs in the heavens and this will be talked about in more detail in regards to the constellations Virgo and Leo on September 23rd, 2017 and the alignment of these stars for the first time in history. What are the pillars of smoke? Is it referring to nuclear explosions that will happen at the end of time? Could be. The sun being turned into darkness and the moon to blood is related again to when the Lord returns to the earth to gather His people and set up His everlasting kingdom. Look at Matthew 24 again:

Mat 24:29 "**Immediately after the tribulation of those days shall the sun be darkened, and the moon shall not give her light, and the stars shall fall from heaven, and the powers of the heavens shall be shaken**:"

Mat 24:30 "And **then shall appear the sign of the Son of man in heaven**: and then shall all the tribes of the earth mourn, and **they shall see the Son of man coming in the clouds of heaven** with power and great glory."

Mat 24:31 "And **he shall send his angels with a great sound of a trumpet, and they shall gather together his elect from the four winds, from one end of heaven to the other**."

This all happens at the end. Jesus confirms that Isaiah 24 and Matthew 24 (interesting both chapters are 24) are both talking about the same event! Both these chapters are describing what will happen right before the Lord comes, the rapture happens, and the Lord sets up His kingdom. What would cause the moon to turn to blood and the sun to be darkened? What could cause the earth to stagger and be moved out of its place and be turned upside down? Could it be a heavenly body on its way to earth? More about this later.

Stop! There is a glimmer of joy or of hope for somebody. We skipped over four verses. Let's go back and pick those up:

> Isa 24:13 "When thus it shall be in the midst of the land among the people, there shall be as the shaking of an olive tree, and as the gleaning grapes when the vintage is done."

> Isa 24:14 "They shall lift up their voice, **they shall sing for the majesty of the LORD**, they shall cry aloud from the sea."

> Isa 24:15 "Wherefore **glorify ye the LORD** in the fires, even **the name of the LORD God of Israel** in the isles of the sea."

> Isa 24:16 "**From the uttermost part of the**

earth have we heard songs, even glory to the righteous..."

The rest of this chapter is talking about the bulk of the people, but this is talking about the righteous, as mentioned in verse 16. It must be inserted here that it doesn't say "Israel" or "the Jewish saved". It says in general terms "the righteous" and up above it also gives a hint of where it comes from (again, not the land of Israel) "...cry aloud from the sea." and "...in the isles of the sea". Some have said that the "isles of the sea" are referring to the United States, but we could definitely say that it was outside the territory of the Middle East! The children of God will be singing in the midst of the destruction. How can that be? It is because God's people will know what is going on and that the Lord is about to return and save them. Remember what Daniel said in chapter 12, in the last chapter of his book:

Dan 12:10 "... and **none of the wicked shall understand; but the wise shall understand.**"

It says the "wise" will understand. The people of God will know what is going on. That is why you, the reader, have a copy of this book in your hands! This book will give you the knowledge of what will happen. Yes, it is scary, but to be "forewarned is to be forearmed". We can sing because why? Because we know that the Lord will appear shortly to give us our inheritance of eternal life and a glorified body and we will rule and reign with Him in His kingdom that will never end. "Look up for your redemption draweth nigh"!

ISAIAH 13

This chapter deals with the very same end time scenario as the 24th chapter of this book.

> Isa 13:5 "They come from a far country, from the end of heaven, even the LORD, and the weapons of his indignation, **to destroy the whole land.**"

> Isa 13:6 "Howl ye; for the **day of the LORD** is at hand; it shall come **as a destruction** from the Almighty."

> Isa 13:7 "Therefore shall **all hands be faint**, and **every man's heart shall melt**:"

> Isa 13:8 "And they shall be afraid: pangs and sorrows shall take hold of them; they shall be **in pain as a woman that travaileth**: they shall be amazed one at another; their faces shall be as flames."

> Isa 13:9 "Behold, **the day of the LORD** cometh, cruel both with wrath and fierce anger, to **lay the land desolate**: and he shall **destroy the**

sinners thereof out of it."

Isa 13:10 "For **the stars of heaven and the constellations thereof shall not give their light: the sun shall be darkened in his going forth, and the moon shall not cause her light to shine.**"

Isa 13:11 "And **I will punish the world for their evil**, and the wicked for their iniquity; and I will cause the arrogancy of the proud to cease, and will lay low the haughtiness of the terrible."

Isa 13:12 "I will **make a man more precious than fine gold; even a man than the golden wedge of Ophir.**"

Isa 13:13 "Therefore I will **shake the heavens, and the earth shall remove out of her place**, in the wrath of the LORD of hosts, and in the day of his fierce anger."

Isa 13:14 "And it shall be as the chased roe, and as a sheep that no man taketh up: they shall every man turn to his own people, and flee every one into his own land."

Isa 13:15 "Every one that is found shall be thrust through; and every one that is joined unto them shall fall by the sword."

Isa 13:16 "Their children also shall be dashed to pieces before their eyes; their houses shall be spoiled, and **their wives ravished**."

Isa 13:17 "Behold, I will stir up the Medes against them, which shall not regard silver; and as for gold, they shall not delight in it."

Isa 13:18 "Their bows also shall dash the young men to pieces; and they shall have **no pity on the fruit of the womb;** their eye shall not spare children."

Some would say that, "No, this is a prophecy against Babylon as it is addressed in verse one." Yes, it is addressed to Babylon as verse one states, but it is amazing how the Lord can sandwich a word of prophecy to the whole world right in the midst of Isaiah 13 in a prophecy to Babylon. How do we know this? There are seven reasons:

1. Two times it says this is the "Day of the Lord". We know that the day of the Lord happens at the end of the world. The day of the Lord is talked about in the Old and New Testament and tells us it is an event that

will come upon the whole world and everyone needs to prepare for it.

2. The phrases in verses 10 and 11 are very similar to phrases used to describe the end times, that being "...stars of heaven and the constellations thereof..." and "...the sun shall be darkened...and the moon shall not cause her light to shine." And, again the end times will affect the whole world.

3. Verse 11 also says He will punish the "world" for their evil—not just Israel or the Middle East. This is a worldwide event.

4. The phrase, "...be in pain as a woman that travaileth", is a phrase used in regards to the end times.

5. The phrase, "...make man more precious than fine gold..." is repeated in chapter 24 and inferred in other places and all dealing with the end times and the scarcity of people who will be left.

6. The phrase in verse 13 says, "...I will shake the heavens, and the earth shall remove out of her place..." is very similar to what chapter 24 says in regards to the world.

7. In verse 16 it uses the phrases, "...children also shall be dashed to pieces before their eyes; their houses shall be spoiled, and their wives ravished." are words used to

describe the end times especially in regards to the battle of Armageddon.

This gives several reasons why this chapter is dealing with the end times. Since Isaiah 24 follows this chapter in chronology in the Bible, chapter 24 becomes the second witness that these events will happen at the end. Revelation 8 and 9 continues the end time narrative, telling us how bad it will get.

REVELATION 8 & 9
WHICH ARE 6 OF THE 7 TRUMPETS

Six of the seven Trumpets that will sound will give more details of the end times. This passage will include a discussion of meteors falling to the earth causing great destruction. See what it says:

> Rev 8:6 "And the seven angels which had the seven trumpets prepared themselves to sound."

> Rev 8:7 "The first angel sounded, and there followed **hail and fire mingled with blood**, and they were cast upon the earth: and the **third part of trees was burnt up, and all green grass was burnt up**."

The last time there was hail and fire mixed together was back in Moses time (Exodus 9:23-24). In this passage in

Revelation the hail is mingled with blood instead of fire, but understand, both are red. There is a correlation here, but let's continue:

> Rev 8:8 "And the second angel sounded, and as it were **a great mountain burning with fire was cast into the sea: and the third part of the sea became blood**;"

> Rev 8:9 "And the third part of the creatures which were in the sea, and had life, died; and the third part of the ships were destroyed."

Irving Baxter with Endtime Ministries tells us that this has already happened and maybe it has to a degree. It all has to do with Fukushima falling into the ocean and contaminating the Pacific Ocean and killing off much of the sea life and vegetation. It all has to do with the island of Japan, which actually is the top of a gigantic mountain coming up off of the ocean floor. It's interesting, huh?

> Rev 8:10 "And the third angel sounded, and **there fell a great star from heaven, burning as it were a lamp, and it fell upon the third part of the rivers, and upon the fountains of waters**;"

> Rev 8:11 "And the name of the star is called

Wormwood: and the third part of the waters became wormwood; and many men died of the waters, because they were made bitter."

Astronomers have spotted a meteor heading toward planet earth. They call it Apophis and more will be given about this below.

Rev 8:12 "And the fourth angel sounded, and the **third part of the sun was smitten, and the third part of the moon, and the third part of the stars; so as the third part of them was darkened, and the day shone not for a third part of it, and the night likewise.**"

Now it continues into chapter 9 and includes the whole chapter:

Rev 9:1 "And the fifth angel sounded, and I saw **a star fall from heaven unto the earth**: and to him was given the key of the bottomless pit."

Rev 9:2 "And he opened the bottomless pit; and there arose a smoke out of the pit, as the smoke of a great furnace; and the sun and the air were darkened by reason of the smoke of the pit."

Rev 9:3 "And there came out of the smoke **locusts upon the earth**: and unto them was given power, **as the scorpions of the earth have power.**"

Rev 9:4 "And it was commanded them that they should not hurt the grass of the earth, neither any green thing, neither any tree; but **only those men which have not the seal of God in their foreheads.**"

Notice that the locusts only had power to hurt those who didn't have God's seal on their foreheads. There is protection here for the servants of the Lord!

Rev 9:5 "And to them it was given that they should not kill them, but **that they should be tormented five months: and their torment was as the torment of a scorpion, when he striketh a man.**"

Rev 9:6 "And in those days **shall men seek death, and shall not find it; and shall desire to die, and death shall flee from them.**"

There is coming a time for five months when people won't be able to die, even if they wanted to.

Rev 9:7 "And the shapes of the locusts were like unto horses prepared unto battle; and on their heads were as it were crowns like gold, and their faces were as the faces of men."

Rev 9:8 "And they had hair as the hair of women, and their teeth were as the teeth of lions."

Rev 9:9 "And they had breastplates, as it were breastplates of iron; and the sound of their wings was as the sound of chariots of many horses running to battle."

Rev 9:10 "And **they had tails like unto scorpions, and there were stings in their tails: and their power was to hurt men five months**."

Rev 9:11 "And they had a king over them, which is the angel of the bottomless pit, whose name in the Hebrew tongue is Abaddon, but in the Greek tongue hath his name Apollyon."

Rev 9:12 "One woe is past; and, behold, there come two woes more hereafter."

Rev 9:13 "And the sixth angel sounded, and I heard a

voice from the four horns of the golden altar which is before God,"

Rev 9:14 "Saying to the sixth angel which had the trumpet, Loose the four angels which are bound in the great river Euphrates."

Rev 9:15 "And the four angels were loosed, which were prepared for an hour, and a day, and a month, and a year, for **to slay the third part of men**."

Rev 9:16 "And the **number of the army of the horsemen were two hundred thousand thousand**: and I heard the number of them."

Rev 9:17 "And thus I saw the horses in the vision, and them that sat on them, having breastplates of fire, and of jacinth, and brimstone: and the heads of the horses *were* as the heads of lions; and out of their mouths issued fire and smoke and brimstone."

Rev 9:18 "**By these three was the third part of men killed**, by the fire, and by the smoke, and by the brimstone, which issued out of their mouths."

Two times it tells us that a third of the men or a third of the population, 2.5 billion will die and it seems to happen in this war that is going to be fought and more will be given about this below. The number of the soldiers in this army are 200 million. They say that China is the only country in the world that could field 200 million men.

> Rev 9:19 "For their power is in their mouth, and in their tails: **for their tails were like unto serpents, and had heads, and with them they do hurt.**"

> Rev 9:20 "And the rest of the men which were not killed by these plagues yet repented not of the works of their hands, that they should not worship devils, and idols of gold, and silver, and brass, and stone, and of wood: which neither can see, nor hear, nor walk:"

> Rev 9:21 "Neither repented they of their murders, nor of their sorceries, nor of their fornication, nor of their thefts."

As one can see, Revelation and Isaiah gives us many of the details of what will happen at the end of this present age. Daniel 12 wraps it up in one verse—being the first verse of that chapter:

> Dan 12:1 "And **at that time** shall Michael stand up, the great prince which standeth for the children of thy people: and **there shall be a time of trouble,**

such as never was since there was a nation even to that same time:...."

APOPHIS

Much of the details of what the end of the world could look like can be found on You Tube sights. One of those sights carries a live interview from Fox News hosted by Shepherd Smith from studio B. He does an interview with Dr. Michio Kaku, the theoretical physics professor at City University of New York. He is author of PHYSICS OF THE FUTURE. He tells us that there is a giant meteor or asteroid headed toward the earth and could hit the earth or make a near pass by. Some call it Apophis. He is so bold to say that Friday April 13th 2029 will be the first pass by and the second one will be in 2036 (Notice there is seven years between those two dates). He says if it hits the earth, it will be a nation buster such as Germany, France, or the entire Northeast part of the United States. According to Russian Scientists it is on its way toward the earth. If it hits the earth, it will hit with a force of 100,000 Hiroshima bombs. He says the force of this thing is beyond human comprehension. NASA is saying that the "chance of this asteroid hitting the earth is minuscule." (In Hebrew NASA means deception and their logo has two red lines going across it like the fangs of a snake. Could they be lying?) They say it is the size of the Rose Bowl or about a 1000 feet across. It will be closer to our earth than our satellites and will be able to be seen by the human eye. Is this in the Bible? Yes!

Rev 8:10 "And the third angel sounded, and **there fell a great star from heaven, burning as it were a lamp, and it fell upon the third part of the rivers, and upon the fountains of waters;**"

Rev 8:11 "And the name of the star is called Wormwood: and the third part of the waters became wormwood; and many men died of the waters, because they were made bitter."

In my chapter, "The End, When Is It", I have revealed that the end will take place somewhere between 2028 and 2048. The arrival of Apophis will be well within those dates. One thing is for sure, the end is coming and the best way to be prepared is to be saved and to be right with God. This is important because the Bible says few people will survive. More about that below.

PLANET X or NIBIRU or WORMWOOD

As big a deal as Apophis is, planet X is just as big a deal or bigger. This needs to be mentioned because it is all over You Tube. David Meade has written a whole book on the subject, PLANET X THE 2017 ARRIVAL. (It was published by eBookIt.com in 2016, but there are also hard copies available which is what I have and use). In this book he gives a lot of facts and has done a lot of research about this planet and its arrival. The total eclipse that took place August 21, 2017 was just a precursor to the great event that was to come in September. He describes with great clarity the constellation of the stars and planets that took place September 23rd, 2017. He explains that the once in a life time alignment was the literal fulfillment of the 12th chapter of Revelation that discusses the woman with child. He believed that was when Planet X would come and the rapture would happen and Jesus would set up His kingdom, but as you can see it didn't happen. He, like many others who tried to pinpoint the day of the Lord's return was disappointed, but that doesn't mean there isn't a lot of information in his book that is important to take seriously. Nonetheless, these were all signs in the heavens that were truly a "kiss of mercy" from heaven in which God is letting us know that the end of all the world is close at hand. (By the way, in his book, Meade also gives some good instructions about being prepared for any disaster.)

General facts: Planet X is also referred to as Nibiru. The Vatican refers to it as Wormwood. It has a diameter of 179,028 to 183,191 kilometers which is 3.34 times the mass of Jupiter, (Planet X, page 75). This makes it 14.4 times the size of the earth. That is big. If the earth is 25,000 miles around, that puts Nibiru at 360,000 miles around! It is no wonder that it has such a strong gravitational pull.

"Planet X is not going to destroy the earth but it's going to affect for a period of years every living person on the planet." (page 75). How devastating will it be? Russia has just finished 5,000 shelters in Moscow. David Meade estimates the US probably has over 150 Deep Underground Military Bases (some in every state) that have been under construction since the 1980s when Planet X was discovered. Remember it was reported in 2001 that $2.2 trillion was missing from the Pentagon's budget. Could this be where that money went (page 74)? Why all the preparation? Look at the You Tube video: Nibiru planet X Pole shift 2016 Latest Update Rt. 5. They say there would be a three mile high tsunami hit the coast lines at the same time. It is called the Destroyer, or Nemesis for good reason. 80 percent of the world population (seven billion people) lives within 100 miles of the coast line, which would be about five and a half billion people, they say would die. Those in authority have been trying to keep this secret, but it's all over You Tube. If everybody moved away from the coast and or started abandoning their homes, it could collapse the whole banking system.

Not everybody is looking at You Tube or reading this kind of book though, so it is not clear how much this kind of information will affect the actions or the attitude of the populace. Know this: there are a lot of scoffers that don't believe a thread of this talk. They believe it is just a bunch of propaganda. You can read some of their comments at the end of some of the You Tube videos. Some of the comments read something like this: Mark Lac "Fake news. There is no Nibiru. These planets we see one minute and gone the next are a hologram, part of the great delusion." Onyx says, "Hope you guys realize that people are just doing this for views...so fake". Grey Olive Black: "Never clean your camera and allow dirt and water to pollute the lens, you should see Planet X , Sasquatch, and UFO's." This is just a few of some of their reactions. Hey, there were scoffers in Noah's day and they perished when Noah survived. Everyone will have to make up their own mind.

In the 1950s science magazines covered these types of stories. Nibiru was reported as coming and with it seven planets around it. (Is this the red dragon talked about in Revelation 12:3 with seven heads, because it is like red oxide, another sun between five to ten million degrees hot. It could be why Revelation 16:8-9 talks about people being scorched with great heat.) It is coming with a tail of debris (Revelation 12:4 says he has a tail with the 3rd part of the stars of heaven and did cast them to the earth.) It is bringing asteroids with it as big as 500 miles across. Much of the debris will weigh 70 pounds as heavy as iron and thousands and thousands landing and hitting the earth. They could take out houses, cars, buses, farm equipment, for food production, farms themselves, and you name it. They say this planet could cause the pole shift that we have been talking about and could all happen within 28 minutes. Some ask, "Is this really real?" Michael Snyder, as of January 13, 2019 just posted an article on Infowars.com entitled, "Signs of the times? A Plague of Locusts Hits Mecca and Earth's Magnetic Pole is Experiencing a 'sudden Shift'". He says in the past the magnetic North Pole has been moving away from Canada towards Siberia, Russia at about 15 km a year, but the speed has now increased to 55 km per year. He says,

"At the same time, Earth's magnetic field has been getting weaker and weaker, and this has many experts deeply concerned that we could soon experience a catastrophic pole flip." He continues, "...scientists tell us that Earth's magnetic field has flipped before, and that it could soon happen again."

Nibiru will shake the earth like a drunkard as Isaiah 13 and 24 tell us. The earth will shift on a different axis. On the outside edge of the globe where it turns, the winds will probably exceed 200 miles an hour. Every high sky scraper and building will come crashing down and who knows how many residential houses. This is the judgment of the Lord and it is coming. Some say you are too negative. Okay, let's be positive—you will die, but the best way to be ready is to be saved. You can get started on that today.

The Dooms Day Seed Vault in Greenland, situated on the latitudinal line between Norway and the Arctic Circle has been placed there because after the pole shift it will be in warmer climate (from You Tube "Insider speaks out about Nibiru, Planet X , and Elenin"). (From this video, you can see they believe in the pole shift.) This seed bank is 130 meters inside a mountain safe from earthquakes, flooding and nuclear warfare. They store over a million seeds at -18 Celsius which will keep for over a thousand years. They say there are over 1400 seed vaults worldwide and are managed by the Global Crop Diversity Trust Fund. They are all 300 feet above sea level. Why? They say if all the ice caps melted sea level would rise 200 feet worldwide. They are not just protecting seeds, they are protecting DNA. The Frozen Ark Project in the UK is collecting the DNA of every species and storing them. (You Tube: Apophis 2029 the Most Dangerous Asteroid for Earth (Full Video). It is obvious that after the pole shift the seed vault will be close to the equator.

Another You Tube, "NASA Quietly Admits Pole Shift Nibiru to Blame", explains Nibiru is responsible for the pole shift. "It is like two magnets that of the same polarity comes together one flips. It explains meteors hitting the earth, and explains climate change. There is proof everywhere of a pole shift from the past: sea shells on Mt. Everest—shows pictures—in mountains there are clams and mussels, and remains of sea life" and what about the mammoths frozen in the ice in the Arctic with tropical vegetation in their mouths?

It's admitted that Planet X is real. You Tube "Dr. Michio Kaku Predicts the End of World from Nibiru, Planet X . May 23, 2017." To understand the following quotes, keep in mind that ten years ago Pluto was demoted from being a planet (to a meteor). Washington Post says, "New evidence suggest a ninth planet lurking at the edge of the solar system." New York Times said, "Ninth planet may exist in solar system beyond Pluto, new evidence suggest." USA Today said, "Researchers find evidence of ninth planet in solar system". (Now we go back to comments before Pluto was demoted.) Ray T. Reynolds said, "Astronomers are so sure of the 10th planet they think there is nothing left but to name it." Zecharia Sitchin writes about it in his book, THE TWELFTH

PLANET. Yes, Planet X (or planet IX as our quotes have labeled it) is real and it could be how the scriptures in Revelation and Daniel are fulfilled.

As stated earlier, many authorities have tried to keep this quiet and in the USA under presidential mandate. President Ronald Reagan signed an executive order, Nibiru Secrecy Act of 1983. It is an obsolete regulation imposing stiff penalties: 50 years imprisonment and unspecified fines on Nibiru whistle blowers. The order, they say, was controversial. A source said the order went overboard. It forbade any public servant, scientist, or persons with true and accurate information about Nibiru from ever mentioning the word. This could be why Jim Gray, the manager of Microsoft Research's eScience Group went missing. It could also be why Dr. Robert Harrington, the chief astronomer of the U.S. Naval Observatory died mysteriously after his published interview with Zecharia Sitchin discussing Nibiru.

Reagan even had the word Nibiru removed from the dictionary. Trump made a statement shortly after taking office, "We will untap the mysteries of space." Many believe that was a direct reference to the Nibiru cover up. Right after he took office, it is said, he signed an executive order stopping the cover up. With the stroke of his pen, he ended 30 years of this secrecy. Besides all of this, how do they take Isaiah 24 out of the Bible? It is there and has been there since 732 B.C. to read and know that judgment is coming to this old earth! This chapter is describing how this judgment will look.

SEPTEMBER 23, 2017 and MORE

> Rev 12:1 "And there appeared a great wonder in heaven; **a woman** clothed with the sun, and the moon under her feet, and upon her head a crown of twelve stars:"

> Rev 12:2 "And **she being with child cried, travailing in birth, and pained to be delivered.**"

There is a constellation in the heavens called Virgo and is well known by astronomers as representing a virgin. There is another constellation called Leo the Lion and this one is right above Virgo's head and has 9 stars in it. Notice above in verse one that it states that there are twelve stars upon her head. For the first time in history, never to be repeated, on September 23rd, 2017 three planets in perfect alignment moved into Leo, thus appearing to have twelve stars! Those planets were Mercury, Mars, and Venus. Wait, there is more. There is a royal or kingly planet known as Jupiter. This planet entered the womb area of Virgo in December of that same year and stayed there for 42 weeks. The normal gestation period for a baby's birth is 40 weeks. Actually, some have said that it will remain there a little less than 42 weeks so that one could say that she was great with child and in pain to be delivered. Jesus is the King and is the Lion of the Tribe of Judah! This is a symbol of Jesus' birth and when Jupiter exits the womb area, it is a type of Jesus returning to this world to set up His kingdom. Revelation 12 tells us that this is a wonder in heaven, so it is a sign in heaven, but there are also signs in the earth and in the oceans. Luke 21 mentions all three of these things:

> Luk 21:11 "And **great earthquakes** shall be in divers places, and famines, and pestilences; and fearful sights and **great signs shall there be from heaven.**"

> Luk 21:25 "And **there shall be signs in the sun, and in the moon, and in the stars**; and upon the earth distress of nations, with perplexity; **the sea and the waves roaring**;"

> Luk 21:26 "Men's hearts failing them for fear, and for looking after those things which are coming on the earth: for **the powers of heaven shall be shaken.**"

> Luk 21:27 "And then shall they **see the Son of man coming in a cloud** with power and great glory."

> Luk 21:28 "And **when these things begin to come to pass, then look up**, and lift up your heads; for **your redemption draweth nigh.**"

The September phenomena is a sign in the stars! Is the "sea and the waves roaring" referring to Hurricanes Harvey, Erma, Jose, Maria, and Lee and other ones? It appears that 2017 was the worst hurricane season in decades. Is Planet X, Apophis, and the pole shift referred to as the "powers of the heaven" being "shaken". The first total eclipse over the United States in 38 years August 21, 2017 was another sign in the heavens of the Lord's soon return. The Special Anniversary Issue of The Old Farmer's 2017 Almanac page 134 says another total eclipse April 8, 2024 will imprint another shadow across this country. The Almanac doesn't tell us that this shadow will cross the path of the last shadow making the sign of the cross upon the face of our country, but it will. An eclipse happened in Jonah's day and it helped bring Jonah's message to bear to the inhabitants of Nineveh. Will these eclipses and the rest of these signs bring this world to repentance? Probably not, but it is all happening to let us know that the end is near! It is God's mercy and His kiss to us on earth to warn us that the end of all things is about to happen. Are you ready for the King of Kings to return to this earth?

FEW MEN LEFT

In our world today is there such a thing as world planners? Yes, I believe there are world planners, but they are better known as globalists. Globalists do not believe in Nationalism. They believe nationalism is selfish and that all countries should be working together to make this world better and not just their own countries better. Sounds good, huh? The question is by whose standards? In other words who decides what is better and not better? And another question is who are these world planners or globalists? Who appointed them to be the "big honchos" and dictators? Are they self-appointed or appointed by their own cronies? What if I don't agree with them? In other words, to get to the point, are their standards based on Biblical standards or humanistic standards? Let's center in on one topic for illustration purposes, and follow it to its logical conclusion. Let's talk about population control as that is what this section deals with.

The globalists believe that there are too many people on this planet and a lot of people need to be eliminated. This ideology was illustrated by a movie called Dante's Inferno, starring Tom Hanks, and was based somewhat on a book written by Dan Brown. Almost the whole movie has to do with a guy who wants to bring about this population reduction by introducing a super virus that will kill off most of the population of the world to accomplish this. The rest of the movie has to do with how they stop him. The truth is, it is not just one man and his girlfriend that wants to do this. It is a whole group of people that are globalists that want to do this. Folks, Huma Abedin's husband, Anthony Weiner, had his computer confiscated and examined and they discovered on it plans to reduce the population of several nations, including the United States of America. The plan was to reduce this country's population by 300 million! That means they are wanting to almost annihilate this whole country. This is real, but is reducing the world population right? No, not according to the word of God. There is enough room on this earth for a lot more people and it is not man's responsibility to figure out how to kill off millions of people. Actually this group has already introduced multiple viruses and bacteria to do this and was the coronavirus released on purpose in 2020 for this reason? Was the HIV introduced into the world to help reduce its population? They have also determined that war is a good vehicle to accomplish their goals, so they inspire war, but who are they to make such determinations? The Christians believe it is God who should determine such things, not man. But if the globalists are in power and are in the "driver's seat" then that is what is going to happen, no matter if the Christians like it or not.

Is population reduction really a part of globalism? Yes, and let me offer a couple more points to confirm this. Many know about the mysterious Guidestones found in Elbert county, Georgia, near the South Carolina Border. This large monument declares that "their" goal is to maintain the population of the earth at 500 million people. The monument is there and no one knows who put it there, but it spells out "somebody's" goals. Basically, they want to reduce the population to less than ten percent of 7.5 billion people. Sort of scary huh? Believe it or not, there is an association set up to help reduce the population of this country. It is called NPG, Negative Population Growth, Inc. Founded in 1972, they have a president, secretaries, treasurers, an executive vice president, and 24 members of the Advisory Board. Twenty of these members are doctors and professors across the globe—very intelligent and influential people. Anyone can contact them and get their newsletter. Their address is 2861 Duke Street, Suite 36, Alexandria, VA 22314 and their phone number is 703-370-9510. Their website is 222.npg.org. It appears that their whole purpose is to help facilitate a reduction in population of the United States and thus lower the population of the world. They offer a "down to earth" four step plan to accomplish their goals, but their goals seem to tie into the goals of those who set up the Georgia Guidestones.

The question is, "Does the Bible talk about the population of the world?" The answer is, "Yes!" And we have already given several passages that mention it, but to make it easier, they are listed below. Let's look at Isaiah 13:

> Isa 13:12 "**I will make a man more precious than fine gold**; even a man than the golden wedge of Ophir."

Earlier in this chapter it is talking about the Day of the Lord and punishing the **world**. This isn't just a judgment against Israel as mentioned earlier in this chapter. There are some prophecy experts who say that the tribulation is just regional and doesn't affect the whole world, but passages like this and others in this section debunk that interpretation. Look at Isaiah 24:

> Isa 24:1 "Behold, the LORD maketh **the earth**

empty, and maketh it waste, and turneth it upside down, and **scattereth abroad the inhabitants thereof.**"

Isa 24:2 "And it shall be, as with the people, so with the priest; as with the servant, so with his master; as with the maid, so with her mistress; as with the buyer, so with the seller; as with the lender, so with the borrower; as with the taker of usury, so with the giver of usury to him."

Isa 24:3 "**The land shall be utterly emptied**, and utterly spoiled: for the LORD hath spoken this word."

Isa 24:4 "The **earth** mourneth and fadeth away, the **world** languisheth and fadeth away, **the haughty people of the earth do languish.**"

Isa 24:5 "**The earth also is defiled under the inhabitants thereof**; because they have transgressed the laws, changed the ordinance, broken the everlasting covenant."

Isa 24:6 "Therefore hath **the curse devoured the earth, and they that dwell therein are**

desolate: therefore the inhabitants of the earth are burned, and few men left."

Again, notice that this is global, but how few is few? Zechariah 13 narrows it down even further:

> Zec 13:8 "And it shall come to pass, that in all the land, saith the LORD, two parts therein shall be cut off and die; but the third shall be left therein."

At this time that means that over five billion will die. Does the scripture get more graphic than this? Yes. Look at Isaiah 6:

> Isa 6:9 "And he said, Go, and tell this people, Hear ye indeed, but understand not; and see ye indeed, but perceive not."

> Isa 6:10 "Make the heart of this people fat, and make their ears heavy, and shut their eyes; lest they see with their eyes, and hear with their ears, and understand with their heart, and convert, and be healed."

> Isa 6:11 "Then said I, Lord, how long? And he answered, **Until the cities be wasted without inhabitant**, and the **houses without man**, and the land be utterly desolate,"

Isa 6:12 "And the LORD have **removed men far away**, and there be a great forsaking in the midst of the land."

Isa 6:13 "But yet in it shall be **a tenth**, and it shall return, and shall be eaten: as a teil tree, and as an oak, whose substance is in them, when they cast their leaves: so the holy seed shall be the substance thereof."

After looking at the goals of the world planners, the Georgia Guidestones, and what the scripture has to say, it appears that their plans are going to come to pass. Many times God uses the wrath of Man to accomplish His own goals. In Noah's day only eight people were saved out of a whole world. Here the Lord lets us know that there are going to be a lot more than eight people saved this time. He says there will be a tenth saved. That's not many people, but praise God for a tenth! It is also possible that the ones who are spared are the ones who are saved and right with God. Look at Revelation 9:

Rev 9:13 "And the sixth angel sounded, and I heard a voice from the four horns of the golden altar which is before God,"

Rev 9:14 "Saying to the sixth angel which had the trumpet, Loose the four angels which are bound in the great river Euphrates."

Rev 9:15 "And the four angels were loosed, which were prepared for an hour, and a day, and a month, and a year, **for to slay the third part of men**."

Rev 9:16 "And **the number of the army of the horsemen were two hundred thousand thousand**: and I heard the number of them."

Rev 9:17 "And thus I saw the horses in the vision, and them that sat on them, having breastplates of fire, and of jacinth, and brimstone: and the heads of the horses were as the heads of lions; and out of their mouths issued fire and smoke and brimstone."

Rev 9:18 "**By these three was the third part of men killed**, by the fire, and by the smoke, and by the brimstone, which issued out of their mouths."

The world planners seem to think that war is a good vehicle to use to reduce the population and in this passage, it appears that God allows their plans to work. There is coming to the forefront an army of two hundred million soldiers and when the dust settles a third of the men of the world will be killed. This is another reason why the Bible tells us that there are few men left. A third of them have been taken out by war. The rest of them seem to be taken out by all the catastrophes that are happening on the earth.

EARTHQUAKES

In the end of the world there will be earthquakes. It is first talked about in Isaiah which we quote above, but repeated here for your convenience:

> Isa 24:18 "And it shall come to pass, that he who fleeth from the noise of the fear shall fall into the pit; and he that cometh up out of the midst of the pit shall be taken in the snare: for the windows from on high are open, and the **foundations of the earth do shake**."

> Isa 24:19 "The earth is utterly broken down, the earth is clean dissolved, **the earth is moved exceedingly**."

> Isa 24:20 "**The earth shall reel to and fro like a drunkard, and shall be removed like a cottage**; and the transgression thereof shall be heavy upon it; and it shall fall, and not rise again."

This theme is taken up in the New Testament by Jesus in Matthew 24 (similar wording is found in Mark 13:8 and Luke 21:11):

Mat 24:7 "For nation shall rise against nation, and kingdom against kingdom: and there shall be famines, and pestilences, and **earthquakes, in divers places**."

John then takes up the mantra in Revelation 6:

Rev 6:12 "And I beheld when he had opened the sixth seal, and, lo, **there was a great earthquake;** and the sun became black as sackcloth of hair, and the moon became as blood;"

Rev 6:14 "And the heaven departed as a scroll when it is rolled together; and **every mountain and island were moved out of their places**."

John continues in Revelation chapters 8, 11, and 16:

Rev 8:5 "And the angel took the censer, and filled it with fire of the altar, and cast it into the earth: and there were voices, and thunderings, and lightnings, and **an earthquake**."

Rev 11:13 "And the same hour was there **a great earthquake**, and the tenth part of the city fell, and in the earthquake were slain of men seven thousand: and the remnant were affrighted, and gave glory to the

God of heaven."

Rev 11:19 "And the temple of God was opened in heaven, and there was seen in his temple the ark of his testament: and there were lightnings, and voices, and thunderings, and **an earthquake**, and great hail."

Rev 16:18 "And there were voices, and thunders, and lightnings; and there was **a great earthquake**, such as was not since men were upon the earth, **so mighty an earthquake, and so great.**"

It talks about an earthquake in each one of these passages. Do you think in each case in Revelation it is a different earthquake? No, it is the same earthquake. If the earth is shaken exceedingly and there is a pole shift, that could be the earthquake that these verses are talking about and it could very likely be the earthquake that sets off the supervolcano in Yellowstone. (More about that below.) When the mountains are moved out of their place and the islands disappear that's the earthquake, and it will happen at the end.

VOLCANOES

Mat 24:29 "Immediately after the tribulation of those days shall **the sun be darkened, and the**

moon shall not give her light and the stars shall fall from heaven, and the powers of the heavens shall be shaken:"

The scriptures over and over again talk about the sun and the moon darkening over and over again. What is it referring to? It could be referring to the blowing of a supervolcano and it might just be referring to Yellowstone! I was in Yakima, Washington May 18th, 1980 when Mt. St. Helens erupted. They say it went 12 miles high. Yakima was down wind and was one of the largest cities hard hit by the fallout. It was on a Sunday and our Sunday Night church service was cancelled. I was driving to the pastor's house and it was in the middle of the day. Everybody had their headlights on. The street lights were on. The sun could not break through the haze. There was a creepy feeling in the air. When the moon came out it barely shown through, but it looked funny. People were wearing masks and within a couple of days were either on their roofs or having someone on their roofs sweeping, shoveling, scraping, or spraying the ash off. This was a small volcano. What would it have looked like if it had been Yellowstone?

Supervolcanoes, like the one in Yellowstone don't have domes on them like Mt. St. Helens had and they may not look very daunting, but don't be fooled, their potential for destruction is very great. (Much of the material from this section comes from a You Tube article, "Michio Kaku— Yellowstone will Devastate America!" It was dated 7/24/17 and it was written by Amy S.) According to professor

Stephen Self, a volcanologist at the Open University, said such like volcanoes "...could result in the devastation of world agriculture, severe disruption of food supplies, and mass starvation." The caldera of the Yellowstone supervolcano is 53 miles by 28 miles—big enough to encompass Tokyo, the largest city in the world. As you can see, that is big!

The article mentions the eruption of Tambora in Indonesia in 1815, the worst in history, Krakatoa in 1883, and Pinatuba in the Philippines in 1991. They were not supervolcanoes from what we can understand, but they still interrupted global climate a whole year following their explosions. If that is true, which it is, what would happen if Yellowstone blew 2,000 million tons of sulphur acid into the sky. It could cause a worldwide blackout causing temperatures to plummet to between 50 to 68 degrees Fahrenheit during the summer. There would be enough ash to burry an area the size of Great Britain under 13 feet of ash. That's enough ash to crush every building for miles around. If that happened what could FEMA do? FEMA could hardly deal with its largest disaster ever, the 9/11 tragedy. How could it deal with something 10 million times larger than that? Everyone would be on their own and what's more, the chances are 5 to 10 times greater that it would happen compared to the earth being struck by a giant astroid.

There is a lot of information on the internet about the history of volcanoes world-wide. The internet covers the dangers of the possibility of volcanoes blowing from many parts of the world. The Drudge Report carried an article on April 7, 2018 that was very informative. It could be pulled up by entering the following: zerohedge.com/news/2018-04-06/ring-fire-becoming-more-active. More information is given on "Skywatch Media News". There was a video posted April 5, 2018 called, "Extreme East Coast Tidal Retreat-West Texas is shaking and sinking-China's massive Weather Control". The speaker on this video says that the chances of a massive volcano exploding somewhere in the world is very likely. He continued, "...if history is any indication, this will happen again, and it cannot be prevented. If statistics are accurate, of a 95% probability of a massive irruption, and we have no reason to believe otherwise, then we have five years or less until the next VEI 5 or higher eruption takes place." (VEI stands for Volcanic Explosivity Index.) As you can see, they believe it could happen at any time.

There is another angle on this whole scenario. There are volcanoes in the oceans. In fact there are signs that a volcano in the Gulf of Mexico could explode in the near future. Documentaries are on You Tube (enter in the search bar, "Volcano in the floor of the Gulf of Mexico.") The waters in this gulf are heating up to 80 degrees Fahrenheit, which is unheard of. There is flesh eating bacteria in the waters and it is everywhere. Everyone is warned not to swim in the waters. There is an underwater caldera that has the scientists on high alert. It could blow. Does the Bible talk about this? Yes!

Rev 8:8 "And the second angel sounded, and as it were **a great mountain burning with fire was cast into the sea: and the third part of the sea became blood**;"

Rev 8:9 "And the **third part of the creatures which were in the sea, and had life, died; and the third part of the ships were destroyed**."

A mountain can be on the bottom of the ocean floor. It says it was burning with fire. That could definitely be a volcano and could include the lava and the sulphur ash that would be cast upward into the sea. It would very likely poison the waters and along with the heat could kill all sea life. The acidic content, present in the ash could cause the bottoms of boats to be eaten up and sink and everybody on the ship would perish. Besides this, it could turn all the waters red like blood and thus this verse would be fulfilled. Are you ready for the end? It's coming and it could be upon us at any time. Get right with God while there is some time left.

THE UNITED STATES WILL BE DIMINISHED

The previous chapter talked about Jerusalem in Israel being Mystery Babylon the Great. As I stated earlier my third book gives 33 proofs why this is correct. Revelation 18:11-17 talks about goods and produce that typically would be traded on the New York stock exchange floor. Is it possible that the stock market could collapse? How bad would the collapse be? Could it be so bad that the world stock market could switch to a city and country other than New York City in the United States of America? Could it be that Israel would be the future home of the world stock exchange? Could Israel be the future home of the One World Trade Center replacing the new one, 1776 feet high, in New York City that replaced the twin towers? At this point it doesn't seem at all likely, but let's continue. Will the US greenback tumble from its lofty position of being the world reserve currency? There could be a currency crash and the United States fall from being the greatest country in the world. In many people's minds it is not very likely, but it is possible and it might result from judgment that God will pour out on this country for all the abortions, idolatries, and atrocities that have been committed between her two seas. If Revelation 18 is referring to Jerusalem THEN it just might be possible!

It appears that the Antichrist will set up his headquarters in Jerusalem. How do we know this? Look at Daniel 11:

> Dan 11:45 "And **he shall plant the tabernacles of his palace between the seas in the glorious holy mountain**; yet he shall come to his end, and none shall help him."

Why would the Antichrist set up his headquarters there? It will be the economic center and capitol of the world. The magazine, *Israel Today*, in it's January, 2017 issue had some astonishing things to say about this small, in physical size, but large in many other ways, country. On page 36 the heading reads, "Why Israel Is the World's Startup Nation". They say, "More than 300 multinational companies including Google, Facebook, Microsoft and Intel have hired engineering teams in Israel to find ways of improving their products." They quote Google developer Don Dodge as saying, "I've been to every corner of the earth. There is no other country on earth that thinks the same way that we (at Google) do like Israel does." Adi Soffer Teeni, the CEO of Facebook Israel said, "The atmosphere in Israel is comparable to that in Silicon Valley." Intel employs 11,000 in Israel and has been there for 40 years and is a microchip giant. (Is it possible that the mark of the beast will be a microchip and be manufactured in Israel?) Roy Ramon, managing director said, "This is one culture that you can't get anywhere in the world." Zack Weisfeld, the general manager of Microsoft Global Accelerators agrees with that statement and has been in Israel for 25 years and employs presently about 1,000 people.

In the same issue of *Israel Today* on page 37 the heading reads, "Jerusalem's New Commercial District". Jerusalem's mayor Nir Barkat said, "This project we are initiating is a game-changer for Jerusalem. It is the biggest, most significant and essential project for the future of the city." This is going to be a 700,000 square-meter Gateway Project at the entrance to the city and it's expecting to provide 40,000 new jobs. Great things are happening in Israel and in almost every issue of this magazine it is reporting on the goings on there.

In the August-September issue they cover more success stories. Again on page 36 the heading reads, "South America Looks to Israel for Cyber and Border Defense". This article tells the story how a group of Israeli cyber-security firms won a contract worth "tens of millions of dollars" to set up an end-to-end cyber defense system for a country in Latin America. They say this was reported in the "Times of Israel". Not only that, but page 37 of this issue covers "The Story Behind Mobileye". Mobileye, three years ago, became the most valuable Israeli stock ever on the US stock market setting a new record of being acquired by Intel for over 15 billion dollars! In case the reader didn't know it, God is blessing Israel like never before.

Let me repeat, is it possible that America could lose her position as the greatest nation on earth? Could it be the result of an EMP (electromagnetic pulse)? Will Yellowstone blow? Some reports say that if it did blow, it could wipe out America and affect the whole world. I am not saying that Dumitru Duduman is a true prophet, but it is possible that the ten great cities of America that he talked about will be nuked. Kim Clement and Mark Taylor say that America will be returned to her former glory, so to speak, because of Donald Trump. Jonathan Cahn has said that America will be judged, but after Trump's election he has modified his predictions. He was interviewed on Dr. James Dobson's Family Talk and linked the life of the Old Testament Israel

King Jehu to the presidency of Donald Trump. With that in mind it is possible that a time of restoration could precede the strike of judgement based on America's response to the Lord. Maybe they are right, but after America is restored, is it possible that she will eventually fall? I believe it is very possible. The new world trade center will likely be finished and the New York Stock Exchange will possibly continue for quite a while, but somewhere, sometime, someway, Israel will come out on top, as the Bible indicates. The main thing is, are you, the reader ready? Are you saved? You can be.

CONCLUSION

The Lord began telling us about the end of the world at the beginning of the world by the prophet Enoch. There are many prophecy experts who tell us, "Don't worry, Jesus will come and rapture us away before we see the AC and the wrath of God. Noah's generation didn't think it would happen in their day, but it did. The prophets in Jeremiah's day said, "Don't worry, God will defend His glorious city and will not allow Judah to be carried away captive nor His temple to be destroyed", but they were wrong, too. A time of trouble is coming and we need to start thinking about how we might prepare for it after we and our families get saved.

We get a pretty grim picture of the future and how bad things are going to get just by looking at the scriptures between Isaiah, Daniel, and Revelation. Apophis, Planet X, the Georgia Guidestones, the great earthquake, volcanoes covering half the United States with ash, and the possible fall of the United States coupled with few men left to face the future from all the devastation should shake us to our knees. My next book will prove that this is the kind of future we will be left to face. The one bright spot in it all is that somehow, someway, there will be a remnant of God's people left standing and surviving that will welcome the coming of our Lord. The people of the Lord at that time will be reading, quoting, and/or repeating Psalms 91:

> Psa 91:1 "He that dwelleth in the secret place of the most High shall abide under the shadow of the Almighty."
>
> Psa 91:2 "I will say of the LORD, He is my refuge and my fortress: my God; in him will I trust."
>
> Psa 91:3 "Surely he shall deliver thee from the snare of the fowler, and from the noisome pestilence."
>
> Psa 91:4 "He shall cover thee with his feathers, and under his wings shalt thou trust: his truth shall be thy shield and buckler."
>
> Psa 91:5 "Thou shalt not be afraid for the terror by night; nor for the arrow that flieth by day;"

Psa 91:6 "Nor for the pestilence that walketh in darkness; nor for the destruction that wasteth at noonday."

Psa 91:7 "A thousand shall fall at thy side, and ten thousand at thy right hand; but it shall not come nigh thee."

Psa 91:8 "Only with thine eyes shalt thou behold and see the reward of the wicked."

Psa 91:9 "Because thou hast made the LORD, which is my refuge, even the most High, thy habitation;"

Psa 91:10 "There shall no evil befall thee, neither shall any plague come nigh thy dwelling."

Psa 91:11 "For he shall give his angels charge over thee, to keep thee in all thy ways."

Psa 91:12 "They shall bear thee up in their hands, lest thou dash thy foot against a stone."

Psa 91:13 "Thou shalt tread upon the lion and adder: the young lion and the dragon shalt thou trample under feet."

> Psa 91:14 "Because he hath set his love upon me, therefore will I deliver him: I will set him on high, because he hath known my name."
>
> Psa 91:15 "He shall call upon me, and I will answer him: I will be with him in trouble; I will deliver him, and honour him."
>
> Psa 91:16 "With long life will I satisfy him, and shew him my salvation."

Jesus is coming back and a new day will break forth. He is coming and bringing His holy city called New Jerusalem, with Him. Before the New Jerusalem comes the present day Jerusalem must be removed to make way for the new one. We that belong to Jesus shall rule and reign with Him as kings and priests in His kingdom of righteousness that shall never end. Look at Daniel 7:

> Dan 7:14 "And there was given him dominion, and glory, and a kingdom, that all people, nations, and languages, should serve him: his dominion is an **everlasting dominion, which shall not pass away, and his kingdom that which shall not be destroyed**."

Will you be among them? You can be, but it's up to you. It is in your ability to obey the Acts 2:38 gospel message to believe and be saved as the scripture has said. The greatest way to be ready is to be saved. My greatest prayer for everyone, whether they read my book or not is for them to be saved. The choice is yours.

Around September 2012 Janet Parshall shared this on her daily radio program "In the Market Place". People called in or emailed her whenever they saw an interesting sign. One sign read the following:

A word, like Facebook, can mean one thing to you and it can mean something different to someone else. That applies to the Lord in the same way. When God gives us a word in scripture, let's not automatically assume His meaning is always our meaning.

"THE END, HOW BAD WILL IT GET?" STUDY QUESTIONS
(*Open Book Quiz*)

1. Which Old Testament prophet talked about the end from the beginning?

2. Which Old Testament prophet dealt specifically with false prophets, saying, "...my people love to have it so"?

3-4. What repeats itself and give the passage where it is found?

5-6. In Noah's day, according to I Peter 3:20-21, what saved eight souls and what does that prove to us today?

7. The wrath of God is mentioned early in the book of Revelation. Which chapter first mentions it?

8-10. What three descriptive words or phrases are used to describe the earth in Isaiah 24:1?

11. In Isaiah 24:13 what will the people (of God) do that will bring majesty to the Lord and a glimmer of hope in the midst of devastation and destruction?

12. Which "day" is described in Isaiah 13 and named in verse 6 which is described as a day of destruction?

13. In Revelation chapter 8 how many times is the word "third" used?

14. In Revelation 9 at the time of the fifth trumpet, what happens to those who desire to die?

15. What is the name of the asteroid that is supposed to hit the earth or have a near pass by April 13, 2029?

16. When was the, once in a life time, alignment of planets and stars that many believe was the fulfillment of Revelation 12:1-3?

17. Where is the Dooms Day Seed Vault?

18. Which president signed an executive order to keep Nibiru secret?

19. How long did Jupiter the kingly planet stay in the womb area of Virgo?

20. The shadows of the August 21st, 2017 eclipse along with the future shadow of the April 8, 2024 eclipse will imprint what sign across the face of the United States?

21-22. What two chapters in Isaiah tell us in so many words, few men are left on the earth?

23. What large monument is found in Elbert County, Georgia near the South Carolina border?

24. How does Revelation 16:18 describe the great earthquake at the end of time?

25. What kind of volcano is Yellowstone?

Bonus Question:

26. What Old Testament Israel King was linked to the presidency of Donald Trump?

"THE END, HOW BAD WILL IT GET?"
(Quiz Answers)

1. Enoch

2. Jeremiah

3-4. History repeats itself, Ecclesiastes 1:9-10

5-6. Water saved eight souls. Baptism does also now save us.

7. Chapter 6

8-10. Empty, waiste, turneth it upside down

11. Sing

12. The Day of the Lord

13. 12

14. They will seek to die and will not be able.

15. Apophis

16. September 23, 2017

17. In Greenland between Norway and the Arctic Circle

18. Ronald Reagan

19. About 42 weeks

20. They will imprint the sign of the cross across the face of the United States.

21-22. Isaiah 13 and 24

23. The mysterious Georgia Guidestones

24. The earthquake was "such as was not since men were upon earth, so mighty an earthquake and so great."

25. It is a supervolcano.

Bonus Answer:

26. Jehu

STUDY GUIDE

Chapter 1: How Important is Prophecy?

- What is Prophecy? Explains it and gives its purpose.

- The Earliest Prophets. The Lord gives the first prophecy in Genesis 3 and Enoch is next.

- Abraham Believed God's Prophetic Word and was Rewarded. God showed Abraham the future.

- God Wants You to Know and Believe the Prophecies of the future Like Abraham.

- Dangers. There are dangers in trying to know the future outside of God's power.

- Lessons from the Past. Israel as a nation missed their Messiah because they misunderstood prophecy. Could we miss the second coming of Christ by doing the same?

- How did Prophecy save Joseph and his Family? Joseph always had dreams of the future, and these dreams showed him how to save his family, and all of Egypt.

- How did Prophecy Save Daniel's Life? It was through interpreting Nebuchadnezzer's dream.

- Objection to Knowing the Future. Though one verse says it is not for us to know the times, other verses tell us we can know the future.

- What is the Key to knowing the Future. It takes a strong desire.

- Only the Lord Can Reveal Secrets. The Lord wants us to seek Him with all our heart and believe Him with all our soul, and who knows how many insights into the future we will get.

Chapter 2: The Four Beasts and Four and Twenty Elders.

There are nine ways to know their identity:

1. In the Old Testament Jewish leaders are called elders, and Gentiles are referred to as animals.

2. Revelation lets us know that both these groups are round about the throne, as the saints are.

3. The Beasts in Revelation 4 were in the midst of the throne, as the saints are.

4. Both the Beasts and the Elders are worshiping God, as the saints are.

5. The Beasts provoke the Elders to jealousy, as the Gentiles do to the Jews.

6. The Elders cast their crowns before the throne, as the saints also do.

7. The Elders and the Beasts prayed, as the saints do.

8. The Beasts and the Elders are redeemed, as the saints are.

9. The Beasts and the Elders are made kings and priests as the saints are.

Chapter 3: Who Are The Two Witnesses?

Who they are:

- Four Possible Interpretations. The four different theories are given.

- Their Timing. They are present during the reign of the Antichrist.

- Their identity, the Two Olive Trees. They are the two Olive Trees and the two Candlesticks.

- Zachariah and John Are Supposed to Know Who They Are. Why are there no introductions who they are? We are supposed to know them—they are the saints.

- Now the Verses I Left Out. Not everything is in chronological order. The Lord hides the meaning between the verses.

- The Two Anointed ones Are the Church. The Church is anointed, as the Two Witnesses are.

- The Two Olive Trees Are the Church. Romans 11 gives us the wild and the good olive tree, as the Gentile and the Jewish saints of God.

- The Two Candlesticks Are the Church. Revelation 1 tells us this and these are the two witnesses.

- The Saved Jew and Gentile Are Also the Temple. In Revelation 11 John was to measure the temple, or expose the temple which Paul tells us is made up of Jews and Gentiles, and that is what Revelation 11 does— tells us who the Two Witnesses are in a parabolic form.

- The Jew and Gentile Are Called Witnesses. Old and New Testament references are given to verify this.

- The Number Two Is a Big Deal. A discussion how often the numbers two and four (double two) are repeated in scripture. Two in scripture is the number of "witness"!

- Why Does God Need Two Witnesses? None can be condemned to death without two witnesses and during this time many will die for their rejection of the Messiah of God.

- The Jews As a Nation Will Be Grafted Back into Their Tree. The Jews as a nation will be saved.

- Are You One of the Elect? Acts 2:38 tells us how to be saved.

- Why So Long? The pre-tribulation rapture theory has limited the scope of putting it together.

- In Review. A list of twelve things we have seen in this chapter.

- Objections Answered. The persecution and resurrection of the Two Witnesses is promised to the Church.

- More Questions. Revelation 10:11 is addressed in why there are not two literal people.

Chapter 4: Who Are the 144,000?

Is the Church Found in Revelation 5-18?

- Does the Rapture Take Place in Revelation 4:1? The phrase "come up hither", is repeated in various forms in four passages and we know the rapture only happens once!

- To Whom Was the Book of Revelation Addressed? The opening and closing of the book was written to the seven churches, or you could say to the Church, which hints to their identity.

- The Word "Church" is not used in Revelation 5-18. But 33 other phrases are used—all referring to the church! Does that mean the Church is not there? No

- Who Are the 144,000? The twelve descriptions of them in chapter 14 are descriptions of the saints. In chapter 7 they are the "servants of our God" and are "sealed" which is true of all God's people.

- Another Group: A Great Multitude. There are TWO groups of people in chapter 7 like it is a repeat of the chapter on the Two Witnesses. Chapter 14 does NOT say this group is just Jews, but the twelve descriptions of them, in a sense match the twelve descriptions of the great multitude found in chapter 7—they are all typical of the body of Christ!

- The Two Groups of Revelation 7: Sealed and Arrayed. The 144,000 were sealed, and the Great Multitude was arrayed. Both of these things is typical of the whole body of Christ.

- Sealed "From" or "Before" Tribulation. It is shown how both groups will have to go through the tribulation, confirming that this is the church which will be going through it.

- 12 the Number of the City. 12 tribes and 12 apostles indicates the city is for both Jews and Gentiles who are in the body of Christ from all ages.

- The Wall of an Hundred and Forty and Flour Cubits. How is the wall of the city derived? It isn't 12 plus 12, but 12 TIMES 12. God wasn't going to ADD to Abraham, he was going to multiply him exceedingly, by giving him the seed of the Gentiles and the city is for both groups.

- If the 144,000 is Literal it's Too Restrictive. Since there were really 13 tribes, 12 is a figurative number because in the list of the tribes, invariably there was always one tribe omitted. Does that mean there is one tribe that has none saved from it? No. And more proof that 12,000 saved from each tribe is too little. This represents the whole body of Christ from ages past to ages to come.

Chapter 5: The End, When Is It?

- Which Calendar Now? The Mayan is complete so which one now? Does God have one?

- When is the End? The most general indicators speak in thousands of years not millions.

- The Study of Calendars. Sir Robert Anderson's figures disagree with the Jewish ones. We're in the year 6156 not 5775!

- The Third Day Indicator. There are three passages in the O.T. and one in the N.T. that indicate the Lord is coming after 2000 years.

- When Does the Clock Start Ticking? At the beginning or the end of Jesus' ministry?

- How Long is a Generation? We go back to Genesis to find the meaning of the fourth generation.

- The Possible Events of the 70th Week. 33 possible steps until the 1,000 year reign.

- A Seven Year Peace Treaty Will be Signed. Daniel tells us Israel is our time indicator.

- 42 Months, 1260 Days, A Time and Times and the Dividing of Time, and Three and a Half Days. The saints will be persecuted three and a half years by the Antichrist. Some will be protected.

- The Great Persecution, the Great Tribulation, and the Wrath of God. The differences and similarities are briefly explained.

- The Abomination of Desolation. Why we don't accept preterism. Three passages in the N.T. and four in Daniel refer to it as a timing indicator. Why the 70 A.D. Destruction of Jerusalem wasn't the final one.

- The 2300 Days. 220 days after the peace treaty is signed, the temple will be built and the sacrifices started and 2300 days later the Abomination of Desolation will be set up.

- This is Not What has Been Taught and the 1290 Days. Five proofs why the Abomination of Desolation does not happen when the sacrifices cease.

- So, What is the Abomination of Desolation? We look at six references to it, three in the O.T. and three in the N.T. and some possibilities how they can be played out.

- Jerusalem Destroyed. Eleven single-space pages of more proof why the 70 A.D. Destruction wasn't the final one.

- The Antichrist Destroyed. This is after his reign of 1260 days as the World Ruler.

- The 1335 Days. Proof why this is referring to the return of Jesus.

- The Return of Jesus. Some very apparent reasons why this happens after the tribulation.

- The Crux of the Matter. If the timing of the Abomination of Desolation is off, it throws everything off (seven things).

- The Time Line. Six time frames are given in scripture: 7 years, 1260 days twice, 2300 days, 1290 days, 1335 days. Two graphs demonstrate from these six time frames when seven events will transpire during the seven years, after the starting of the peace treaty and including: 1. the starting of the sacrifices, 2. the ceasing of the sacrifices, 3. the World Ruler begins, 4. the Great Persecution begins, 5. the Great Tribulation and wrath of God begins, 6. the Abomination of Desolation is set up, and 7. the Return of Jesus.

Chapter 6: The End, How Bad Will It Get?

- Much of this book says when it will happen, but how bad will it get at the end?

- In Noah's day, people were warned, they prepared for it, and few men were left.

- Revelation 6 and the 6th seal brought an earthquake, stars fell, and the wrath of God came.

- Isaiah 24 shows the earth turned upside down as in a pole shift, people are burned and few left.

- Isaiah 13 shows the earth moves out of its place, the sun and moon are darkened and few left.

- Revelation 8 and 9 gives us the 6 trumpets; a meteor hits the ocean, vegetation is consumed.

- Apophis meteor could hit in 2029 or 2036 with the force of 100,000 nuclear bombs.

- Planet X has been verified and could cause the pole shift. Seed vaults set up due to the sea rising.

- September 23rd, 2017, a one-time event in the stars and planets letting us know the end is near.

- Few Men Left, is verified by the Georgia Guidestones and by the Bible.

- Earthquakes, are talked about in the Bible and the greatest and last one before the end.

- Volcanoes

- The U. S. will be diminished before Jerusalem becomes the capital of the world.

ALTERNATIVE READING

Wrath by D.R. Roquemore: A fictional story about Christians surviving after the Antichrist takes over.

The Islamic Antichrist by Joel Richardson. Could the Islamic savior, the Mahdi be to the Christians, the Antichrist?

What On Earth is about to Happen…for Heaven's Sake? by Kent Hovind: One view of Post-tribulation, pre-wrath rapture concept.

The Rapture Verdict by Michael T. Snyder: Another view on Post-tribulation, pre-wrath rapture concept.

The Blessed Hope by George E. Ladd: An older book on Post-tribulation, post-wrath rapture, written by a professor from Fuller Theological Seminary.

A Message for the President by Irving Baxter, Jr., 1986: Absolute proof that the U.S. is in the Bible.

Understanding the Endtime, 1995, Endtime, Inc.: A prophecy home Bible study, post-tribulation presentation. P.O. Box 940729, Plano, TX 75094-0729.

Endtime Magazine, published by Endtime Ministries, www.endtime.com, 800-363-8463.

Soon-coming World-shaking Events! Christian Missionary Society, P.O. Box 4097, Phoenix, AZ 85030. An older book, no publishing date. Book on post-tribulation.

The Final Victory: The Year 2000 by Marvin Byers, 1994, Treasure House. Book on post-tribulation.

LIST OF QUOTES

Note: Please, keep in mind this material has not been hastily thrown together in a couple of months. It is the result of approximately 50 years of research and examination. The following references represent a fraction of that research. I have listened to and read a lot of material from many people, yet I still maintain they are incorrect in their interpretation of end time events. My personal views have been greatly altered to embrace the "Revelation of God" (as they may also claim), but it is up to you, the reader, to determine how many of them are from Him and are supported by the scriptures themselves. One may ask, "How could so many men of God be wrong?" I don't know, but I do know it was like that in Jesus' day and in Paul's day. Also, remember David started his kingship close to age 30, and he penned the following words in Psalms 119:99-100: "I have more understanding than all my teachers; for thy testimonies are my meditation. I understand more than the ancients because I keep thy precepts." Even though this is true, and God has given me a lot of answers I must claim the words of Mark Hitchcock on page XIV of the introduction in his book, THE END, as a disclaimer, "I do not have all the answers, nor do I have every puzzle piece in place. To claim otherwise would be arrogant and foolish." But as you can see, the following list proves I have looked at and considered many of their opinions.

about.com, 364

Anderson, Kerby, 18

Anderson, Sir Robert, 279, 287, 297, 434

Apophis 2029: The Most Dangerous Asteroid, video, 478, 484, 488, 506

Armageddon News, 367

Baxter, Irving, with Endtime Ministries, 472

Bible Answer Book for Students, The 319

Bright, Randy, 366

Bullinger, E.W., 249

Byers, Marvin, 285, 294

Cahn, Jonathan, 505

Cayce, Edgar, 266

Clement, Kim, 505

Dante's Inferno, Dan Brown, movie and book, 489

Coming Prince, The, 279, 287, 297

David, Elihu Ben with Tyson Ministries, 136

Decoding Doomsday, 291

Detering, Hermann, 362

De Young, Jimmy, 289

Discover Publications, 379

Dixon, Jeane, 266

Dobson, Dr. James with Family Talk, 263, 505

Doomsday seed vault, The 483

Doukan, Jacques B., 337

Dr. Michio Kaku Predicts the End, video, 484

Drosnin, Michael, 383, 384, 396

Drudge Report, 501

Duduman, Dumitru, 385, 386, 505

Equilibrium, movie, 369

Eusebius, 380

Exo Vaticana, 369

Final Victory: the Year 2000, The 286, 294

Frozen Ark Project, The 484

Freidman, Matti, 131

Georgia Guidestones, 490, 491, 494, 507

Global Book Publishing, the Middle East, 361

Global Crop Diversity Trust Fund, 483

goodnewspirit.com/goodnewsprophecy.com, 285

Gray, Jim, 485

Green, General James, 312, 316, 334

Hagee, John, 274

Hagia, Sophia, 366, 367

Hanegraff, Hank, 317, 319, 320

Harrington, Dr. Robert, 485

Hedrick, Gary with Messianic Perspectives, 395

Heitzig, Skip, 10, 120, 131

Hill, Kenneth, 289

Hinds, John T., 168

Hitchcock, Mark, 60, 98, 159, 289

Hocking, David, 154, 274

Hollywood, 369, 384, 385

Horn, Tom, 369

Hutchings, Noah, 173, 274, 289, 420

Insider Speaks Out About Nibiru, video, 483

Interlinear Greek-English Lexicon, George Ricker Berry, 417

Interlinear Greek-English Lexicon, Jay P. Green, Sr., 342, 417

Israel Today, 278, 365, 504, 505

Jackson, Wayne, *Christian Courier*, 167, 168

Jehovah Witness, *Watchtower*, 167

Jenkins, Jerry, 154

Jeremiah, David, 154, 159, 274

Jericho, TV series, Jon Turteltaub, Steven Chbosky, Josh Shaer, Johnathan E. Steinberg, 385, 386

Kaku, Dr. Michio, 478, 499

Kampen, Van, 274

Kirban, Salem, 274

Krakatoa, 500

LaHaye, Tim, 154

Last days, 285

Last Days According to Jesus, The, 318

Late Great Planet Earth, The, 266, 290, 291

Lazarus, David, 278

Leavenwoarth III, Ted D., 285

Lindsey, Hal, 154, 266, 290, 291

Lindsted, Robert, 289

Lucas, Jerry, 255

MacArthur, John, 60, 279

McGee, J. Vernon, 113, 133

Meade, David, 291, 479, 480, 481

Medina, G. Jorge, 319

Miller, William, 337

Millerites, 337

Missler, Chuck, 26, 141, 154, 291, 442

NASA Quietly Admits Pole Shift, video, 484

New York Times, The, 484

Newton, Sir Isaac, 154

Nibiru Planet X Pole Shift, video, 479, 481, 488, 506

Nostradamus, 266

Negative Population Growth, Inc. (NPG), 490

Numbers in scripture, 249

Obama, Barack 365, 366
Old Farmer's Almanac 2017, The, 488
Pack, David C., Restored Church of God (Armstrong), 364
Parshall, Janet, 420, 510
Pentecost, Dwight, 154
Perkings, Donald, 318
Perry, Richard, 274, 285
Pinatubo, 500
Poland, Larry, 274
Price, Randall, 289
Putnam, Chris, 369
Reagan, President Ronald, 485
Reynolds, Ray T., 484
Roberts, J.W., 168
Rhodes, Ron, 420
Search for Truth #2, Jerry Twentier, Marcella Willhoite, 382
Secrets of Daniel, Jacques B. Doukhan, 337
Self, Professor Stephen, 499, 500
Seventh-Day Adventists Believe, 337
Seventh-Day Adventist book brochure, 336, 337, 338
Shoebat, Walid, 365
Shopenhauer, Arthur, 155
Sinistrari, Ludovico Maria, 369
Sitchin, Zecharia and his book, 484, 485
Skywatch Media News, video, 501
Smith, Chuck, 285
Smith, Shepherd, 478
Snyder, Michael, 482
Sproul, R.C., 153, 317, 318, 416
Stedman, Ray, 378

Swindol, Chuck, 440

Taylor, Mark, 505

Theomatics, 255

Thomas, I.D.E., 289

Titus, 362, 374, 375, 376, 378, 380, 381, 385

Tondering, Claus, 279

Trump, President Donald, 485

Tulsa Beacon, 366

Twain, Mark, 95

Twentier, Jerry, 382

Tyndale, William Bible Translation, 417

U.S.A. Today, 484

Umayyad Caliph, Abd al-Malik ibn Marwan, 362

Unger's Bible Dictionary, 362, 363

Upholding Our Future Hope, an Apostolic Response to Preterism, 319

Van Impe, Jack, 154, 274

VEI, volcano explosive index, 501

Visible remains of the temple, 380

Volcano in the Floor of the Gulf of Mexico, video, 501

Walvoord, John, 159

Washburn, Del, 255

Washington Post, 484

Webster's Dictionary, 322

Why I Still Believe These Are the Last Days, 289

Wikipedia, 337, 362, 363, 396

Willhoite, Marcella, 382

Woodward, S. Douglas, *Decoding Doomsday*, 291, 407

Yellowstone, 499, 500, 505

Yerbury, Ray, 289

Youngbrandt, Chuck, 352
Zondervan Pictorial Encyclopedia of the Bible, 361

www.ingramcontent.com/pod-product-compliance
Lightning Source LLC
Chambersburg PA
CBHW030211170426
43201CB00006B/57